Letters from Italy

A Transatlantic Love Story

Mario Dell'Olio

Black Rose Writing | Texas

4050045

Second printing

This book is a memoir. It reflects the present recollections of the author's
mother, members of his family, and their experiences over time. Since so
many family members share the same names, some have been changed to
make it easier to follow. Dialogue has been recreated.

ISBN: 978-1-68433-894-8 (Paperback); 978-1-68433-949-5 (Hardcover)
PUBLISHED BY BLACK ROSE WRITING
www.blackrosewriting.com

Printed in the United States of America
Suggested Retail Price (SRP) $22.95 (Paperback); $26.95 (Hardcover)

Letters from Italy is printed in Garamond

Cover design by Matthew David Roberts

To my mother and father, Nicoletta and Orazio Dell'Olio.

By your example of unwavering love in the face of adversity, during times of uncertainty, and through joy and laughter, you have taught me the meaning of unconditional love. For all immigrants who risk everything in hopes of a better life, or to fulfill their dreams, honoring your cultural heritage while embracing and contributing to the fabric of a new country—Letters from Italy is your story too.

Praise for

Letters from Italy

2022 Maxy Awards Runner-Up - Bio & Memoir

"Letters from Italy is an astonishingly beautiful work of art. I encourage everyone to read it. Brimming with romance, comedy, drama, history, and family lines. It's everything."

**–Jeannie Gaffigan, Writer, Producer,
New York Times Bestselling Author**

"Mario Dell'Olio's *Letters from Italy* is a wonderful book that proves once more that writing a memoir is not only important for one's own family but may be valuable for society at large.*"

–*L'idea Magazine*

"The masterful weaving of the story, punctuated by the letters between family members, creates a realistic and intimate image of numerous periods of life in both southern Italy and in America."

–*The Italian Tribune*

"Mario Dell'Olio is a well-connected first-generation American, but his Italian roots are evident, they are strong, and they emerge clearly in the story of a difficult yet unshakable love that accompanied the life of his parents."

–*L'Edicola del Sud*

"An American Story, told in a time of tumult, with love and laughter. Whether you trace your family to Italy, Ireland, or South Africa, this story hits home."

–*The Connecticut Post*

"A rich family story immersed in the history of Italy and the United States told with aesthetic beauty to make it the film of a lifetime, of many lifetimes, of the pursuit of happiness and opportunities."

–*Nuovo Quotidiano di Puglia*

Acknowledgments

Letters from Italy is a passion project—a story of family, love and adversity that flowed from my heart like no other tale possibly could. I could not have written it without the support of so many, and I must thank them all with adoration and admiration.

First, I thank my mother, Nicoletta, an Italian immigrant, who spent countless hours reading these letters to me, recounting stories long forgotten. Those precious moments together transported me back through time and into the hearts of both my parents. I came to know them more intimately than I could have dreamed. Nicoletta revealed a glimpse into their loving hearts.

To my sister, Maria Roberts: Your many readings of this manuscript transformed my words into a cohesive narrative that remains true to our shared history. Little did you know back when you proofed and typed my elementary school essays that you would take on such a pivotal role in writing our family history. You inspire me every day.

To my nephew, Matthew Roberts: Thank you for spending countless hours scanning, repairing, and editing old photographs. I know that it was a labor of love. The cover design you created truly captures this love story. From my first book to this very special project, your generosity of time and talent has been freely given. You have been with me every step of the way, with technical advice and artistic, creative design.

To Dr. Matthew Speiser: You have single-handedly convinced me that I am a writer. Your historical insights and suggestions greatly influenced the body of this work. Letters from Italy took its form largely due to your counsel and it is all the better for it. You were the first stop on my writing journey, you asked the difficult questions that prompted refinement, and you were fundamental to my process. I am grateful to count you as my friend.

To my dearest companions from Fairfield University, Eileen Pollack and Diana Filiano: I can't express how much I value your opinions, critical eyes, and encouragement. Life-long friends, you make me a better person by being in my life. To Anthony DeFilippis: Thank you for believing in me and being my biggest champion in getting Letters from Italy noticed.

To Bethany Ciullo and Joanne Paulson: Your editorial prowess and expertise helped me to see what my eyes could not. Your hands helped refine and shape this manuscript into a book.

To my Twitter family, who have followed me along this path and never allowed me to doubt my abilities, I can't thank you enough. The Writing Community Chat Show, Story of a Story Teller, Boomers on Books, The Shadow's Project, and my QueerIndie family have become a significant force in my literary experience. Thank you to Halo Scot, T.T. Banks, Ash Knight, A. C. Merkel, Christopher Aggett, Christopher Hooley, Conor Bredin, Tim Curry, and Vince Stevens.

A final note of thanks to my husband, Jim Alexander, for his continual support and love. Because of you I can honestly say that I understand the *immenso amore* that my parents shared. Your constant love and support in all my creative endeavors buoys my soul and lifts me to ever greater heights. There is no one else in the world with whom I'd rather sail life's storms.

Letters from Italy

"Amor, ch'a nullo amato amar perdona.
(Love, that exempts no beloved from loving in return.)"
–Dante Alighieri, *Inferno***, Canto 5, line 103**

Dell'Olio Family Tree

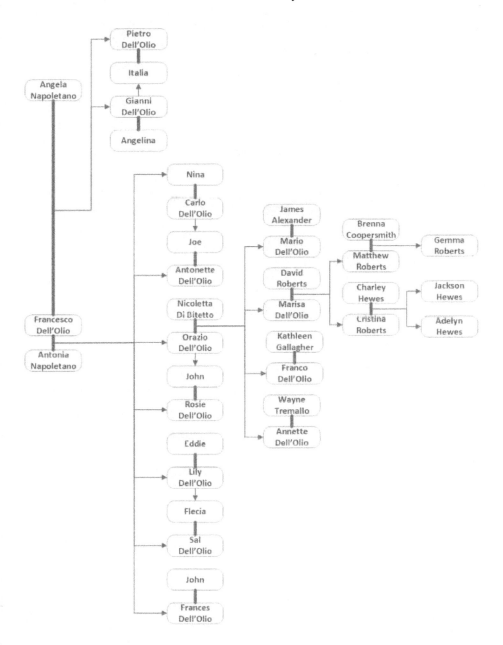

Di Bitetto Family Tree

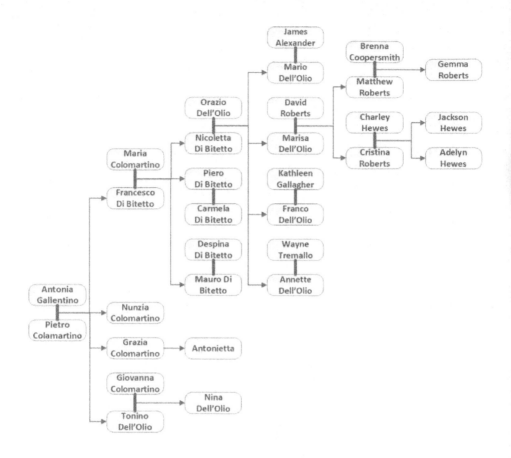

Introduction

I was brimming with anticipation. I had finally made it to the Greek island of Rhodes in search of information regarding my *Nonno* (grandfather). Mom had been sharing stories of him for as long as I could remember. His image loomed large in my imagination—a bigger-than-life hero in my mother's heart. The previous summer, Mom spent a week with us, during which I prompted her to tell me about herself as a child. I wanted to know more about our family history. She is the only one in her generation who has the presence of mind to remember, and fortunately, she has always told tales of her childhood in great detail. We have always given her a hard time when she would tell a story, any story. There were so many minute details and tangents that we would often lose the thread of the original anecdote. But not her, thirty minutes later, she would wrap it all up neatly, giving us an in-depth understanding of each character involved.

"Oh, wow, I had forgotten what you were talking about. How did you find your way back to the original story, Mom?" I'd say, laughing.

"Never mind," she'd say with playful annoyance. "Details matter!"

We have beautiful photos of both of her parents taken by professional photographers. One is of her mother, Maria, in a long dark dress with a white lace collar and a long necklace. The photo of Francesco, my grandfather, has him standing at an easel painting that very image of his wife. Mom's eyes sparkled when she would speak about him. There was reverence in her voice as she told us of his intelligence and artistry. I knew he had left their home in Italy and traveled to the Island of Rhodes in Greece to find work during the Italian occupation. To this day, there is little documentation regarding his death six years after his departure.

My husband and I vacationed in Turkey one summer and visited with friends in Marmaris. From there, the island of Rhodes is a short ferry ride away, and we took the opportunity to find where my grandfather worked.

Upon my return to New York, I visited my mother to tell her of my journey to Rhodes. Her memories sparked, and she pulled out a pile of letters that she and my father had written to one another during the early years of their courtship. Never having met, these letters told the history of my parents' relationship and the love that grew through the written word. The longing for a better life and dreams of a bright but uncertain future fill the pages. A family history unfolds as they came to know one another and fell in love.

The following years were filled with my mother reading their precious letters to me. Each line would spark more memories and tales of family drama. During those sessions, I got a glimpse into the eighteen-year-old girl whose dreams were well beyond her imaginings and the reality of her life in the small town of Bisceglie in southern Italy. I discovered that my father, who rarely showed emotion, was a hopeless romantic who swept Mom off her feet with his heartfelt poetry written on elegant stationery. Revealed in decades of oral history and now in letters long forgotten were tales of two idealistic dreamers that I had only ever known as Mom and Dad.

My mother had told me hundreds of stories, and before his death, my father did as well. Having both parents weaving yarns of our culture and heritage gave me an invaluable gift. I came to know Nicoletta and Orazio as individuals who grew up during the second world war, fought to survive in a country mired in economic ills, and took a leap of faith traveling thousands of miles to create a life in a foreign land. They learned a new language, worked in factories, starting from nothing as they built a new life together. They were Italian immigrants during the 1950s whose struggles and determination helped shape and form them into the parents who raised me and my three siblings. I discovered that there is so much more to who they were and are than what I experienced as their youngest child.

Through the letters to and from Italy, I tell their story. However, the story of immigrants seeking a better life in the land of opportunity is ubiquitous. Names and details change, but the dream remains the same. Taking tales I heard hundreds of times and placing them in history provided insight into the gravity of wartime, the horrors of Fascism and

Nazism. I found myself researching the causes of Italy's economic crises during the early twentieth century—trying to understand how a brutal dictator came to power and won the adulation of ordinary citizens. I learned more about my own country and the opportunities it offered to hungry immigrants as well as the prejudice and pitfalls they encountered by pursuing their dreams. Their story is immersed in the history of Italy and the United States. In learning about my parents' past, I've learned what it means to be a first-generation American and whose shoulders I stand upon.

In the following pages, I have recounted stories heard hundreds of times during my youth. As I have come to know my mother as an adult, many more stories have been revealed, some are painful to tell, but they are stories of flawed people trying to find their way in the world. They are stories of dark times obfuscated to protect the children and to keep the family together. These are stories of real people with all their flaws exposed. Through it all, there is one common thread—love.

Tina Dell'Olio reminiscing with the letters and holding her wedding album after reading the completed manuscript.

Letter One
The Beginning

New York City
Jan 4, 1950
Orazio to Tina
Dear Signorina,

I truly hope that you permit me to write to you because I feel in my heart that I am so in love with you. That is why I pray that you accept this dream of love that has yet to begin between us. I would be so proud to have you write to me.

I have written directly to your cousin, Antonietta, to ask for her permission, and I pray that you accept my declaration of love. You should know that I have always dreamed of having a beautiful girl from my hometown—and see how that destiny has come to pass. I would love to write many beautiful words, but I cannot, since this is the first time I write to you. I would love to have a family, and my dream is to buy a home here in New York—not an apartment. It would be filled with fine furniture, a radio, television, and many beautiful things one can find in America. So to fulfill my dream of love, I pray that you accept this profound love that is open to us both.

When you come to America, you will see that I will take you anywhere you like. There is little left for me to say. Please give my love to Nina, Carlo, and my loved ones.

I send you my cordial regards, your dear friend,
Orazio Dell'Olio

I hope that you will write to me soon and that you will send me a photograph of yourself—and tell me your name.

New York 4-1-950

Dear S. g.

Mi scusi se mi permetto
a scriverti perché sento
nel mio cuore che sono molto
Innamorato di Lei perció
la prego cara di accetare
questo sogno D'amore
che é nato fra noi
quel sono cosi fiero
di a essere scritta
da te sei una
scrivo diret-
tamente a
tua cugina
perché a
molto fiduicia
serso di

Chapter One
The First Photo—The Ask

Orazio's first letter to Nicoletta, January 1950
New York City

He saw her face for the first time in New York City. The photo fell out of the airmail envelope that came from his brother, Carlo. Orazio hadn't even read the letter when her smiling face entranced him. Walking beside his brother and his fiancée was a beautiful young woman. Her smile and joie de vivre came alive as if it jumped out of the photo from his hometown in Bisceglie. Without knowing who she was, he was utterly taken with her. There were two young men and three women walking arm in arm in the main *piazza*.

Gazing at the photo, memories of his childhood home flooded his mind. The girl from the photo looked awfully familiar, but he couldn't place her. He tried to picture her several years younger when a faded memory came into focus. Each evening after work, as he wound his way through the ancient city streets, Orazio would see her leaning out the window. She waited with pasta in hand until she spotted her brother coming down the road, at which point she would disappear into the apartment to throw the pasta into the boiling water. Each night he would watch her as he passed by, but if she caught his eye, he'd quickly look away. Though he desperately wanted to talk to her, he was too shy to act on his desire. He contented himself with seeing her beautiful face in hopeful anticipation. *Could this be the same girl at the balcony that I pined over as a teenager?* he wondered.

In an age when arranged marriages were no longer in vogue, he hoped it might work for him. After all these years, his mystery girl reappeared in the photograph Carlo just sent. It had to be a sign. He immediately grabbed paper and pen.

Dear Sister-in-law,

Congratulations on your engagement. As you know, I am Carlo's brother. The photo he sent includes a young woman. I believe I know her from my youth. I remember her waiting at her window for her brother to come home from work. Who is she? What is her name? Would you kindly ask her if I may write to her? She is beautiful, and I would like to correspond with her.

Cordially,

Orazio

He included a note for this beautiful young woman in his letter. Nina read his words and ran right over to her cousin Nicoletta's house.

"Here, look what you got from America. Read it. It's for you."

"Me? I don't know anyone from America. What are you talking about, Nina?" Nicoletta replied.

"It's Carlo's brother in New York. He saw your picture and wants to write to you. Read it for yourself."

"Why would I want to read that? I don't even know him!" Nicoletta said with annoyance.

"He knows you. He used to see you at the window, waiting for Piero."

"That's ridiculous! Why would I want to correspond with someone so far away? What could come of that? I'm not going to read that letter. You can take it back."

"Suit yourself, Nicoletta. I'll just leave the letter right here," she said as she placed it beside her. "You can do whatever you like with it. But don't be so rash. Just see what he has to say."

Nicoletta stared at the letter after Nina left and shook her head. *Why would I read a letter from a complete stranger?* she thought. But her inquisitive nature would not let her be. *What harm can come from simply reading it?* She was under no obligation to respond. Finally, her curiosity won out. She opened the letter and read Orazio's declaration of interest.

"I pray that you accept my declaration of love. You should know that I have always dreamed of having a beautiful girl from my hometown—and see how that destiny has come to pass."

Despite herself, his candor moved her. *He thinks I'm beautiful.* She folded the letter and inserted it back into the envelope, holding it in her hands as she gazed toward the window. Try as she might, Nicoletta could not conjure memories of this man. She ambled onto the balcony and placed her hand gently on the rail. *This was where he first noticed me,* she thought.

Carlo, Orazio's big brother, was very solicitous of Nicoletta when he learned of Orazio's interest. While she appreciated his constant attention, she was not willing to write to his brother just yet. One afternoon, Carlo brought her several photos of Orazio from New York City. He was so handsome, with a thick mane of black hair, smiling at the camera, the city skyline as his backdrop.

"Nicoletta, he's a nice boy and a hard worker. Trust me. Write him back."

She eventually relented. She wrote a formal letter of introduction and anxiously awaited his reply. She wasn't sure what she expected from him, but Nicoletta pictured that handsome photo of him and knew she had nothing to fear. Not long after, Carlo brought a photo album to introduce Nicoletta to the rest of the Dell'Olio family. She spotted a photo of a teenage boy and asked, "Who is he?"

"You silly girl, That's Orazio."

"But he looks so different," was all she could say.

This young man was a world away from the sophisticated man she saw in his recent photos. In New York City, he was dressed in a suit and tie. His thick black hair shimmered in the sun, and his smile was beaming—he looked like a fashion model. Whereas the photo before her was of a shy boy, seemingly afraid of his own shadow. Nicoletta scanned her memories and recalled seeing that handsome boy walking by each day. He passed by their house as she waited on the balcony for her brother, Piero, to come home from work. Although he seemed shy, he'd always pause to look up at her. She recalled thinking he was very sweet and gentle, not like so many other guys whose bravado steamrolled anyone in their way. No, Orazio was different.

As the memories washed over her, Nicoletta rested in her decision to correspond with this man in New York. Suddenly, he was familiar to her, no longer a stranger from a faraway place. He was the same boy who gazed at her from afar. Somehow, it seemed less crazy to write to him and carry on this love affair of words.

And so, this orphaned girl dared to dream. *Perhaps there are happy endings after all.*

The photograph that started it all. From left to right:
Carlo, Nina, Nicoletta, Carmela, Piero

Chapter Two
Francesco Di Bitetto

Bisceglie, Province of Bari, Italy 1938

Many years before that first letter arrived, Nicoletta looked to an uncertain future. Barkers at the fish market echoed boorishly under the stone canopies as her father, Francesco, stepped out of the house and walked into the crowd.

"Hey, Francesco, come. We have a beautiful baby octopus today. Maria will love it," a fishmonger called out.

"*Buon giorno*, Nicola. Maybe later, I have a few errands to run."

Francesco walked past the fish market and headed towards the main *piazza* to grab a cappuccino. A few blocks away, the narrow alleys of the southern Italian town opened to a spacious square surrounded by palm trees. The *piazza* was in the heart of the city where young lovers strolled and older folk gathered to visit. They held the annual carnival celebrating the patron saints of Bisceglie in the *piazza* every August. Colored lights were strung along the surrounding streets, and the aroma of delicious delights filled the air. Citizens of all ages packed the open space listening to live bands, tasting the focaccia from one of the many vendors, and treating themselves to creamy gelato.

But early that morning, the piazza was still. Francesco could barely hear the muted conversations as he strolled to his regular cafe. The usual crew of friends sat with furrowed brows at tiny tables discussing the economic problems of the country. Many of these men had lost jobs and were looking for work. Some had given up hope. Francesco joined the gathering and jumped into the conversation.

"We can't give up hope, friends. No, we must do whatever we have to do to support our families," he encouraged them.

"Don't you think we've been trying?" Enzo replied. "I've knocked on every factory door in the region. No one is hiring."

"Then, you must go farther—maybe up north."

"How can we do that? Mussolini's government has an anti-immigration policy. They don't want us *terroni* to take jobs away from the northerners," Enzo replied.

"No one pays attention to the law," Francesco said. "If there's a job, and you are qualified, they'll hire you. It's basic supply and demand."

"There you go, talking all that fancy garbage. So they hire us, then what? We live all by ourselves, far from home? Who wants to leave their wives and children to find a job?"

"No one wants to leave home, Enzo. But if the choice is between starvation and traveling for work, the solution is quite clear."

Jobs were scarce during the 1930s in southern Italy. Industry was slow to arrive in the provinces south of Rome. If one lived out in the country, there were vineyards and vegetable farms to work on. But in the cities and towns similar to Bisceglie, work was nowhere to be found. What made the economic hardship worse were the policies put in place by the fascist government of Benito Mussolini.

Mussolini's rise to power after World War I was swift and calculated. The elite ruling class refused to recognize the newly formed political parties and largely mismanaged the deterioration of the postwar economic crisis. A transition from a monarchy to a modern democracy might have mitigated the rise of nationalism. But Mussolini seized upon the discontent of ordinary citizens seeking a voice in their government. Mistrust of the ruling class exploded. Italy was left with massive economic debt as a result of the war. Although it emerged victorious, the government could not capitalize on that victory.

The massive redistribution of wealth was made possible through official contracts affecting smaller farms in rural areas. Many of Francesco's friends traveled to the industrial north, which experienced a boom for factory owners such as FIAT and Italy's largest steel producer, Ilva. But Francesco had no intention of giving up his trade to work in a factory. Besides, although the owners amassed great wealth, the ordinary worker and farmer suffered. Strikes, unlike any Italy had seen before, became commonplace. Disruption of business and lost wages worsened an already tenuous economic environment. After leaving family and friends in the south, many laborers found themselves without jobs once again. The socialist government was hesitant to intervene, which created a vacuum of power. The ordinary citizen, as well as business owners, sought a powerful voice to lead them forward. Mussolini was that voice.

Mussolini was a charismatic leader who rose through the ranks of the Italian military. Although Francesco mistrusted his fascist rhetoric, he hoped Mussolini would bring jobs back to his city. Instead, Mussolini fanned the flames of discontent and quickly gained a loyal following. Wearing black shirts, which became their distinctive uniform, squads of militia swept through the countryside, burning down union offices and terrorizing the local population in Puglia and the Po Valley. Extreme nationalism and anti-Bolshevism spread throughout the country. Local citizens of Bisceglie were terrified of what might happen to them if they spoke out against him and that shadow darkened their gathering at the café that morning.

During the early years of his reign as prime minister, Mussolini's popularity grew because of the establishment of order and work projects that employed many. However, his charisma was no match for intelligent economic policies. His bluster appealed to the nationalist sentiment. He spoke animatedly about a new Italian Empire, reminiscent of Ancient Rome. Initially, his conquests proved successful, and he caught the eye of an emerging political leader to the north. Hitler took note of Mussolini's rise to power, and a relationship was soon established.

Mussolini planned to reinvent southern Italy. He instructed the farmers to plow over the vineyards and olive groves to plant wheat, which didn't grow well in the local climate. Then in 1935, Italy invaded Ethiopia. The military action and slaughter of thousands of Ethiopians outraged countries around the world. The League of Nations responded with significant sanctions that sunk the Italian economy deeper into recession. The southern cities suffered the most unemployment, where skilled workers were not in high demand. There wasn't much new construction, let alone a need for artists. Men considered themselves fortunate if they gained jobs as day laborers. It wasn't uncommon for men to leave their homes and families to find work in other countries.

The despair that pervaded the recent conversations with his friends disheartened Francesco. He agreed that southern Italy was in rapid decline, but he would not give up hope. However, he had reached his limit in Bisceglie as well. Temporary work laying bricks had been sporadic, and he longed to use his sculpting skills and tap into his creative energy. As worrisome thoughts swirled in his mind, his feet took him to the seaport when he bid goodbye to his compatriots at the cafe. He always loved strolling along the water's edge. While the piazza was in the heart of the city, the port was the heartbeat. The ancient port had been the access point for centuries of foreign invaders, especially the Saracens. The Normans, who had ruled Bisceglie for over a hundred years, built two watchtowers to warn the villagers of an imminent attack. The town got its name from the Latin, *Vigiliae*, to keep vigil.

Port of Bisceglie, Bari

For generations, a seaport and fishing village, the local fishermen packed their wooden boats with nets and fishing gear before daylight. Each morning, a procession of brightly colored boats sailed out into the Adriatic Sea to capture a bit of its bounty. The local tradition was ages old, and little had changed over the years. It was mid-morning by the time Francesco arrived, and the fishermen had long since returned with their catch. He stood watching as they put their nets in order and rinsed the boats. *You can clearly see the Norman influence here in the port,* he thought, noticing the handsome faces and beautiful, clear eyes of the children playing. Families of fishermen were fair-skinned with green and blue eyes. Citizens of Bisceglie looked distinctly different from many other southern cities.

Gazing out at the port and the azure Adriatic Sea just beyond it, conflicting thoughts filled his mind. He felt a great affection for Bisceglie and its rich history, as he stood watching the daily routine of life on display before him. His heart ached for the rich history of their town but he knew that, although these traditions hadn't been altered in years, something had to change. In many ways, his hometown was stuck in a rut—progress had forgotten his tiny village. Francesco couldn't allow himself to do the same. He had to find a fresh way to make it in the world. He owed it to Maria and his children. As the sun rose higher in the sky and reflected on the placid water, he formed a plan for their future.

During the Italo-Turkish War in 1911, the Kingdom of Italy annexed the Dodecanese islands of the South Aegean Sea. By 1923, Italian control was firmly established. During the 1930s, Mussolini, developed an Italianization campaign for the former islands of the Ottoman empire. The island of Rhodes, now part of Greece, was the largest and most historically significant Dodecanese island. Its history dates back to ancient times, including legends of the Colossus of Rhodes; a statue of the Greek sun god, Helios was erected in 280 BCE. Although only the remnants remain, it is considered one of the seven wonders of the ancient world.

Mussolini's plan included the restoration of the ancient walled city, the construction of civic buildings, and Catholic churches. His campaign sought to promote tourism and economic growth. They needed Italian workers to build roads, schools, and churches. For so many Italians, Mussolini brought a sense of national pride. However, his campaign aimed to purify the island, eliminate the Greek language in favor of Italian.

Francesco Di Bitetto was a sculptor and artist who longed to work his craft once again. Tales of the idyllic beauty of Rhodes called to him. If the rumors of its booming economy were true, perhaps he could send for his entire family once he got his footing. Hope glimmered with the sun's rays on the sea before him. Francesco knew what he must do. He would leave his little town of Bisceglie in the Province of Bari, using his skills to build Roman Catholic Churches in Rhodes. Time away from Maria and the family would be a considerable sacrifice, but the promise of a brighter future would make the struggle worth it.

On June 18, 1938, he kissed his loving wife, Maria, goodbye and promised her he would be back as soon as he could. His oldest son, Mauro, was away serving in the Italian military, so he gently took his fourteen-year-old son by the shoulders.

"Piero, take care of your mother for me. You know she is not well, so it's up to you to make sure she is mindful of her health."

"Of course, *Papá*. Though I can never be as great a man as you, I will try to fill your shoes as best I can."

"You have always made me proud, Piero. Although," he laughed, "we nearly spent our entire budget trying to quench your enormous appetite." Francesco ruffled Piero's hair affectionately. "You've always worked hard to help our family. Now it's time to take the lead with your mother."

"Papá, Papá! Dové vai? Where are you going? Don't leave us?" His six-year-old daughter called out to him with her arms outstretched.

"Cara Nicoletta, ti amo, I love you, my beautiful girl. Don't worry, my angel, *Papá* will be back soon. Promise me that you will mind your Mamma and be a good girl," Francesco said as he kneeled down to the floor to hug and kiss her.

La Reginella, he called her—the little queen—and they treated her as such throughout her early childhood. Maria always dressed her in embroidered collars and bows in her hair. If she made a fuss about anything they denied her, Francesco would give in. He was strict about education and manners, but he was soft-hearted about his daughter's comforts. Francesco, enamored with classical music, attended concerts as often as possible. One evening, there was a performance of a Mozart symphony at *Il Teatro Garibaldi*. As he and Maria dressed, Nicoletta pleaded to let her come with them.

"*No, no cara Nicoletta, é troppo tardi per te*. It's much too late for you, dear one. Stay with your cousin, Antonietta. You don't want to leave her alone all evening, do you?" Maria said, trying in vain to persuade her to stay.

"No, *Mamma*, I want to come with you and *Papá*. You look so pretty, and I want to dress up too!" she whined.

"But it is not a show, *carina*. There won't be any other children there to play with. They will simply play music, and it will bore you," Francesco tried to reason with her.

"*Voglio venire!* I want to come with you," she said as she crossed her arms and curled her lip. Then she ran into the other room.

"Now, she is upset. Perhaps we should bring her along. I can hold her when she falls asleep," Francesco suggested.

"She'll be fine at home, *caro*. Just let her be, and she will get over it," Maria said. She was used to Nicoletta demanding her own way. Not wanting to spoil her, Maria continually set boundaries for her daughter. But Nicoletta was Daddy's little girl—he hated to see her cry.

A few minutes later, she entered her parents' bedroom, donned in her pretty new dress, and a hair-band with a pink rose on it. Her cousin, Antonietta, followed directly behind her.

"What can we do with her? She is unstoppable," Antonietta apologized both hands raised in surrender.

Francesco turned to Maria. "She'll get over it, eh?" Then he kneeled on the floorboards, placed his hands around her face and said, "*La mia Reginella,* my little queen, you look beautiful tonight. Of course, you can come to the concert with us. But you must promise to sit quietly and listen to the music; no crying or talking. *Hai capito?* Do you understand?"

"*Si, Papá, Si!*"

He adored that little girl with his whole heart. Nicoletta was their miracle baby. There was a seven-year difference between Piero and Nicoletta. Their eldest child, Mauro, was fifteen years older than she. Nicoletta adored her father, and she wanted nothing more than to please him—well, that and going to the concert that evening. She sat looking up at him, imitating his every reaction as he nodded his head with the beat of the music. Not long into the program, Nicoletta's eyelids grew heavy, and rather than nod her head to the music, she nodded into a contented sleep in her father's lap. His hand stroked her hair as he looked at his little queen adoringly.

His heart ached with the knowledge of what lay ahead for him. Images of his little girl and his loving wife danced in his head as he walked home from the port that morning. He had made his decision. They would come to realize it was for the best. Maria and Francesco had always been equal partners in their marriage. Working together to build their life, they stood apart from many of Bisceglie's small-minded people. He knew she would support his idea and do all that she

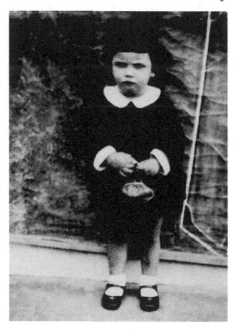

Nicoletta at age three

could to keep the family together while he was away. They would have a long, happy life together. His journey to Rhodes was only the beginning of their dreams for the future.

A few short weeks later, Francesco's departure was upon them. Amber rays of the sunrise colored the sandstone *Torre Normani*, the Norman Towers that distinguished Bisceglie from the other towns along the Adriatic coast of southern Italy. Maria and Piero solemnly walked to the port to see him off. She spied the fishing boats lined up and ready to go. The fishermen were barking commands at each other and their helpers. Everything appeared ordinary, but Maria knew it was anything but. She spotted the large ship that was to take her beloved to a distant land, and she sighed. Looking beyond at the beautiful, clear water of the sea, she thought,

"You have deceived me. Oh, beautiful Adriatic, you always brought me peace and comfort, but now you will take my Francesco away."

She knew that he had no choice and that he would suffer their time apart as much as she. She realized they could not survive without his income and, as was her way, she stoically accepted their fate. However, her heart ached at the thought of being apart. It was in June 1938. Francesco had gone with his luggage to board the ship earlier that morning. Maria and Piero, drew near to the dock with Nicoletta hand in hand with her cousin, Antonietta, just a few steps behind. When she spotted Francesco, his broad smile radiated his love. His expression changed when he noticed that Nicoletta was with them. He had expressly asked that she stay home. Normally, she'd still be asleep at this early hour. His departure was going to be challenging enough. Maria understood that saying goodbye to his little queen would be heart-wrenching. She knew that seeing their daughter cry might make him question his decision to leave and melt away his resolve. But Nicoletta was insistent and, Maria agreed that they should all be together at the port to bid him goodbye. Those last moments together as a family were precious, and each of them would carry the memories in their hearts forever.

Finally, the captain called for passengers to board the ship, transforming the almost festive atmosphere at the dock. Francesco looked deeply into Maria's eyes. Few words were necessary. As they embraced, he whispered in her ear.

"Sei il mio immenso amore. Ti amo, Maria." You are my great love, Maria.

With tears in her eyes, she kissed him on both cheeks and turned him to his children. Piero's face was stoic, but his eyes showed fear. Francesco pulled him into his arms.

"I am very proud of you, Piero. Take care of your mother and Nicoletta."

At six years old, his little girl had no sense of the finality of their goodbye. Nicoletta was filled with excitement as she watched her father embark and waved the white handkerchief in her hand. The dock was full of families and friends waving to their loved ones on the departing ship. People were shouting words of encouragement, wishing good luck, and some sang love songs. Once onboard, Francesco leaned against the rail and waved at his family.

Nicoletta shouted, *"Papá, Papá, arrivederci, Papá!"*

In her exuberance, she was totally unaware of her surroundings. When her handkerchief slipped from her grasp, she instinctively leaned over the dock and reached out to catch it. Panic transformed her smiling face as she lost her balance and began to fall. Francesco watched the entire scene play out from the deck of the ship. There was no guardrail to keep her from falling into the rocky water below.

"Nicoletta!" he shouted.

Just then, Piero reached out to grab her arm and pulled her to safety. Realizing what had almost happened, she began to cry in her brother's arms. With tears streaming down her face, she continued to wave goodbye to her father as the ship pulled away from the dock.

Francesco thought to himself, *this couldn't have been worse.* His heart was already broken in two but ached all the more at the realization that there was little he could do to protect his family, even from such a short distance. He'd soon be hundreds of miles away—even less able to help them. As the waving handkerchiefs faded in the distance, Francesco slowly walked away from the deck and made his way to the cabin. Shaking his head, he tried to convince himself that he was doing the right thing.

"I have to provide for my family. There is nothing in Bisceglie for me but an occasional job laying bricks, and nothing where I can use my craft. All the churches were built centuries ago; they don't need a sculptor. I can't sit around and wait for people to die in order for me to carve gravestones. This is the right thing to do, and if Rhodes is as beautiful as they say, I will send for the entire family."

His departure ripped Maria's heart in two. The two of them were not merely husband and wife. No, they were best friends who shared a similar vision of life. They stood out in Bisceglie as a forward-thinking and educated couple. Even her own sisters espoused the small-town mentality that held them back from any progress. What would she do without her soulmate? She was acutely aware of the poor state of her own health and worried that something would happen to her while Francesco was away. However, Maria always trusted his judgment. Rationally, she understood this move was the right thing to do, and she certainly wouldn't be the only woman in Bisceglie whose husband had left to find work. Maria, determined to put on a brave face, resolved to support Francesco in every way she could. Although her eyes welled, she wouldn't allow one tear to fall. She smiled her most radiant smile so that his parting memory of her would be filled with happiness.

When the ship faded into the sea, she turned to her children and smiled.

"Your father has begun a grand adventure. What wonderful stories he will share upon his return."

She took Nicoletta's hand in hers and put her arm around Piero's shoulder. He'd grown as tall as she. *When had that happened?*

"Come, let's take a walk to the *piazza*. I think we all deserve a pastry. What do you say?"

Nicoletta squealed with delight. Piero and Antonietta gave Maria a sympathetic glance as they headed away from the port. Although she wore a smile on her face, the tears brimming in her eyes revealed her broken heart.

Francesco Di Bitetto

Maria Colamartino

Letter Two
Letter from Rhodes

Francesco to Maria
Island of Rhodes, Greece, 1938
Cara Maria,
My dearest and ardent love, yesterday your long-anticipated letter arrived. I was so pleased and happy to hear about the good news. I hope that you continue to feel better. Please be scrupulous in your care. Do whatever you must do to continue healing, no matter the cost. The price is irrelevant when it comes to you, my love. Please don't worry about that.

Be sure to eat your meals and drink warm liquids to help with digestion and revitalize your bronchial passages. It will also calm the nerves when you have your asthma attacks. Hopefully, it will help you sleep more peacefully.

I want you to enjoy your life rather than continue to suffer. We must have patience and goodwill, and as you said, we need to remain positive in our intent to become healthy. I hope you maintain your positive attitude so that little by little, you will be completely healed.

Anyway, I understand you must have intravenous injections. Just do as the doctor advises and don't dwell on it—I'm sure it will go well. Ask for a bit of cognac or marsala with a beaten egg to give you strength. Think only of getting well.

Meanwhile, my love, I am doing quite well. One hopes that it will be the same for all of you as well. Please don't fret should my letters be late. It has been taking nine days for yours to arrive. I can assure you because we can see the passage of the steamships that travel to Italy.

It seems that I will have plenty of work this winter. Let's hope this helps us move forward to a better position—or at least that I'll earn enough to maintain our lives. Either way, I am content, and know it will turn out well.

And so, Maria, we must stay balanced—that will lift us up, my dearest. I am pleased to hear of Piero, whose unexpected surprises and success move beyond our imaginings.

My love, when you can, please send me photographs of you and the children. Give my love to the Mastrototaro family. Much love to you and our dear children, to Antonietta and her fiancé, and your dear father and mother.

Infinite hugs.

Yours for life and in faith,

Francesco

Chapter Three
Love Lost

Bisceglie, Province of Bari, Italy 1939

M ussolini's government campaigned to get Italian citizens to move and work in the territories or countries he invaded. Like many of his compatriots, Francesco took to Rhodes immediately. The Italian expatriates called it the *Island of the Roses* because of its incomparable beauty. Conveniently, Maria had a cousin who lived in Rhodes. He and his family took Francesco in and gave him a genuine sense of home. There was a large Italian community in Rhodes, and he felt quite comfortable in the island's "little Italy." In many ways, the historic center of Rhodes reminded him of life in Bisceglie. Surrounded by the warm Mediterranean Sea, there was a vibrant fishing industry, even more so than back home.

With so many Catholic Italians on the occupied island of Rhodes, there was a need for Roman Catholic churches for the many expatriates. St. Francis church was one of the first built during the Italian occupation, and his work there would last years. Francesco was confident that there would be many more opportunities to use his craft after they completed construction of the church. He believed that Rhodes had a great need and appreciation of his work. At long last, he felt like an artist again, and prospects for the future looked bright.

Francesco was firm in his resolve. He wrote to Maria as often as he could. Francesco kept his promise and laced the pages with dreams of their future together. He wrote poems to express his deep love and described how his heart ached for her. And the letters he received from Maria were his sustenance keeping his heart full of thoughts of his *immenso amore*. Unlike most of his friends and family members whose marriages were arranged, he had married for love. Maria was his best friend. They loved spending time together and exploring new ideas. Neither of them bought into the old-world views and traditional practices that were pervasive in Bisceglie. Together they discussed medicine, politics, and social issues. Though he was a sculptor by trade, both he and Maria enjoyed intellectual debate. They were never convinced by the ancient superstitions or gave into the town gossip. When acquaintances in Bisceglie saw him, they addressed him as *Dottore* (Doctor.) They were one of the most respected young couples in Bisceglie.

During an age when it was unthinkable to use artificial contraception, Maria and Francesco kept their own counsel. They would have children when they were ready—not before. Theirs was a happy marriage, and they decided to enjoy each other's company as a couple before becoming parents. When they started a family, they happily anticipated the birth of their first child.

However, Maria's first pregnancy with Mauro was difficult. She was often ill or bedridden, and the labor and birth left her weakened. Not long after he was born, she developed debilitating asthma that plagued her throughout her brief life. With each pregnancy, her condition worsened. Infant mortality rates were high during those years, and their experience did not differ from many other parents. Many couples tried to keep an emotional distance from their newborns until their survival seemed more secure. But in reality, that was nearly impossible to do. Between Mauro and Piero, four more children were born, all of whom died within their first year of life.

There were twin boys, one who lived only three weeks while the other fought with determination for eleven months. Although they knew that his survival was tenuous, they had bonded with him. They reveled in his first solid food, his bright eyes, and his infectious laugh. So, his death was even more difficult to bear. She had two girls that were born between 1920 and 1923. Decades later, Nicoletta's nephew found the death certificate in her brother Mauro's effects and learned that one of them was named Nicoletta.

Each birth left Maria more and more fragile, so, after Piero's birth, she and Francesco began to use birth control once again. It was the only way to safeguard her health and her life. Of course, they were sure to keep that private because it would have been a scandal in the little town of Bisceglie. When she became pregnant with Nicoletta seven years later, it was a worrisome surprise. Francesco was concerned throughout her pregnancy. He worried that Maria's fragile body would not survive the birth of her seventh child. Thankfully, she managed the pregnancy with better health than either of them had expected. Nicoletta was born with no complications, and Maria weathered the labor without an asthmatic attack. It was a good omen, and they looked adoringly at their new baby girl. That Nicoletta grew strong and survived her infancy was a miracle to Maria and Francesco. Although it wasn't evident during her labor, Maria's lungs became even weaker.

Maria and Francesco savored their time with Nicoletta. Daddy's little girl was spoiled, and they enjoyed every minute. Maria finally had a girl whom she could dress up with lace and bows in her hair. With both of her boys years older, she relished every moment with Nicoletta. Those years passed all too quickly, and the economic woes of the country weighed heavily on their family. Walking away from the port after Francesco's departure, Maria knew that life would never be the same.

In his weekly letters, Francesco painted an idyllic scene of life on the beautiful island of Rhodes. He regaled her with dreams of a home on the shore with olive groves and fruit trees dotting the land surrounding their own little hamlet. He poured his love into the letters he wrote, and hope dripped from their pages. The money he sent was substantial, and she maintained their comfortable life in his absence. Even so, she felt the strain of raising a teenaged boy and a demanding seven-year-old girl.

Antonietta was a tremendous help to her, but she was still quite young and lacked the sophistication Maria and Francesco shared. There were no chats about politics or philosophy, nor could they reminisce over their shared history. Although she raised Antonietta as her own after her mother died, she and Maria didn't share a similar mindset. Antonietta never attended school and was pure old-time Bisceglie harboring fears and superstitions that were as extreme as the older generations. Maria missed the intellectual stimulation of her husband. But most of all, she missed his companionship. The letters they wrote to each other were the only comfort to her loneliness.

The added responsibility and stress of raising her family alone took a toll on Maria's health. Her asthma flared up more frequently, and she was often bedridden. Antonietta took over most of the household tasks, caring for Nicoletta as best as she could. Throughout the months that followed Francesco's departure, Maria relentlessly battled her weakening body. However, in March 1939, only nine months after Francesco left for Rhodes, Maria suffered a debilitating asthma attack.

"Antonietta, help me," Maria cried, trying in vain to gasp for air as she leaned against a chair. Her niece reached her just before Maria fell to the floor.

"Zia, I've got you. Come, come to the bed. You must rest," Antonietta said.

Seven-year-old Nicoletta froze at the sight of her mother falling as she wheezed.

"Nicoletta, my child," Maria began before losing strength. She could see the fear in her daughter's eyes.

"Don't worry, Nicoletta," Antonietta said. "Your *Mamma* just needs to rest. Go out and play. I've got her."

Nicoletta knew better. She had seen her mother struggle to breathe before. Somehow, she could see that this episode was severe, lasting much longer than usual. Tears filled her eyes as she watched from a distance.

With Antonietta tending to her mother, there was no one to comfort her or to calm her fears.

Maria was bedridden for weeks, and with her weakened lungs, she soon developed pneumonia. Antonietta acted as a nurse and caretaker. She sat for hours with her after Nicoletta had gone to bed, reading to her and telling her the day's news. She knew that Maria loved to hear stories about her little cherub, Nicoletta, so Antonietta would fill her in on the latest drama in her young daughter's life.

But Maria's health continued to deteriorate. Rather than recovering, she felt herself slipping further into her malady. The weight upon her chest was crushing—she found it difficult to speak without wheezing. Her lungs felt as if they were on fire. One night, sensing that her time was limited, Maria reached out from her bed and called to Antonietta. It was late at night, yet the family had gathered in a death watch. Antonietta flew to her side. Maria took her hand in her own and squeezed it tightly. With a whisper of a voice, she spoke.

"Antonietta, promise me you will take care of my Nicoletta," she said, pleading with her.

"Zia, of course, I always look out for her. You know that," Antonietta assured her.

"No, *figlia*, my child, I mean when I am gone. You must promise me that you will take my place."

"Zia, what are you saying?" And although she feared it was not true, she continued. "You will recover, you'll see. I know that you will be up and about in no time. Please don't talk like that—it's bad luck. You're scaring me."

"No, Antonietta, this time is different. I feel the heaviness in my chest. My breathing becomes more and more shallow with each passing hour. Please, promise me that you will be her mother just as I became yours. Love her as if she was your own. Please, Antonietta, promise me."

"Zia, I can never express the gratitude and love I feel for you and Zio Francesco. You are the only mother that I really know. You opened your home and your family to me when I was only six years old. More than that, you opened your hearts to me. I have never felt more loved by anyone; I need you to understand that."

Maria nodded her head in reply as a single tear fell from her eye. Antonietta continued as she wept silently.

"Zia, I love Nicoletta as if she were my own child. She means everything to me. I think you know that. I promise you she will feel as loved as I have by you and Zio Francesco."

Maria closed her eyes as a soft smile spread across her face, and for the first time in weeks, her breathing seemed less labored. Relieved, Antonietta hoped she would finally have a more restful night. But soon, fear took hold as she gazed at Maria. Moments later, with her hand still clasped between Antonietta's, Maria let out one final labored breath. A hush came over the room. Maria was gone at only 44 years of age.

Antonietta stared in shocked silence, immobilized by her sadness. Grasping Maria's hand, still warm to the touch, she held it to her heart. Then she lay her head on Maria's chest and wept.

Not long after, Maria's body was dressed and laid in state on her very own bed. Family members milled around, each stopping at her bedside to say a prayer. Nicoletta wandered from person to person, not knowing what to do. Everyone was so consumed with their own grief that no one took notice of this newly orphaned girl. Finally, *Papa Nonno*, her grandfather, caught her eye.

"My poor little one. We have lost our shining star, and all seems dark right now," he said as he pulled her into a hug. Nicoletta clung to him and her tears finally came. After she calmed, he took her face in his hands. With his thumbs, he wiped the tears from her cheeks.

"Have you gone to see your mother?" he asked.

Silently, she shook her head.

"You're afraid, aren't you? Come, I will go with you," he said as he took her hand.

The rest of the family made way, and Nicoletta and *Papa Nonno* stood at Maria's bedside. He looked down at his daughter's pale, lifeless face. As tears filled his eyes, he looked to the heavens and cried.

"Why, why did you take this young girl's mother, oh God? Why not take me? I am an old man—I have lived my life. How could you leave this child alone? How could you be so cruel?"

Nicoletta looked up at *Papa Nonno's* grief-stricken face. She had never seen him cry. She turned to him and hugged him around his legs. Placing his hand on her head, he whispered, "Sweet child." Clinging to one another, their anguish consumed them as they wept at Maria's bed side.

Antonietta poured all her sorrow into caring for Nicoletta. There was nothing she wouldn't do for that child. She held her close to her bosom and stroked her hair when she cried for her mother. Antonietta tried in vain to explain death to her seven-year-old cousin when she herself could not make sense of it. She would tuck Nicoletta in at night and calm her fears. She cooked her favorite meals and attended to her every need. Antonietta's love and affection engulfed Nicoletta in warmth and security. There was not a moment when she thought of herself first. Antonietta's first thought was always for Nicoletta. In return, Nicoletta attached herself to her cousin as a child to her mother. No one could fill the void, but Antonietta's love poured endlessly into the empty space Maria left.

On the day of Maria's funeral, there was a torrential rainstorm. The raindrops were as big as grapes, and the gusts of wind blew their umbrellas inside out. Maria's younger sister, Nunzia, was beside herself, crying uncontrollably. She was very close to Maria, more so than her older sister Giovanna. The capacity for love in Nunzia's was rivaled only by her sense of humor. She loved to joke and laugh and was a spitfire with a playful, mischievous side. Nunzia never understood the point of going to school, and as a result, she never learned to read or write. She relied on Maria to handle all practical matters concerning her household, especially the bills. Maria even wrote letters to Nunzia's husband, Pepino, when he was working in Tripoli.

"What would you like me to tell him, Nunzia?" Maria would inevitably ask.

"You know how I feel. Just tell him what you would say to Francesco," Nunzia replied.

"Oh, come now, Nunzia. That's ridiculous! They should be your words—he's *your* husband."

"I don't have fancy words like you. Write, go ahead. I know Pepino will love it," she responded with finality.

Nunzia believed Maria knew her heart better than she herself. When Maria died, it seemed that Nunzia died as well. Maria was a part of her.

In the pouring rain, Nunzia sobbed. Perspiration mingled with the water as it dripped from her forehead. Wailing, she ran after the coffin as the funeral procession made its way down the boulevard toward the cemetery. There were scores of mourners, but none felt Maria's death more deeply than she. Nunzia was barely aware of anything other than her heart-wrenching grief.

After the interment, she trudged back to Maria's house with the rest of the mourners. The heavy rain soaked Nunzia through to her undergarments, but she didn't have a change of clothes. She shed the water-laden black dress from her shaking body and slipped into Maria's bed. She breathed in Maria's scent as she buried her face in the pillow to cry. The house was full of family and friends, but she paid them no mind. Nunzia let her tears flow until she drifted into a bone-weary sleep. She stayed there for days—wouldn't leave the house because she wanted to be close to Maria. All the while, she continued to sob woefully.

Just a few days later, Nunzia caught a severe cold, which eventually developed into pneumonia. Still, she wouldn't leave Maria's bed or her house. She took to Maria's same sickbed, and almost died of the same ailment as her sister. It was only after she recovered that she returned to her own home.

Seven-year-old Nicoletta was in shock. At fourteen, Piero worried that he would never be able to fill his father's shoes. Antonietta had been caring for Maria, Piero, and Nicoletta for years. At the age of six, she had been orphaned when Maria's sister Graziella died suddenly from an aneurysm. Maria had been her mother figure longer than her very own mother and Antonietta suffered her death as intensely as her cousins did. It was as if she had lost her mother for the second time. Seeing Nicoletta's grief was like watching her younger self suffering, trying to make sense of losing a parent. Her heart ached all the more. Now, with both Maria and Francesco gone, her life was completely altered. Antonietta found herself caring for a teenage boy and a little girl as she battled her grief.

Francesco trusted Antonietta fully and gave her the same authority as Maria had concerning raising Nicoletta. He left all decisions to her; in Francesco's absence, she was the head of the household. He knew she was engaged, and that she had to prepare for her new life as a wife and mother. Francesco treated Antonietta as a daughter rather than a niece. As an adoptive parent, he instructed her to buy whatever she needed to build her trousseau. He sent money to pay for her wedding, and any other expense she had. This was Antonietta's family now, but she never expected the level of his generosity. Francesco was fully aware of the magnitude of her new role and the responsibility with which he entrusted her. She was only twenty-two years old; her married life was just about to begin, and she already had a family to take care of.

Antonietta took her role seriously. Just as her Zia Maria had raised her after her mother's untimely death, she would step in and become a mother to Nicoletta. Maria had taught Antonietta how to be a nurturing parent while setting appropriate boundaries and teaching proper manners. From Maria, she had learned to cook and how to keep a clean home.

In actuality, Antonietta was even more meticulous than Maria. The terrazzo floors sparkled after she had finished sweeping them and washing them down with a mop. There was not a speck of dust on any piece of furniture, and she made the beds so tightly that a coin could bounce on their surfaces. It was her duty to teach Nicoletta how to care for her household properly.

Letter Four
Letter from Rhodes to Nicoletta

Island of Rhodes, Greece, December 1942

Nicolettina, my dearest daughter,

I realize that it's difficult to be apart, especially now that your beautiful mother has passed on. Know that I hold you in my heart each and every moment. Your bright spirit and zest for knowledge remind me of your mother during her younger days. She is always with you, Nicoletta, watching over you in all you do. Please do not spend too much time grieving her loss because you know that she is with God, and both she and God are watching over you and protecting you. Always behave as if they were right beside you.

My wish for you is that you grow up to be respectful and obedient, and that you study and strive beyond what is expected of you. I hope you will feed your fertile mind with as much knowledge as possible. You are a smart and inquisitive young girl. May you never lose your intellectual curiosity, no matter what life may bring to you.

Make the family proud and be obedient to your aunts and school teachers. If you do that, both your mother and I will always be proud of you.

A huge hug and kiss,

Papá

Chapter Four
Grief and Loss

Rhodes, Greece • Bisceglie, Bari, Italy 1939

When the news of Maria's death reached Francesco, he was overwhelmed with grief. Guilt over having left during the last months of her life washed over him like ice water. For days he could not leave his room. The cousins he lived with begged him to join them at the dinner table, but he was inconsolable. *What more is there to live for? Maria is my life,* he thought as he read through her letters again and again. Pulling yet another letter from an envelope, something fell to the floor. He reached down absentmindedly to pick it up—a photograph of Nicoletta with an enormous bow in her hair smiled back at him.

Through his tears, he realized that he did have a purpose, a reason to live. His little girl, though well cared for, was left far away with no mother or father. Nicoletta brought him and Maria great joy during her brief life. Gazing at the photo through watery eyes, he could see Maria's features staring back at him dressed with a precocious smile. A single tear dropped to the picture. Bringing it to his heart, he resolved to bring the family together as soon as possible.

Antonietta begged him to return to Bisceglie, and he considered leaving Rhodes. However, in 1939, the economic landscape had worsened due to the deteriorating political climate in Europe. Francesco needed to earn enough money to carry the family through the hardship of the subsequent years. He committed to working extra hours and save all that he could.

Shortly after Maria's death, their oldest son, Mauro, who was serving in the Italian military, asked for a transfer to Rhodes. Francesco was thrilled to have Mauro nearby. Together, they comforted each other in their grief. At nineteen, Mauro was optimistic and adventurous. During their time together in Rhodes, they looked toward the future, and a different plan emerged.

"When will you return to Bisceglie, *Papà*?"

"I've been in Rhodes for more than a year, Mauro. Nicoletta and Piero need their father. I have to make a move soon."

"You shouldn't delay too long. The rumors coming from my commander is that the war in Europe is escalating. Hitler and Mussolini are already rather friendly."

"A fact that will be the ruin of our country," Francesco said bitterly.

"That may be so, but what other option do we have? The rest of the world is against us as well. Ever since Italy invaded Ethiopia, they have isolated us."

"Exactly," Francesco added. "Why should we go back to Bisceglie, where there are no jobs and little hope for our future? Life in Rhodes is good. The island prospers, and there is no lack of work. Perhaps we should remain here, start a new life."

"Sounds like an exciting plan, *Papà*. But won't you miss Bisceglie?"

"To be quite honest with you, son, I can't bear the thought of returning to our home without your mother. Every corner of our little town is imbued with memories of her. It would be a constant reminder that she is gone. I just can't bear it."

"I'm sorry, *Papà*. But the family will be furious with you if we stay here."

"Let them be angry. Such small-minded people, they never fully understood Maria and me. It would be better for all of us to have some distance."

"Then we should look for a home here in Rhodes," Mauro said with excitement.

"As soon as I save enough money, I will bring Nicoletta and Piero to live here. We will start fresh in Rhodes."

However, when Italy entered the Second World War, Francesco had to halt his plan to unite the family in Rhodes. Communication was slower and travel nearly impossible. When Mussolini and Hitler became allies, there was a sense of impending doom. No one had any idea what was to become of the country they loved. While citizens of the south knew that

Mussolini was a Fascist dictator, he had brought much-needed change to the impoverished region. He made schooling mandatory, built roads and improved the infrastructure. By contrast, the Italians knew of Germany's brutal leader and could see nothing positive about his alliance with Mussolini.

The Nazi troops soon occupied both southern Italy and Greece. The supply chain crumbled, making food and sundry items scarce. Life became even more difficult for the impoverished southern towns. Still, Francesco held onto his dream of uniting his family. He continued to write to Nicoletta to maintain their intimacy and strengthen the relationship with his young daughter. His heart ached to see her again, but they would have to wait out the war.

In the meantime, Francesco committed himself to his daughter's continued studies in Bisceglie. After Maria's death, he kept in touch with Nicoletta's elementary school teacher. She had written to him telling of Nicoletta's significant progress and that she was well ahead of her classmates. She informed Francesco of her intention to have Nicoletta skip the fifth grade and advance her to the sixth grade.

Francesco was so proud of his intelligent little girl. *How proud Maria would have been*, he thought. They made plans for Nicoletta to move ahead in the following years and eventually continue her education in an Italian school in Rhodes. Sadly, none of that would come to pass.

Mussolini's pact with the Axis powers brought Italy into the Second World War in 1940. Francesco's hope to have Nicoletta and Piero join him in Rhodes was delayed indefinitely. Continued conflict with Greece and the former Yugoslavia brought military action to southern Italy. The military transformed a former middle school in Bisceglie into an army hospital. Any students who wanted to continue their education beyond elementary school had to take the train to Bari. It was a forty-five-minute ride to the station, followed by a lengthy walk to the school. That was the moment the sun set on Nicoletta's bright academic future. Only eleven, she could not travel so far on her own, especially in wartime.

Francesco wrote letters to Nicoletta religiously, and in her responses, she asked for advice and sought his counsel. His letters reminded Nicoletta of his expectations of proper behavior. Even though he was not physically present to guide her education, he needed his daughter to know that he was there to help. Without Maria to guide her through her studies, it was up to him to push her forward. Knowing that no one at home could help with her homework, he took it upon himself to do so. In each letter he wrote, Francesco enclosed Nicoletta's previous communication complete with grammatical corrections and comments on her writing. Nicoletta had a passion for learning from an early age. She poured over each returned letter as if it were a corrected essay handed back by a beloved teacher. She loved to see his handwriting superimposed upon hers. It was a symbol of their bond—his script laced over hers was as if he was holding her hand with their fingers intertwined. If they couldn't be together physically, at least they'd be together in her letters.

Antonietta and her mother's sisters tried to fill the void that her parents had left. Nicoletta's favorite was dish *ceci e riso* (chickpeas with rice.) Her two aunts, Zia Giovanna and her favorite, Zia Nunzia, cooked that dish once a week. They made sure to prepare it on separate days so that she would have *ceci e riso* three times a week. Nicoletta was a delightfully spoiled child before her mother died. The little queen was quite picky about her food. Bread was obviously a staple at each meal, but Nicoletta liked only the crispy crust. She pulled out pieces of the loaf's soft white center, rolled them up into little balls, and hid them under the furniture. She hung her head in unrepentant shame when Antonietta discovered the hardened bread balls. Not only was she being wasteful, she messed up Antonietta's clean house.

Nicoletta—First Communion

Up to the age of seven, Nicoletta experienced a privileged life. Her family was well to do and highly respected. Francesco and Maria spoke only the formal Italian. They attended concerts, opera, and went to the theater. The memory of her mother posing for a portrait was imprinted in her mind. Maria wore a beautiful dark gown with a white lace collar and three-quarter length sleeves. She looped a pearl choker around her neck with a glimmering chain of gold that draped down to her waist, where a precious stone hung in its pendant. In her right hand was a luxurious leather purse. Nicoletta dreamed of growing up to be just like her. As the youngest child and only girl, she was treated like a star. She was used to getting anything she wanted, as long as she behaved and used proper manners.

All of that changed when the Second World War began. The relative wealth and comfortable lifestyle that she enjoyed ceased. Francesco could no longer send money from Rhodes, and the rationing of food was a heavy burden to bear. Piero, a growing teenager, returned from working long hours each day ravenous with hunger. Nicoletta adored her brother, who showered her with great affection. When she looked at his weary face, Nicoletta wanted nothing more than to ease his burden. She took only a fraction of her portion of food and gave up her ration of bread so that Piero would have enough to satisfy himself. During those years, they began to take care of each other in the only ways they knew how.

Antonietta often sent Nicoletta to the local grocery store to get their rations. There was little she hated more, but she understood Antonietta was doing all that she could to keep the family together. With the coupons in hand, she walked hesitantly to the *Alimentari* (grocery store). From a block away, she could see the crowd lined up outside the store and slowed her pace, delaying the inevitable. In 1940, she was only nine years old as she stood amid the agitated locals vying for the remnants of the precious food they sought. She took her place in line, and by the time she passed through the doors of the cramped store, the crowd overwhelmed her. Many of the older men would tease her or try to take advantage of her youth by pushing her to the back of the line. They towered over her—at eye level, she could only see their enormous bellies and hairy arms. Hearing their booming voices as they joked and gossiped made the already cramped space feel claustrophobic. The smoke-filled store made her feel as if she would choke, but worst of all was smelling their foul breath and body odor. There seemed to be no escape. However, every now and again, the patron would spot her and chide the other customers.

"Watch what you're doing! You're going to crush her, the poor thing. Come, come to the front, little one. What can I get for you?"

On those days, Nicoletta would feel relief wash over her like a cool breeze on a summer's day. The patron had rescued her from all these old buffoons. Nicoletta handed in her ration coupon and collected the meager allowance it gave her. Fleeing out the door as quickly as she could, Nicoletta turned and scowled at the boorish men before making her way back home.

Letter Five
Letter from Francesco to Nicoletta

December 1942

Dear Nicoletta,

As it is your desire, I have written something to read at your dear cousin's wedding. It isn't a poem, but rather a little discourse for the occasion that you will recite when all the guests are gathered. This takes place before they begin serving dessert. Be careful to read clearly, slowly, and with proper cadence, paying attention to commas and periods. This way, it will produce the desired effect of the written word without undue emotion.

Ok then, I ask you to behave and be a good girl. Don't be capricious or act in ways that might detract from the festive occasion. You know, in the absence of your deceased mother, my loving wife, you are the lady of the house just as your brother, Piero, is the head of the family. Therefore, I encourage you to be kind and respectful. Listen to your aunts and uncles, and follow their counsel. After the wedding, please let me know how well you did and how our combined efforts were received. I pray that our thoughts fly toward those that have gone before us.

Please continue with your education. For now, be sure to learn to be a good homemaker and learn to sew. Are we in agreement? Always go forward with good thoughts and right actions.

Love and kisses to all of you.

Papá

Chapter Five
Wartime Wedding

Bisceglie, Province of Bari, Italy 1942

Early in his career, many Italians considered Benito Mussolini a genius. He had taken a country divided by civil unrest and economic hardship and united it with public works projects that reinvigorated the economy. But his ambitions proved to be his downfall. His goal was to restore, in part, the Roman Empire. His military actions in Spain, Ethiopia, and Albania severely depleted the government coffers. His fascist reign over Italy continued to ravage the country. His government called young Italian men to active duty and sent them to various combat zones.

While the rest of the world decried Mussolini's imperialistic conquests, his friend to the north supported his brutal invasion of Ethiopia. Hitler found a willing partner in Mussolini, modeling some of his political actions on the success he observed in Italy. The Rome-Berlin Axis in 1938 would eventually draw Italy into a war it could not win.

Mussolini took aim at Greece and Albania as Hitler continued his assault on the Balkans, a region Mussolini coveted for Italy. He flexed his military power by moving east, but Greece thwarted him. His failure was an embarrassment not only for his ambitions but also because his military prowess paled compared to Hitler's continued success.

Once looked upon as the most powerful leader in Europe, Mussolini realized he would fall behind Hitler and his brutal decimation of the continent. His alliance with Hitler and the beginning of World War II deteriorated an already fragile economy and took a personal toll on Italy's citizens. Italy had remained neutral despite Hitler's urging. When it became clear that France would fall to Germany, Italy joined Hitler and declared war on France and Great Britain. It was June 10, 1940.

With war raging through the continent, the Mediterranean, and Northern Africa, Francesco Di Bitetto could not travel back to Bisceglie. In the early years of the war, he could still communicate with his children through the letters he wrote. He worried about his little girl the most. But all that changed when Italy entered the war. Those precious letters slowed to a trickle.

Antonietta was like another daughter to him, and the fact that she took on the responsibility to raise Nicoletta in his absence elicited the greatest of love and gratitude from him. There were very few reasons to celebrate during the war. However, Antonietta's fiancé, on active military duty, was granted leave to get married. Although it would not be an elegant affair, it was a joyous occasion for the family. They set the date for December 7, 1942.

Antonietta and Peitro's wedding. Nicoletta, front row, center left

It was a tradition that the youngest member of the family would stand before the guests and read a poem dedicated to the bride and groom. Often, it was a familiar verse that everyone had heard many times. But Nicoletta wanted to present something more special for Antonietta's wedding. Their bond was more profound than cousin, or sister, or parent—it was a combination of all three. And at eleven years of age, Nicoletta wanted to express her feelings but didn't know how. So, she wrote to her father and asked him to compose something original. After dinner, when the guests were seated, and the confections were passed around, Nicoletta stood and addressed the crowd.

The Tribute

December 7, 1942

Spouses! Today is a solemn day, for your hearts are in celebration.

All of us here present, unite in your joy to render it ever greater and more memorable.

Dear honored Bride and Groom,

At this moment, my thoughts fly to my dear ones far away and our beloved deceased,

Mamma.

You that loved them so much, pray to God in Heaven that He will give His blessing,

Oh, Lord God,

Accept our prayer and grant to this newly married couple eternal faith, love, togetherness, peace, and everlasting happiness.

Oh God, bless this joyful husband and wife,

Watch over them, Mamma, that they will merit a good life and that God will grant it to them.

Family and welcome guests, please stand for a moment,

Toast to them, and bless this young couple

Wish them a world of happiness and progeny to serve God and the country.

Dear Bride and Groom,

I have completed my discourse.

I kiss you and bless you,

Nicoletta Di Bitetto

She dazzled the guests who thought this young child read like an actress. When she finished reading, the bride and groom swept her into their arms. Nicoletta knew she had made her father proud.

Chapter Six
During the War

Bisceglie, Province of Bari, Italy 1942-1945

Mussolini's failures in the Mediterranean left Hitler angry and betrayed. As the war progressed, the Fascists lost control of their own country. As a result, the Nazis did not look kindly upon the Italian troops and treated them as second-class citizens. They pushed the Italian soldiers out of their posts and controlled the local governments with force.

Along with the rest of the citizens of Italy, Nicoletta's family had endured the brutal violence of the black shirts of Fascist terror only to be ravaged by the Nazis. Years of economic stagnation and hardship multiplied after the Nazis occupied their towns and villages. Daily life was filled with drudgery and fear. The rationing that took place during wartime was exacerbated by the overall shortage of food. Workers were scarce, and there was little money to pay the considerable expenses of a working farm. Those who could afford to buy their fruits and vegetables found little from the meager yield of crops—barely enough to feed their families. Making matters worse, Mussolini signed legislation that forced local citizens to supply the Nazi soldiers with food. This further incensed the local villagers. In addition, the farmers were forced to pack most of what they grew and load it onto transport for the German soldiers who occupied the north.

The Nazis took over schools and public buildings to use as storage units. They already packed them with canned foods and supplies from Germany. The Nazis had an abundance of everything they could want. But they were in Italy, where the growing season was long. Before the war, Germany received fresh fruits and vegetables exported from Italy. Nicoletta could only dream of the bounty that was grown in the farmland surrounding Bisceglie. To add salt to their wounds, with the Nazis occupying all southern Italy, Mussolini and the Fascists ordered local families to feed the Nazis. Each household prepared and cooked meals they would never taste.

Nicoletta had firsthand knowledge of the food shortage. She went out to the market every day. One never knew what they would find or if they'd even get the essentials. The government strictly rationed bread and pasta. The farmers sold much of the wheat to the government and what little was left on the black market. They allowed every family one tiny roll per person per day. The head of the household was given two buns. Nicoletta's brother, Piero, was a hard worker. Two small rolls to stretch over three meals barely made a dent in his hunger. She adored Piero, so each night, Nicoletta broke hers in half.

"Piero, take this. I'm full already."

"But you ate nothing, Nicoletta. You eat it," he replied despite his hunger.

"Honestly, Piero, I don't want it to go to waste. Take it."

Night after night, they played the same game, and he would take her meager offering. They both knew what she was doing and their bond grew even stronger throughout the war.

The lines for meat were long. Nicoletta waited hours only to find empty shelves. She would have to get an earlier start the following day. Fruits and vegetables were not rationed but most of the harvest went to feed the soldiers. Many times, by the time she got to the front of the line, most of the produce was gone. Fortunately, a neighbor had a tiny plot of land just beside the Church of the Misericordia. He planted a vegetable garden and sold his produce to the locals. One day, Nicoletta went to buy a head of cauliflower.

"*Ciao, Signore.* I would like to buy some cauliflower."

"Sorry, Nicoletta. I have nothing today," he responded.

"But I see a nice head right over there."

"Oh, but I can't sell that to you today."

"Why not?"

"You're a clever girl. Can you figure out why?" he asked.

"No, it makes little sense," she replied.

"Nicoletta, do you see how small that is today. If I wait a few days, it will weigh much more. Then, I will get a better price for it."

"I understand," Nicoletta replied. "What if I pay you the higher price for the head today?"

"No, no, child. That wouldn't be fair to you. You will just have to wait."

That day, Nicoletta went home empty-handed.

Mussolini vacationed in Bisceglie on occasion and stayed at *Villa Ciardi* several times during the war. *Villa Ciardi* was an elegant mansion with expansive grounds. Nicoletta and her cousins dreamed of having their wedding receptions at the beautiful villa. But as the Nazis seized more control, they raided it and took it for their headquarters. Mussolini maintained a bit of influence, and in allowing the Nazis to have control of the Villa, the soldiers looked more kindly on the local citizens. The people of Bisceglie believed that is what saved the city from being destroyed by the Germans.

Italy had been Germany's most powerful ally. When Italy surrendered to the Allied forces, Mussolini's betrayal of Hitler was complete. The Nazi soldiers showed no mercy to local citizens. However, it was much worse for men in Mussolini's fascist army. Hitler's troops perpetrated a campaign of revenge on Italian soldiers.

The citizens of Bisceglie shivered in fear and disbelief when they heard of what happened to Trani, their neighbor to the north. Its grand cathedral with its glimmering white bell tower was built on a point jutting out into the Adriatic Sea. The glimmering sandstone church stood prominently in the Mediterranean sunshine. A jewel on the southern Adriatic coast, it created an impressive panorama on the skyline.

Piero warned his little sister to give the Nazi soldiers a wide birth.

"Nicoletta, I know you are very careful when you are buying food. But you must promise me that you will turn in the opposite direction when you see them. Even if that means you have to step out of the long lines."

"*Sì, Piero.* I don't understand. They've never bothered me before."

"Let me tell you what those animals did to the bishop of Trani. It's a horrible story," he warned. "But I need you to see how dangerous it is right now."

The bishop of Trani was a powerful and wealthy figure in the region. After Italy surrendered to the Allies, the bishop tried desperately to shelter and care for the hunted soldiers. He vowed to protect them from the

Nazis. The Nazis knew of his subversive acts and made numerous attempts on his life.

In an ultimate confrontation, all was lost. The bishop had hidden six Italian soldiers from the retreating Nazis. The Nazis, knowing that the bishop was harboring fugitives, banged loudly on the rectory door, demanding that he release the six men to them. The bishop could not, in good conscience, give these young men up for execution. Instead, he offered himself up in sacrifice. The Nazis soon forgot about the men in the rectory. The bishop was the perfect high-ranking victim for them to send a message to the local citizens. They dragged the defiant bishop out into the square in front of the seaside cathedral. The spectacle alone proved a greater compensation for the Nazis. As a frightened and horrified crowd gathered, the Nazis shot the bishop with a firing squad.

While the war decimated Europe, the Mediterranean, and North Africa, Mussolini attempted to colonize several nations in Eastern Europe and British territories such as Egypt and Ethiopia. With the war zone continuing to expand, Francesco's health waned along with the hope of reuniting his family. He suffered from intestinal issues throughout his adulthood, but they worsened severely in 1944. Access to decent medical facilities in Rhodes was minimal, and there was little hope of traveling back to Italy for treatment. After several botched surgeries, Francesco died in February 1945, just months before the end of the war.

So many years later, Nicoletta recalled a dream she had the night of his death. The expansive cemetery in Bisceglie appeared before her—she was bringing flowers to her mother's grave. Nicoletta began the long walk home down the cemetery's main boulevard through the first set of grand gates. When she looked up, she saw a man dressed in a black suit coming toward her. He was wearing the traditional garb of one in mourning. As he approached, she recognized him—it was her father. She hadn't seen him in years—his weekly letters had trailed off as well; there had been no communication from him in recent months. Nicoletta worried constantly about her father and her brother Mauro during the final months of the war. In this dream she ran towards him with her arms outstretched. But as she got close enough to touch him, he held up his hand to stop her.

"*Cara* Nicoletta, do not touch me," he said to her.

"But why, *Papá*? It has been so long since I've seen you."

"You can't, sweetheart."

"But I want to hug you, kiss you, and feel your arms around me, *Papá*."

"Shhhh, listen to me, my dear one. I am here to counsel you—to tell you that everything will be okay. Pay close attention now. As you grow older, you must follow your own path. But listen carefully, for there will be some that will try to dissuade you. Do not heed their advice. You must follow your heart and do what you know is right. Always be true to yourself, Nicoletta."

She woke with a start with tears streaming down her cheeks. She felt her father's presence just as strongly even after she had awakened. Nicoletta would later discover that her dream came to her the very night her father had died. In her heart, she believed he had come to say good-bye. She understood that the path he spoke of was a prediction of her eventual marriage to Orazio and her decision to leave Italy for a life in America. Her brother Mauro had tried his best to convince her not to abandon her country.

Chapter Seven
Postwar Life

Bisceglie, Province of Bari, Italy 1945-1949

Nicoletta had just begun to recover from losing her mother when news came of her father's death. Her life changed immeasurably after the death of her mother, but she clung to the dream of being reunited with her father. His death crushed her heart and was a decisive blow to her already fractured life. Her daily visits to the Marian altar at her church were balm to her soul. It was the only place where she could let her grief show, where she expressed her sadness and frustration as she kneeled in front of a statue of Mary.

Confronted with the news of her father's death merely five years later, Nicoletta struggled to imagine her uncertain future. Her anxiety was compounded by the thought that she could not be with him in his last days. The last time she saw him was when he departed for Rhodes—only months before her mother died. Nicoletta was only seven years old, and the memories of his face were fading. Her heart ached to feel his touch once again.

Although the war was over and rationing had ended, the family no longer had the means to live as they had in the past. The spoiled little princess no longer had the most beautiful dress or a bow in her hair. Once envied by her cousins, her standing within her own family diminished—she was an orphan now. Nicoletta wasn't the little girl to admire; rather, they pitied her.

She had always imagined that she would go back to school after the war. It was what both her parents would have wanted, and Nicoletta longed to be back in the classroom where she could read and write. She dreamed about graduating and going on to the university to study education. Nicoletta had always wanted to be a teacher. However, her new reality dashed her hopes for the future.

She yearned for the daily routine of attending school and doing homework. The lack of intellectual stimulation ate away at her—mundane chores took its place. She learned to cook and clean the house but pined for something more. She was training to be a homemaker rather than a teacher, and she resented that. As supportive and caring as Antonietta was, she couldn't relate to Nicoletta's desire for education. A woman's place was in the home, caring for her husband and family. That was her priority, and she believed it was her duty to prepare her cousin for the life she would inevitably lead.

Antonietta approached each of her household tasks with purpose. There was a right way and a wrong way to accomplish every chore. For example, after making the bed, she would stand at the foot to see if it was perfectly flat and even. One could not merely mop or dust around furniture; she had to lift chairs onto the table, move objects off countertops to scrub every inch of the room. Her fastidiousness irritated Nicoletta at times. *What did it matter how things were done, as long as the task was completed?* she reasoned.

On one occasion, she was helping to make zucchini patties. Antonietta was busy setting the table for *pranzo,* the main meal of the day. Nicoletta had watched her cousin making the patties dozens of times. She measured each ingredient and placed it into the bowl. Then she picked up the eggs and cracked them against each other over the rest of the ingredients. Just then, Antonietta yelled from the other end of the kitchen.

"What are you doing?"

"What do you mean? I'm mixing everything for the zucchini patties, just like you do," she said defensively.

"No, no, no! You have to beat the eggs separately first; otherwise, they won't mix well. There'll be globs of egg white throughout the mix."

"What does it matter? It all goes to the same place," Nicoletta responded, exasperated. She could do nothing right. Worst of all, none of these tasks truly mattered to her. Nothing she was learning would advance her academic education. Her resentment colored all that she did. It upset Nicoletta that Antonietta had chided her over such a trivial matter. In a fit of anger, she picked up the bowl and threw it to the ground. Her mother's china broke into pieces. The mixture splattered all over the newly cleaned kitchen. Startled, there was silence as they both stared at the broken glass and mess on the floor. *What have I done?* Nicoletta thought.

Antonietta viewed it as a challenge to her authority, believing Nicoletta had thrown the bowl at her. Her face turned red as she waved Nicoletta away.

"Go! Get out of my kitchen now!"

"I'll be happy to," Nicoletta said as she stomped out of the room.

"What is wrong with that girl? All I've ever done was love her and teach her how to be a good wife someday," Antonietta said loudly enough for Nicoletta to hear.

Once tempers had calmed, the two cousins talked through their anger and frustration. Nicoletta apologized, acknowledging she had acted like a child.

"I'm so sorry, Antonietta. I don't know what came over me. It's just that I am so frustrated. This is not what I had imagined my life to be."

"I know, *cara*. Neither of us did. You should be in school, studying for university. No one would have imagined that both *Mamma* and *Papá* would be gone. I will try to be more patient."

"No, Antonietta. I am the one who needs to be patient. I acted like a spoiled brat. I promise to control my temper and behave. You know I love you."

"I love you too."

She pulled Nicoletta into a rough embrace, then playfully pushed her away.

"Enough of this! We have work to do!"

After the War

Zia Nunzia was Nicoletta's favorite aunt. Her gentle, caring nature engulfed her niece as she drew Nicoletta into her loving arms. The intimacy between Maria and Nunzia had created a lasting impression on Nicoletta. After her mother died, there were only two women who even came close to filling her shoes. Antonietta gave the stability and structure Nicoletta needed, and Nunzia gave her the affection she longed for.

"Give your aunt a kiss and tell me what is on your mind," Zia Nunzia said to her whenever she saw worry or sadness in her eyes. After her mother's death, Nicoletta was no longer a happy-go-lucky child.

"*Ciao, Zia.* Hi, Auntie, I was just thinking about *Mamma.* I miss her so much," she cried.

"*Sì, figlia, sì.* Yes, my child, we all miss her. Your mother was an angel, and she is watching over you from heaven. You can still talk to her, you know." Zia Nunzia tried to comfort her beautiful niece. "When you miss her, just tell her so. You may not hear her voice talking back to you, but she is still right here," she said as she pointed to her heart. Nunzia ached with sadness when she saw Nicoletta grieve her mother's death. She still felt the loss of her sister acutely and knew that her young niece could make little sense of the passing of both her parents.

After her little chat with Zia Nunzia, Nicoletta slowly walked up the aisle of the nave of her church. Kneeling at the altar of Mary, she spoke to her mother.

"*Mamma,* I miss you so much. Can't you come down from heaven just once so that I can feel your touch? I want to sit in your lap with your arms around me. I need you to tell me that everything will be all right."

Silent tears streamed down her cheeks in the dark church. When no response came, Nicoletta sighed and looked up to the statue of Mary. Her arms were outstretched, almost calling to her.

"*Maria, Madre di Dio,* Mary, mother of God, you are the mother of us all. Please help me. God took my mother away from me, and I have no one. I have no mother and no father. Oh, Mary, you must be my mother now. Please give me guidance," Nicoletta pleaded, but there was no response. "From now on, I will come to you."

Nicoletta kept her word and visited that statue of Mary every day. The entire extended family couldn't help but notice. They worried about her but hoped that she found the comfort she needed. Unlike the others, Zia Nunzia, always playful, took a unique approach. She stopped Nicoletta on her way home from church one day.

"Nicoletta, *vieni qua.* Come here and talk with me, child."

"*Ciao, Zia.* Hi there, Auntie. How are you today?"

"Good, good. I see that you were in church again today. You've been spending an awful lot of time there." She paused dramatically, and with a mischievous smile, she said, "So, my little Nicoletta, is there something you're not telling me?"

Nicoletta looked at her aunt with a puzzled expression.

"Are you going to become a nun?" Zia Nunzia asked.

"No, Zia, no! I don't want to become a nun!" Nicoletta replied vehemently.

"Ah, I see, so you want a man. You want to get married!" she teased.

Nicoletta blushed a deep red and said, "Zia, what are you saying? I can't think of marrying anyone yet!"

Zia Nunzia let out a boisterous laugh and hugged her niece tightly.

"*Bella figlia, ti voglio bene.* Beautiful child, I wish only the best for you, dear one."

Nunzia was a pure and beautiful soul. Her presence in Nicoletta's life was a godsend. She was a bright light during the dark times after the war.

The postwar years were nearly as difficult as the war. When it became clear that they had lost, the Nazis left a trail of death and destruction throughout southern Italy. They burned everything in their path and killed the livestock. In their wake, the Nazis left behind a ravaged land and a hopeless people desperate for relief. After the soldiers fled the *Villa Ciardi* in Bisceglie, the locals discovered that the storage bins were still filled to capacity. Many people, desperate for food, raided the Villa and took as much as they could carry. Piero ran to join the fray after seeing his friends pass by with arms full of grocery items. Unfortunately, there was little left by the time he arrived.

Zia Nunzia and her husband Zio Pepino opened a grocery store after the war, but neither had a mind for business. Nunzia loved chatting with the customers and getting the latest news or gossip. It was a way to connect with her neighbors. There was such poverty in Bisceglie at the time, and everyone had a story to tell. So many people were searching in vain for jobs that didn't exist.

Everyone knew Nunzia had a soft heart, especially for children. She couldn't resist scooping them up into her arms and kissing them. She loved to make them laugh and to see their happiness. Many mothers would come to her store with six or seven poorly clad and unbathed children. Nunzia could see the hunger in their eyes. Although she knew they did not have the money to pay, she would grab a freshly baked loaf of crusty bread and break off a piece for each child delighting as they gobbled it up. It was likely the only thing they had eaten that day. The mother would thank her profusely, to which Nunzia would say, "*Scrive, Scrive.* Write, write what you owe, and pay me when you can. God bless you." She did this so often, but rarely did the customer return to settle their account. So many never repaid what they had taken on credit, and Nunzia and Pepino soon went out of business.

Chapter Eight
Nicoletta's Youth

Bisceglie, Province of Bari, Italy 1940s

The years passed, and Nicoletta entered adolescence with the added burden of her family circumstances. She never let go of her dream to go back to school. Unfortunately, going on to high school was no longer an option. However, she committed herself to advancing her education in any way possible.

Nicoletta needed something besides homemaking to replace her academic education. Given that a university degree was no longer feasible, her new focus was to learn a skill that was sought after and would garner a decent wage. There was a dressmaker in the *città vecchia,* the old part of the city. She lived in the former summer palace of Lucrezia Borgia, the illegitimate daughter of the infamous Pope Alexander VI. It was a grand building with a rich history. Entering the central portico, a circular granite staircase led to Signora Tozzi's apartment at the very top. She accepted only a few girls in her class, and Nicoletta was lucky to be among them. She learned how to stitch by hand, embroider, and create patterns. Once she got her certification in pattern-making, many doors would open for her. She could then design and create dresses for private clients.

Tasks she abhorred during the war, such as going to the water pump to get drinking water or waiting in lines at crowded grocery stores, became part of her routine. Many years had passed since she was the rich girl with prestigious parents. Nicoletta was simply another girl from a struggling family scarred from the war. The financial crisis and loss of life endured by many Italians during the Nazi occupation hit southern Italy particularly hard. Unlike northern and central Italy, Puglia was not a tourist destination—and there was very little industry to employ the throngs of desperate citizens. Prospects were dismal, and many emigrated from Italy to America or Argentina, seeking a better life.

Losing her social and economic status plagued her most when she was with her cousin, Nina, whose mother, Giovanna, was Maria's sister. The two girls were just about the same age, and given the angst of adolescence, there were many opportunities for her to feel inferior to Nina. Her cousin's privilege grew, while Nicoletta's ended after the death of her parents. Nicoletta found it challenging to watch, and to acknowledge her own bitterness. She couldn't talk to anyone about her envy. It would seem petty, materialistic, and ungrateful to Antonietta, who had sacrificed so much to take care of her.

Nina's father, her Zio Tonino, believed that his brother-in-law, Francesco, had been foolish to take Antonietta into the family. The cost alone was reason enough. But having another person in the house could bring conflict and disturb the family dynamic. There was a great deal of drama with Antonietta's father after his wife, Grazia, died. He made it clear that he had no desire or intention to raise his daughter. Maria and Francesco wanted nothing more than to care for and comfort her. They offered to legally adopt her, but that was too much of a blow to her father's pride. Grazia and Maria were very close, and so, regardless of her legal status, Grazia's daughter was like Maria's own.

Tonino was selfish and miserly. He tipped none of the service people who helped him. He seldom gave gifts or hosted dinners. On the rare occasion when he did host the family on a holiday, he served day-old bread, as well as mortadella and salami that was clearly past its prime. In addition, the wine was cheap with an acidic aftertaste. None of the family enjoyed holidays at their place, which suited Tonino just fine.

In preparation for one of these holiday gatherings, Nicoletta yearned for her previous life. It was customary to wear special or new outfits for Easter Sunday, complete with new shoes and bonnet or bow for her hair. Nicoletta opened the armoire to look at the dresses she'd worn in previous years. She held each one up to herself and closed her eyes as she recreated the scenes in her memory. She knew that there was little money to spend on such an extravagance this year. Her brother Piero was her only financial support, and he gave most of his earned pay to Antonietta to support the household. She resigned herself to wearing a dress from the previous year. After trying it on, it was clear she had grown significantly.

None of her special occasion dresses fit—leaving her with only her everyday clothes.

Zio Tonino ignited her hopes for a new dress when, knowing of her recent graduation and certificate in pattern-making, came to the rescue, or so she thought. He asked if she would design and sew a dress for his daughter, Nina. In exchange, he would purchase enough fabric for two dresses, one for each of them. Nicoletta couldn't have been happier.

"Of course, Zio! I would be happy to sew a dress for Nina. It will be great fun." She believed this would be the perfect opportunity to show off her new skills and gain back a bit of respect from within the family.

Filled with excitement, they strode to the fabric store. The two girls, usually at each other's throats in competition, chatted animatedly about the colors they preferred or the styles that looked best on them. Nicoletta could hardly contain her excitement as they entered the store—it was filled with possibility, and her creative energy flowed. She wandered the aisles, trailing Nina as patiently as she could while waiting her turn. She gave her opinion on types of fabric and colors.

"I love this green fabric," Nina exclaimed. "It feels luxurious, and the color is brilliant."

"Mm, yes, the color is magnificent on you, but the fabric is much too heavy for a spring dress. You'll be boiling in it by noontime," Nicoletta replied.

"Oh, you're right. I hadn't thought of that. But I love the color."

"Look at those bolts by the wall; there's a beautiful green, and the fabric looks much lighter," Nicoletta suggested.

They had found the perfect fabric and color for Nina's dress, and she couldn't be happier. With Nina satisfied, it was finally time to find something for Nicoletta. Zio Tonino, realizing how costly Nina's fabric was, turned to Nicoletta.

"Tina," he said, using her nickname, "look over here on this table. There are some beautiful pieces. I'm sure you can find something you like."

She walked over to the table and read the sign hanging above it: *Scrap pieces, Huge discount!* She looked at him with heavy eyelids and tight lips.

"These are just remnants, Zio. The pieces aren't big enough to make a dress."

"No? Well, perhaps you can use several different pieces," he said as he held up several of them. "You can create a new style."

"I don't think my mother would like this. It doesn't look right."

"What do you mean? She would be happy that I'm footing the bill for your new dress."

"Zio, none of the pieces match, and the fabrics are not the same. It would look terrible—as if I threw together a bunch of scraps to make the dress. I'd look like a pauper," Nicoletta replied indignantly.

"I see. So my gift to you doesn't meet your standards, little one? Things have changed for you, young Tina. Now that your parents are gone, you can't expect the world to bow at your feet."

His insensitive reprimand startled her. Nina stood at a safe distance with a slight grin on her face. She was enjoying this. Anything that knocked Nicoletta down a few pegs seemed to raise her up. Nicoletta knew she must respond to her uncle, but she also knew she must remain respectful so as not to offend him. However, his words stung; she ached and seethed with anger.

"I don't expect anyone to bow to me. My parents always wanted the best for me. I'm sure they would not approve of a dress made of scraps. I'm sorry."

"I see. So what of our bargain? Choose from this table, or our deal is off."

"I'm sorry, Nina," Nicoletta said as she walked past her to the exit. Her previous smirk turned into a frown of defeat. Clearly, she would not be getting her new green dress.

That was the last conversation Nicoletta had with her uncle regarding the dresses, and she didn't design or sew a dress for Nina. Nicoletta's disappointment over not getting the fabric for her own new dress paled by comparison to the aching in her heart. The way Zio Tonino treated her shocked her—as if she were a servant, someone who should be grateful for the scraps from the table of the rich or the higher class. When she returned home, Antonietta could see she had been crying, and although she tried to hide it, the tears flowed with abandon once she was asked about the shopping trip.

"Nicoletta, *cara,* what happened? Didn't you go to the fabric store with Zio Tonino and Nina?"

"*Sì*, Antonietta, *sì*. Nothing happened." She couldn't manage an explanation without crying, so she resolved to remain silent. But Antonietta was not one to give up so easily.

"Those are tears of joy, then?" she said sarcastically. "Where's the fabric for your new dress?"

"There won't be any dress."

"What nonsense are you spouting, Nicoletta? Zio Tonino promised you. He's not one to go back on his word."

"No, but none of us would consider him generous," Nicoletta said honestly as she explained what had transpired in painful detail. Antonietta was furious. Even though Tonino was cheap, she never thought of him as petty or cruel. How could he treat his grieving niece in such an insensitive manner? She was done with him. She promised Tina that she would always put her first.

"You may have lost both your mother and father, but let me be perfectly clear: you are no one's servant, nor are you less valuable or loved than your cousins. You are like a daughter to me. I know I can never live up to your mother, but I will do the best I can to prove to you how much I love you. My heart broke as if they were my parents too. They raised me and loved me from the moment my mother died. I suffer their loss as well. Come, my dearest Nicoletta," she said as she pulled her into her bosom and embraced her. "I love you."

There was no new dress for Nicoletta that year or for several years to come. She continued to sew and make enough money to save a little after contributing to the family. But it only amounted to pocket change. She learned to do with less and made sure not to engage in hurtful arguments with Nina. Tina may not have had Nina's means, but she carried herself with dignity. After all, she reasoned, she was much smarter than her cousin.

Chapter Nine
Despina and Mauro

Rhodes, Greece • Bisceglie, Bari 1940s

Mauro took to Rhodes as quickly as his father. The ancient history of the walled city and the endless seacoast enchanted him. He found the Greek women bewitching with their luxurious hair and dark, mysterious eyes. There was one in particular who caught his eye each day when he was on duty. This dark-haired young woman would pass him by as if she owned the town. She walked with a sense of purpose as she tended to her errands. She was seemingly unfazed by the many men who ogled her as she strolled by. Mauro, always the gentleman, tipped his hat to her and smiled day after day. Taking him entirely by surprise, she stopped at last and spoke to him.

"Good day, soldier. Why are you watching me? Have I done anything wrong? Or is it that you can't resist a beautiful Greek woman?" she asked boldly. Mauro stuttered his reply.

"G-Good Morning *Signorina*. Yes, I mean, no. You have done nothing wrong."

"Ah, then you are taken by my beauty," she said with a mischievous grin. "How do you like my shiny dark hair? Everyone compliments me on it."

"It is beautiful, just as you are, *Signorina*. My name is Mauro."

"Pleasure to meet you, Mauro. I am Despina. So is this what you do all day, Mauro, stand around and ogle beautiful women?" Once again, Despina took control, and Mauro was getting nervous.

"I…I'm working now, keeping guard," he stammered.

"So, you have no other life than this? Not much to draw the interest of any woman, let alone someone as beautiful as I," she said, seductively showing off her figure. Mauro blushed, but could not look away.

"Well, there is not much to do on base," he replied honestly.

"But you are in Rhodes! There are many wonderful ways to pass the time."

She was still engaging him in conversation. *Maybe I have a chance*, he thought.

"Perhaps you can show me around. I would be grateful for your company."

"What a gentleman you are. I may very well take you up on that offer. What time do you get off duty? You can take me to dinner, and then I will give you the executive tour."

Mauro's mind swirled with excitement. He had never met a woman like her. Those he had known in Bisceglie were proper and quiet. No one had ever been as bold as Despina had just been. She led him around that evening with confidence, and he fell immediately under her spell. She took him by the hand and caressed his face. She laughed boisterously and cared little that others took note. He wondered if she craved the attention. After walking her home, she kissed him.

"I approve, Mauro. You were an apt partner in the evening's festivities. You can take me out another time."

Mauro couldn't wait to see her again. That was the beginning of a passionate courtship. After several weeks, once she knew that Mauro was smitten, Despina told him she had something significant to share with him. For the first time, she invited him to her home. He was very excited and believed that this was the next step in their relationship. He was sure that she planned to introduce him to her parents. Instead, there would be an unexpected revelation.

He stood with flowers in his hands and knocked. When the door opened, the cutest little boy stared up at him with piercing blue eyes and a timid smile. He couldn't have been more than five or six years old.

"Well, hello there, young man. How are you today?" Mauro asked.

He immediately backed away and hid behind Despina's skirt, peeking at Mauro from a safe distance.

"I see you've met my son, Franco," Despina said, gauging his expression.

"Your son? Oh," he said, and without skipping a beat, he continued. "He's as beautiful as his mother."

"I didn't know how to tell you, Mauro. I am raising him on my own. My husband left me just after we got married. He went off to Africa to explore, but he never came back. I was fourteen years old when we married, only a girl."

Mauro was moved to compassion for her unfortunate circumstances. Her story only drew him closer to her. There was nothing she could do that could chase him away.

Despina loved to tell the story of her parents' courtship. She described her Turkish father as a true man's man. His macho swagger kept potential rivals at bay. If he saw something he wanted, he took it by force if necessary. As a young man, a young Greek girl on the island had captured his interest, and he pursued her aggressively. When her Greek parents discovered his efforts, they became enraged. There was a great deal of animosity between the Turks and the Greeks, which lasted for centuries. Beyond the historical conflicts between the two countries, there was the matter of religion. There was no way that they would let their Greek Orthodox daughter marry a Muslim man. It would be an indelible mark on her soul. They guarded her as best they could so that there could be no contact between them. Despina's mother was in her early teens at that time, and she was infatuated with a man she had never met. Each day, she gazed out her window at the swarthy young fellow below. Although she was afraid of him, she found him exotically attractive.

When he discovered that her parents forbade their courtship, the suitor developed a plan. He bided his time—waiting weeks before taking action. He realized he could not be seen anywhere near her home and kept his distance. As he laid in wait, he could see her parents' diligence begin to wane. That is when he struck. He climbed up the trellis to her room and entered through the window. She was shocked and about to scream when he placed his hand on her mouth. She froze in fear as he pulled her out the window and kidnapped her. They married immediately, and her parents disowned her for marrying a Turk. This was the type of man Despina admired. She raved about her powerful father. She wanted nothing to do with a man who showed any weakness.

Determined not to leave her daughter's future to chance, Despina's mother took the reins and began her search for a suitable husband as soon as Despina reached puberty. Prospects were slim for girls of marrying age on Rhodes. When her mother heard of a handsome Italian explorer who was in town, she jumped at the opportunity. She sought to give Despina a future away from the island. His name was Lorenzo, and although he was nearly twenty years older than her daughter, he was dashingly attractive. Well educated and suave, Lorenzo had traveled abroad for many years and had never had time for a wife.

Despina's mother convinced him that her daughter would be the perfect wife: obedient, kind, and independent. She would never curb his enthusiasm for exploration. She set up a meeting in her kitchen while she served him strong coffee and baklava. Her argument was persuasive, and he agreed to meet his potential mate.

Despina was out playing with her friends when her mother called her into the house. She reluctantly left the group of laughing girls to heed her mother's call.

"Despina, say hello to Signore Parlatore."

"Good morning, Signore. It's nice to meet you," she said dutifully.

"Please call me Lorenzo. It's lovely to meet you, Despina."

She had barely turned fourteen and was eager to get back to her friends. When introductions were finished, she asked, "Can I go out and play now? The girls are waiting for me."

Lorenzo was intrigued by the young spitfire he'd just met. She was willful and had a forceful personality. Despite their brief encounter, Lorenzo liked what he saw. "Perhaps she's right," he thought. "Maybe it's time for a wife."

That very afternoon, as Despina played games with her girlfriends, her mother arranged and planned her marriage. Within two weeks, they married. However, Lorenzo was never a husband to her. Although her youthful exuberance excited him during their first months together, he soon tired of her childish behavior. He thought Despina was vain and selfish. Lorenzo longed for the freedom of his travels once again. Less than a year after the wedding, he left for good, but not before Despina became pregnant.

At the birth of her son, her life changed forever. She never mourned the loss of Lorenzo; he was but a blip on the radar for her. However, when Franco was born, she poured all her energy into caring for him. Her son was the center of her universe and she doted on him constantly. Despina would do anything for him— he was everything to her. There was little room in her heart for anyone but Franco.

Despina needed affection too and loved to flirt with handsome men. But ultimately, no one could interfere with the life she wanted for her son.

Planning the surprise meeting of Franco was going to be Mauro's true test. If he did not accept him and treat him as his own son, there would be no future relationship. Mauro couldn't have passed her test with higher marks. He loved children, and Franco reminded him of his little sister at that age. Mauro felt the loss of his family during his years in the military. He mourned his deceased mother and missed his brother and sister terribly. Despina and her son filled the void they left in his heart.

Despina couldn't care less about what family and friends thought. When they called her selfish, she retorted, "So, what? Everyone is selfish. At least I'm honest about it." Despina was proud of her devious mind and frequently concocted plans to cheat others out of money or ridicule anyone she viewed as a threat.

After they had been together for a while, she told Mauro one of her favorite stories. Sometime after her marriage to Lorenzo and before she met Mauro, her mother became seriously ill. From her hospital bed, she grasped Despina's hand.

"Despina, I don't think I will leave this horrible place."

"Mamma, don't talk like that. I know you will live for years just to torture me with your nagging."

"Enough of that, Despina, listen to me," her mother said, looking directly into her eyes. "I have a set of antique gold coins. They are worth a fortune. I planned to will them to you and your sister upon my death. I need to tell you where to find them should I die from this awful illness."

Despina's ears perked up, and she listened intently.

"Please tell your sister about our conversation. You should divide these coins evenly between you. At least I will die knowing my daughters are well taken care of."

Despina went directly to the hiding place her mother spoke of. The glittering beauty of the gold coins bewitched her. There were hundreds of them. Figuring that her mother would die in the coming weeks, she took half for herself. She planned to show her sister the remaining coins at her mother's death. She would tell her of her mother's wishes to divide the gold between them. No one would be any wiser to her theft. With a self-satisfied grin, she returned the remaining coins to their hiding place.

Despina's plan was thwarted, however. After a protracted stay in the hospital, her mother survived, and upon her return home, she discovered that half the gold coins were missing. Despina denied knowing anything about it, but her mother knew how devious her daughter was. She immediately kicked her out of the house and disowned her. Despina didn't have any regrets. She felt justified in doing what she had to do to get ahead. After she and Mauro moved to Bisceglie, he could not find a job. Those gold coins ensured their financial survival until he secured a position. Before the war, Mauro was one course shy of getting his teaching certificate for grades one through eight. His academic aspirations were thwarted when he was called to service. Upon his return, he lost interest in teaching. Instead, he finished his degree in civic affairs. He began his career in city government, which would eventually lead to his election to vice mayor of Bisceglie.

During those two years, they tried in vain to contact Despina's husband, Lorenzo. Unless they petitioned him for divorce, Mauro and Despina could not marry. Ultimately, they returned to Bisceglie without the divorce. They would simply tell the family that they had married in Rhodes. In reality, theirs was a common-law marriage because Italian law did not recognize divorce, and she was still legally married to Lorenzo. Many years later, when laws changed, they were civilly married.

Despina loved to tell a romantic story about how they fell in love. After Italy had surrendered and joined the Allied forces, the Nazis hunted down the Italian soldiers. Despina took Mauro into her home to hide him. As she told it, Despina saved Mauro from certain torture and death at the hands of the Nazis. During the months before the fall of Hitler, she kept Mauro safe. And that is when they fell in love.

Eventually, Mauro and Despina had a daughter together, and he couldn't have been happier. He doted on his little girl, just as he had done with Nicoletta. She had thick chestnut hair and eyes that glowed when she laughed. Despina reminded Mauro that they had another child and that just because Franco was from a different father, he was very much his son. Mauro couldn't agree more, but nothing he said or did would convince her. She believed he favored his daughter, and resented their bond.

When he looked at Lucia, it filled him with joy. He couldn't help but think of Nicoletta. She had the same round face when she was a toddler.

"Lucia, you are so beautiful. Do you know that?"

"She can't understand you, Mauro," Despina said. "You are acting like a fool."

"Perhaps I am, and whether or not she can understand me, she likes the attention. Look at her smile," Mauro replied. "You know, she looks just like Nicoletta."

"What? You're crazy! Lucia is beautiful. Your sister is ugly, hideous! How can you compare the two?" she said with anger.

Mauro was used to her outbursts and ignored her as he continued to coo at Lucia. But Despina wouldn't let it go.

"Look at the proof. That little photo you carry in your wallet tells a different story."

While serving with the Italian military, Mauro and his two siblings wrote many letters to one another. One of the letters included a photo of Piero and Nicoletta. It had blemishes on it, but it was a beautiful reminder of his precious sister. He missed her so. At last, he had a photo of his siblings to show Despina. Mauro ran over to her apartment as soon as his shift ended. With the picture in hand, he burst into her parlor, where he saw her gazing into a mirror, looking at her hair from different angles. He knew Despina was obsessed with her looks; if she passed a mirror, she would stop and primp. She turned to him and asked, "Aren't I beautiful? Look at my smooth skin and thick dark hair."

Mauro was filled with excitement and gave her a perfunctory response. Then he placed the photo before her.

"Despina, my love, Piero sent a photo. Now you can see my wonderful family. Look at my cute little sister. Isn't she adorable?"

"Humph! I don't know. Look how thin her hair is. She is ugly!"

Mauro was taken aback when he first heard her cruel words. But here she was repeating it. He worshiped Despina, but he could not understand how she could be so heartless. She clearly knew that her insensitive words cut deeply. Her jealousy regarding his affection for his sister was absurd.

"How could you say such a thing, Despina? She is only a girl."

"But it's true, Mauro. Look how thin her hair is compared to mine. See how thick and shiny it is? You have to admit that I am much prettier than she is," she said, utterly unaware of how offensive her statements were.

"Of course you are beautiful. You are the only woman for me. But Despina, after we marry and move to Bisceglie, Nicoletta and Piero will be your family too."

"I know that, but that's no reason to pretend that your little sister is a beauty queen. Let's not deceive ourselves. She will have a lot of trouble finding a husband," she said, knowing it would wound him deeply. She had to make sure that she was the only queen in Mauro's life. His adoration of Nicoletta had to stop now, before they moved back to Italy, lest she would be assimilated in the existing family culture. Despina planned to show to all of Mauro's family that she was the elder. She would make the rules from that point on. She glanced at Mauro and could see the pain in his face and was satisfied that she had made her point.

"Now, Mauro, where are you taking your beautiful girlfriend for dinner tonight?"

And that is how it remained. Despina was the vainest person he had ever met, but he was smitten; her strength and independence captivated him. It was a testament to that strength that she had flourished after her first marriage, raising a child on her own. Mauro knew he would do anything to keep her happy, even if it meant letting go of the many hateful statements she made about his family. Despina was the center of his life. There were sacrifices to be made in all love relationships, and he couldn't bear losing her.

She made good on her promise to take charge of the family, regardless of whom she offended. The resentment towards her grew on every front. The only one who seemed oblivious was Mauro.

Sadly, their precious Lucia died at two years old, and they were both distraught. For Mauro, Lucia was the embodiment of their shared love. Despina was often combative, but when there were any concerns regarding Lucia, she softened, and the two of them seemed to work in harmony. Those were rare moments, and he cherished them. After Lucia died, Despina wanted no more children.

Antonia Napoletano

Francesco Dell'Olio

Chapter Ten
The Dell'Olio Family

West Virginia 1912-1930

Orazio was one of twelve children. His parents Francesco and Antonia, lived apart for many years during the war. Eventually, Antonia was able to join Francesco in the United States. Antonia was his second wife. Francesco had been happily married to Antonia's older sister, Angela, a gregarious woman who loved to joke around and was always the center of attention. Francesco and Angela had two sons together, Gianni and Pietro.

By contrast, her little sister, Antonia, was demure, rarely raising her voice—she was content to remain unnoticed. The two women could not have been more different.

Circa 1912, many men in southern Italy traveled abroad to find work to support their families. Francesco joined his brother, Pantaleo, and sought work in Buenos Aires. They rented an apartment and found jobs as laborers. Francesco earned enough to pay his expenses while sending money to Angela to support the family. But his landlord was dishonest, continually trying to swindle him and asking more for rent. His distrust had grown so much that he left Argentina completely.

Francesco first traveled to the United States during the third wave of American immigration, when more than twenty million Europeans came to America. Like many of the Southern Europeans, Francesco was a laborer who found work during a time of industrial expansion. He sailed to North America, where he got a job with a mining company in West Virginia. During the first World War, coal production was used to fuel the war machine. By the mid-1920s, Scotts Run, part of the Fairmont coalfield, boasted approximately forty active coal mines with an output of over four million tons of coal in 1921

The need for laborers was so great that companies relied on immigrants and black Americans. Over sixty percent of the inhabitants of Scotts Run were foreign born. Immigrants from all over Europe worked in the coal mines. The work was back-breaking, the hours were long, and breathing in the coal dust proved deleterious to Francesco's lungs. However, he could live comfortably while sending the better portion of his income to Angela in Bisceglie.

Angela felt his absence deeply, just as many women missed their husbands who had traveled for work. All the same, her life was full—she had a large extended family and many friends to fill most of her emotional needs. There was always some occasion to celebrate—births, engagements, and weddings.

Angela was delighted to be the maid of honor for her girlfriend and was busy preparing dinner for the party on the night before the wedding. Everyone's spirits were high and the wine flowed freely. The groom's brother, Enrico, was a terrible flirt and was playfully enjoining Angela in his horseplay throughout the evening. After dinner, only a few guests remained, but the festive atmosphere continued into the early part of the morning. Always pushing the limits, Enrico pulled out a gun and twirled it around in his hand.

"Look, Angela. Have you ever seen such a skillful marksman as me?"

"Marksman? Just because you can twirl a gun like a show-off doesn't make you a marksman," Angela responded.

"What do *you* know, Angela? I'm an excellent shot. If I wanted to, I could shoot you right in the ass!" He laughed, glancing at the other men gathered around. They joined in the laughter and looked at Angela, knowing she'd be quick with a retort.

"Is that so, Enrico?" she said as she rose from her chair, looked at him with a mischievous grin, and bent over. "Here it is. I bet you couldn't hit my big ass if you tried!"

The room roared with laughter. No one ever bested Angela—her quick wit always won out. At that point, the jeering began. Enrico's face flushed red. He raised the gun and took aim. He only meant to scare her and get everyone to shut up. Angela looked at him, defiant. Surely he wouldn't pull the trigger. They were just having fun.

Perhaps it was the alcohol or his pride; no one will ever know. In a flash, Enrico pulled the trigger. Shock reverberated with the deafening bang. Angela fell as blood stained her beautiful dress. *No, no, no, this can't be happening,* she thought as the agony pulsed through her body.

Enrico had a look of shock on his face as everyone rushed to Angela's side. He sat there, gun in hand, as the room erupted into chaos. *What had he done?*

In moments, they tackled Enrico to the floor. Bewildered, he watched as his gun went sliding across the floor. He gave no resistance as the men dragged him out of the hall and held him until the police arrived. He didn't mean to shoot her. It was just a game; they were having fun. How did it all go so wrong?

Angela struggled to stay alive during the following days. The doctor dressed her wound as best he could, but she was bleeding profusely and he couldn't stanch it. As the hours passed, Angela grew weaker. Her younger sister, Antonia, was at her side the entire time, placing warm compresses to her forehead and holding her hand. As comforting as her sister was, the one person Angela wanted most was thousands of miles away in America. She longed for his touch and his quiet strength. As Angela felt life slipping away, she asked for her boys. Antonia brought Pietro and Gianni to her bedside immediately. She needed to say goodbye to them while she was still coherent.

Antonia took the boys by their hands and kneeled before them. At only two and three years old, they could barely comprehend illness, let alone their mother's death. With her arms around each of them, she said, "Pietro, Gianni, your Mamma doesn't feel well, but she wants to give you a kiss goodnight."

"What's wrong with Mamma?" Pietro asked.

"She has a bellyache, and it won't go away," Antonia explained. "So you mustn't jump into bed with her or make loud noises. You don't want her to feel worse now. Do you?"

The boys nodded their heads and let her lead them to their mother's bedside. Angela reached out and stroked their hair. With a wan smile upon her face, she tried to reassure them.

"Mamma is very sick, but don't you worry. You have another mother right here with you," she said as she motioned to Antonia. "She will always take care of you. Will you promise me you will be good boys, yes?"

They nodded tearfully and leaned into her. They had not seen her since the accident, so they clung to her. They could not get close enough to their mother. Angela looked up at Antonia pleadingly—she could no longer bear it. How could she die and leave her helpless boys? Just a week before, Angela had looked forward to her future in America with Francesco. Now she faced the fact that she was leaving all this behind. Antonia lifted the boys from the bed, and they reluctantly followed her as they stifled their tears. They knew something was terribly wrong as she led them out of the room. Returning to her bedside, Antonia took Angela's outstretched hand in hers. Angela looked pleadingly into her sister's eyes.

"Antonia, those boys mean everything to me. You know that."

"Of course, Angela. Don't you worry, I will take good care of them."

"I know that, Antonia. But I want you to be their mother now. Francesco will need your help too. He can't raise them alone."

"Angela, you know I will do everything in my power to help. I will love them and take care of them as you would have done. Please don't worry."

"I know that. But I need you to take care of Francesco as well. I want you to marry him; become his wife and mother of my children. Won't you do that for me, Antonia?" Angela pleaded.

"Angela! What are you saying? Francesco is your husband. He won't want to marry me; he loves you."

"Antonia, he will need you, and he will grow to love you, and you will love him. He is a good man."

"Oh, Angela, how can you ask me to do that? I am not vivacious and beautiful like you. My quiet and reserved personality can never match up to you."

"Promise me, Antonia. Please. You must marry him; take my place."

Antonia could do nothing but acquiesce. The sight of her dying sister was almost too much to bear.

"Shhhh, don't you worry, *cara mia*. I will take care of all of them. I just hope I can give them a fraction of the happiness you've given them. I don't know how I'll measure up, but rest assured, I will marry Francesco and become their mother in your place," she said with tears streaming down her red cheeks.

They sent a telegram to Francesco in West Virginia, informing him of his wife's death. The shock of the news was rivaled only by the announcement of Angela's wishes that he marry her sister Antonia. Francesco knew she was a good woman who was kind and gentle. Antonia would make a fine mother to his children. But she was not his beloved Angela. No one could ever take the place she held in his heart, and his grief was all-consuming. He could hardly bear the thought of his wife thousands of miles away at the moment of her death. He never got to say goodbye. Ultimately, the most critical issue was the care of his sons. Pietro and Gianni needed a mother immediately. They were much too young to be sent off to relatives, not that they could afford to support them. He knew of Antonia's bountiful love and trusted her to care for them as her own children, especially in his absence.

They were married by proxy in 1914, just a few months after Angela passed. Antonia never dreamed that her wedding day would be so banal. She sat in the office at the city hall, signed the marriage certificate, and watched as they stamped it several times. There was no white gown, no walk down the aisle, no wedding party. Sitting in the cramped office, she realized she was a married woman with two children, and she had never been with a man. She had never even had a boyfriend.

Life took on a different hue after that. She moved into Angela and Francesco's apartment and continued the routines of a new mother. Gianni clung to her in his mother's absence; he never let her out of his sight. But Pietro was resentful—he was too young to understand that Angela had died. His grief over the loss of his mother grew into anger, and Antonia was the recipient of his wrath. Somehow it was her fault that his mother was gone. As he grew older, his contempt for Antonia only grew. But what happened next would permanently sever their relationship.

Several months later, Antonia traveled to the U.S. to join Francesco. As she prepared to join him in West Virginia, her mother, Rosa, begged her not to go. America was so very far away, and she feared she would never see her again.

"You'll go and never return! I've already lost one daughter; I can't bear losing you as well."

"*Mamma*," Antonia insisted, "Don't say that. Of course I will come back. This is my home."

"No, your sister Francesca is there now too. She never even writes to me," Rosa cried. "My children are all abandoning me, leaving me to languish in this godforsaken village!"

"There's no need for dramatics, *Mamma*. We all love you. But you must understand that a wife's place is with her husband. And these children need their father."

With that, Rosa wailed in agony, "Not only are you abandoning me, but you are taking my grandchildren from me, too. How cruel can you be?"

"*Mamma*, please!"

"No, you must leave the boys with me," Rosa insisted.

"No, *Mamma*. Our family has been separated enough. It's time for us to be all together again."

"At least leave Pietro with me. At two years old, he's old enough to miss his home here in Bisceglie. It will be such a disruption in his life. I will take care of him, and he will remain in the home that his mother lived in. That will comfort him."

"*Mamma*, I am his mother now. Pietro already resents me. You see how he won't even let me hold him. How will he feel if I leave him behind?"

"Antonia, you see how close we are. Pietro will be grateful to have some stability. At least if you leave Pietro with me, I know you will come back. Please, child, please leave him with me."

Antonia was beside herself with grief, and now she faced an impossible decision. How could she leave him? He was a troublesome child, but she loved him with all her heart. He had been through so much pain. Losing one mother was bad enough. But Rosa was relentless, and

Antonia, always the peacemaker, finally gave in. After that, the rift between Pietro and her grew wider. His resentment grew more bitter and lasted throughout his life. Antonia was not his mother and never would be.

Antonia Leaves Italy

The journey across the sea with four-year-old Gianni was arduous; they both experienced their fair share of seasickness, but what made it more difficult was her anxiety. Meeting Francesco for the first time as her husband was frightening. He had always been loving and kind to her sister, Angela, so she knew it would be fine. However, she was afraid of what married life would be like in a strange land with a man she hardly knew. Although her older sister was already in Virginia, she worried about how they would get by. Neither of them knew how to speak English. Neither she nor Francesco had had much schooling so they didn't speak proper Italian. The local dialect was all they knew, and she was afraid that English would be impossible to learn. Antonia resolved to do her best in a country where she did not speak or understand the language.

From the very start, Francesco and Antonia found comfort in each other as they grieved Angela's death. Each could share their profound loss with the other—they bonded over their pain. What could have been an awkward union grew into a warm intimacy with mutual respect and care. Within the first year, she was pregnant with their first child. It was the perfect tribute to the new family they had created. But it wasn't meant to be—Antonia had a miscarriage. Poor living conditions and inadequate healthcare provided a fertile environment for infections and disease. Losing children during pregnancy or as toddlers was a common occurrence during that time.

Before long, Antonia was pregnant once again. In 1916, Antonia gave birth to her first child, Orazio. He was a joyful distraction during a tough and lonely period.

Life in West Virginia was difficult for them. Francesco's work on the railroad was back-breaking—he would return each evening exhausted and sore. Antonia doted on his every need, made sure the dinner table was overflowing, and that there were many loaves of bread. In the span of seven years, Antonia had three more children. Angela (Lily), named for her sister, was born in March 1918. Antonia (Antoinette) was born in 1919, named after Francesco's mom. And they named Rosa, born in October 1921, after Antonia's mom.

The naming custom, which has continued into present-day Italy, is that the firstborn male is named for the paternal grandfather—or the firstborn female for the paternal grandmother. The second male and female children are named for the maternal grandfather and grandmother, respectively. Some of Bisceglie's most common family names are Francesco, Antonia, Maria, Mauro, Angela, Giovanni, and Nicola. There are male and female versions of each of those names, making the occurrence of each dizzying. Given the naming tradition, there were always multiple cousins with the identical names. Often, nicknames took precedence—it was much easier to keep track.

Antonia and Francesco took comfort because although they were thousands of miles from their homeland, they had family in Virginia. Francesco's brother, Orazio, after whom their son was named, lived there with his wife, Francesca. She was Antonia's older sister. The two brothers had married two sisters. The close family ties comforted and sustained them so many miles from their homes in Italy. Together, they could speak the Biscegliese dialect and carry on their customs and traditions.

However, that brought other problems since Francesca was a busybody who loved to stir the pot and then sit back to watch the ensuing drama. A selfish woman, she looked out for no one's interest but her own, often to the detriment of her sister. The two couples lived in an Italian ghetto where little English was spoken, but Antonia relied on Francesca for translation when necessary. She lived nearby and was always free with her advice and counsel, and as always, self-serving.

Francesco had traveled to America to find work and a better life for his family. For many years, his work in the coal mine provided a good living for his young family. Laborers were in high demand. But when work dried up, many immigrants returned to their native lands. Francesco resolved to find another job in the US, even if they had to move away from West Virginia. Hearing that, Antonia's sister painted a picture of gloom and doom.

"Antonia, what are you going to do? You can't follow him from town to town as he looks for work."

"What do you mean, Francesca? My place is with my husband. What else would I do?"

"Antonia, be reasonable. You have four children to care for. How will you find a place to live that's large enough? How will you take care of them as you travel? That is no life for a child, let alone four of them."

Francesca's argument swayed Francesco. "Well, Antonia, maybe your sister has a point. You know I will worry about you constantly when I'm away. It wouldn't be right for you to be alone with the children."

"No, Francesco, why would I be alone? I have my sister here, and I don't want to leave you."

That's when Francesca chimed in again. "Antonia, listen to reason. What if my husband loses his job and we have to move as well? You'll have no one here. At least in Bisceglie, you'll be with *Mamma*. I know she misses you so. Besides, just think of how happy she will be to meet her American grandchildren!"

"*Sì*, Antonia, she's right. Life for us here is so uncertain. In Bisceglie, they'll be able to meet Pietro, their big brother. I know he misses us all."

"But where will you live, Francesco? You can't live alone. Who will cook and clean for you?"

"Oh, don't you worry, Antonia," Francesca offered. "He will live with us. At least both of you will be with family."

There was no way she could refuse at that point. Against her better judgment, she began to make plans to travel back to Italy with the children. Antonia's heart ached at the thought of leaving her husband. Their bond had grown stronger throughout the years, and they came to depend on each other for support and intimacy. Antonia was shy and reserved while Francesco was more gregarious and loved to tease her. Watching her face blush bright red brought giggles of delight. Their affection for one another had grown over the years.

However, family finances dictated he could not support her and five children in the United States. They believed that being back in Italy with her mother and the rest of the family would provide the support she needed. And Antonia couldn't argue with the fact that she missed her mother and little Pietro. She wished Francesco could return with her, but believed that their decision was for the family's well-being.

When the day of departure arrived, she boarded the ship with Orazio and the three girls but left eleven-year-old Gianni with his father. At the time, she didn't know she was already pregnant with Carlo, who was born in Bisceglie in December 1922. Her homecoming was bittersweet, but Antonia was content to be surrounded by her loving extended family. The girls were young and basked in the playful attention they received from their *Nonna*. Orazio, however, never adjusted to Italy after the move. He missed his father terribly and felt out of place. Orazio had already learned to speak English and found it difficult to understand most of the Biscegliese dialect. Tragically, he would never reach adulthood; he died of rheumatic fever at the age of four. Regardless of his diagnosis, Antonia always said that Orazio died of a broken heart. The only time he recaptured his joy was when his father visited from America. Each time Francesco left Italy to return to his work, Orazio pined for him until his next visit. Years after his death, they named my father in memory of him.

After Antonia's departure Francesco discovered that his sister-in-law had an ulterior motive. She informed him that he would pay for room and board. Francesca convinced Antonia to leave to make extra money. But Francesca's game didn't end there. Month after month, he would put the money on the kitchen table when payday arrived. And although he knew she was lying, Francesca would frequently tell him he had missed a payment.

"Eh, Francesco, you forgot to pay the rent this month. You know we have to buy food for the table, don't you? And you like your bread!"

"What? I put it there last week. Didn't you see it?" he'd ask.

"No, you must have forgotten again."

He never forgot. Rather than begin an argument within the family, he ended up paying her a second time. Each time she tried to deceive him, he became more dispirited. He realized that his living arrangement was not sustainable. If his sister-in-law lied about this, how much more was she doing behind his back?

Given that Francesco's work was not steady, he had to move around a lot. Working in the coal mines, Francesco experienced difficulty breathing. The coal dust had impacted his lungs. It was time for a change, and he believed that there would be better opportunities in a big city. Before the year was up, he made the decision to move to New York City.

Chapter Eleven
An Ocean Apart

West Virginia • New York 1920-1950

Gianni stayed with Francesco after Antonia returned to Italy and could not have been happier. West Virginia was the only home he could remember and leaving it to go back to a country where he didn't understand the language held no allure. Zia Francesca had been an integral part of his life from the very beginning. Having her as his surrogate mother seemed perfectly natural. Both Francesca and Antonia were his birth mother's sisters—it always seemed that he had three moms. Zia Francesca took care of Gianni as if he were her own son. During that time, he became closer to her than Antonia, who had been absent during his most formative years.

When Gianni got older, Zia Francesca decided it was time for him to marry. Her cousin had a lovely daughter who was just a year older than Gianni. She was a lovely young woman who loved to cook and keep a nice home. Zia Francesca thought she would be a perfect match. But Gianni was more interested in her younger sister, who was full of life — a spitfire who liked to go out and have fun. Marrying her would have been out of the question, because the older girl had to be married off first. But Gianni was not ready to get married yet. He was young and handsome and enjoyed all the attention he got. Settling down hadn't even occurred to him.

Try as he might, he could not fight Zia Francesca. Her will was mightier than anyone he had ever known. Gianni reluctantly agreed to an arranged marriage to Angelina but made it clear he was not happy. Angelina was a dutiful wife and hoped that affection between them would grow.

Francesco traveled to Italy whenever he could to bring money and spend time with Antonia. They missed each other terribly, but this was the reality of life for the working poor. You did what you had to do to find work and support your family. They were not in the minority. In many southern Italian towns, it was commonplace to have families split up due to lack of work.

Francesco managed to get back to Bisceglie every eighteen months or so, and it seemed that Antonia became pregnant each time he visited. Three more children were born and lived with her in Bisceglie. The second, Orazio (Larry), was born in 1926, Sal in 1928, and the youngest, Francesca (Frances), was born in 1931. Essentially, the younger siblings, Carlo, Orazio, Sal, and Francesca grew up as Italians in southern Italy.

Orazio at 2-years-old
holding his baby brother Sal's hand.

Born in the United States, Lily, Antionette, and Rosie were American citizens and could travel back to the U.S. at any time. By their early teens, they sought to escape the poverty of Bisceglie and longed for the land of opportunity. As American citizens, they were free to travel, so Francesco paid their fare and they grew into adulthood in New York City. The four Italian siblings referred to them as the *Americani*.

Life in America was not the dream they had expected. They lived with their Zia Francesca, Antonia's sister, and she was particularly hard on the girls. She nagged them about cleaning the house or setting the table for dinner. Lily, being quiet and shy, endured her ire. Francesca's sharp words often wounded Lily, though she never responded to her insults. It seemed she reserved all the worst household tasks for Lily, who resented her aunt. The youngest of the three, Rosie, was a spitfire, and whenever Zia Francesca would make a backhanded comment, she would fire right back with sarcasm. Francesca liked the challenge and enjoyed their sparring. With all the attention placed on Lily and Rosie, Antionette seemed to skate by with little trouble. She was affable and friendly to everyone—she approached everything with a smile and let negativity roll right off her back.

"Lily, don't let her bother you so much," Antionette said. "You know how she is."

"Yeah, she's a nasty old woman who hates her life," Rosie added. "Just be glad you're not her."

"Easy for you to say," Lily shot back. "Zia Francesca doesn't harp on you two like she does on me. And why do I always get the worst chores? She loves to see me suffer."

Lily found it hard to follow her sisters' advice. She was more sensitive and took Zia Francesca's insults to heart. The constant barrage of negativity cut her. She couldn't wait to get out of the apartment. The sooner she could marry, the better. When she met Eddie from Naples, she loved his gregarious personality. He was a butcher's son with a secure income. Although she got pushback from the family because he wasn't from Bisceglie, butchers were considered a good catch because of their financial status. They dated briefly and married shortly thereafter. Together with Gianni and his wife, they moved away from New York City to raise their families. Just an hour and a half train ride away was Bridgeport, Connecticut, which had a booming industrial economy. There were numerous factories, and the job market was roaring. The two couples ended up living within walking distance to each other. They lived in modest houses with backyards perfect for vegetable gardens and ample room for children to play.

Rosie and Antionette married but raised their families in New York City. Rosie met a young fellow who worked in a factory that made fine china. His parents were from Sicily, however, John was born and raised in New York. Antionette married a kind, affable man named Joe whose parents were also from Sicily. Joe was quick with a joke and always put people at ease. Both couples lived downtown and became real New Yorkers.

Young Orazio

Bisceglie, Province of Bari, Italy 1930s

Orazio always dreamed of joining his siblings in America and knew he'd be on his way as soon as he saved enough money for the voyage. When he was only eight years old, Antonia and her brother took the train up to Naples with her four children. Francesco had sent word that his job was stable enough for her to join him. The children couldn't have been more excited. Life in America was a dream. Knowing they had brothers and sisters they had never met served as a constant draw. At last, they were going to America. Antonia packed bags for each of the children and bought tickets for the train.

Antonia and her three youngest children walked from the station to the harbor with hurried anticipation. When they arrived at the port, Orazio lifted his head to see the massive hull of the ship that was to take them to a new land. His excitement and fear mingled, making his constant patter nearly unintelligible. He had so many questions: When would they leave? How long would it take? Where would they sleep? Would *Papá* be waiting to greet them upon their arrival?

Antonia patiently put her hand on his shoulder to calm him as she searched for the correct office. She had her tickets in hand but was told that the children would have to undergo a medical examination to board the ship. She never trusted doctors and adding this stipulation to their travel plans did not sit well with her. But Antonia was a quiet and meek woman who never questioned authority. She simply put her head down and did what was necessary to support her family. Raising four children on her own with little money taught her perseverance and gave her the tenacity to make things happen.

Her youngest, Francesca, was separated from the three boys for her examination. She was an ebullient little girl, full of life and always laughing. She didn't show a bit of fear as she entered the room filled with young girls standing in line. She looked toward her mother and said, "Don't worry, *Mamma*! I am fine. Go with the boys, and I'll meet you on the other side." Antonia smiled and thought, *What a delightfully precocious child.*

In a separate room, the boys stripped to their underwear and lined up with many others. They had twenty or so people ahead of them. Carlo and Sal were always cutting up, joking with each other and teasing Orazio. While he was quiet and shy, they were gregarious and mischievous, constantly preying upon his fears.

"Orazio," Carlo said to him, "they will stick you with a huge needle."

"Yeah, I saw it too," Sal chimed in. "They're going to pull down your underwear and poke it in your butt." They pealed with laughter while Orazio shuddered in fear.

Orazio was anxiously waiting for his turn. Carlo and Sal had passed the exam with no issues. When he was finally called, Orazio timidly approached the doctor with his head lowered.

"All right, young man, let's take a look at you," the doctor said as he placed his stethoscope on his chest and listened intently.

"Your heart and lungs are in fine shape. Let's see those eyes."

He lifted Orazio's chin with his hand, and his expression changed.

"Does your eye hurt? Did you notice that it's all red?"

"No, no, it's fine. I was crying earlier. My brothers were teasing me," Orazio lied.

"This isn't from crying. You have an infection. I'm sorry, but you can't travel like this."

The doctor diagnosed him with pink eye, and they denied him his travel papers. When Antonia heard the news, she was heartbroken. She had waited so long to be reunited with Francesco and her four oldest children. She longed to have all of them in one home. How could this be happening? She resigned herself to traveling back to Bisceglie with her children to try again after Orazio fully recovered. Her brother, who had accompanied them on their journey, offered to bring Orazio home and send him after he got better.

"Absolutely not! How can I leave my son? He would be the only one left in Italy. Orazio is a sensitive boy; he would be lost without me. No, my place is with the children."

"But Antonia, listen to reason," her brother tried to convince her. "If you don't take this ship now, who knows when it will be possible to travel again? You have the tickets. Just go. Orazio will be fine with me. I promise."

"No, either we all board the ship together, or nobody goes!" Antonia was a mild-tempered woman, but she was fiercely protective of her children. Her decision was final. As expected, the boys did not take the news well, and they were mercilessly cruel to Orazio.

"It's all your fault," Carlo accused.

"Yeah, what's that gross stuff in your eye? No wonder they didn't want you on the ship," Sal said.

"Get away from us!" Carlo said as he walked away.

Francesca and Orazio were very close. She immediately put her arm around him and said, "Don't listen to them, Orazio. They always try to hurt your feelings. *Mamma* will bring us back to Naples as soon as you get better. You'll see. Then we will all be living in America together."

Orazio hung his head in shame and didn't say a word during the entire trip back to Bisceglie. They didn't know it at the time, but many years would pass before the opportunity to travel to America would come again.

Growing up in Bisceglie was an adventure. If your family worked in the countryside, you learned to tend the olive or almond groves. Similar to other farming communities, as soon as a child was old enough, he or she would contribute what they could. They added more responsibilities as children grew older. But for the city folk, if your child was not academically inclined, he would learn a trade. There were no truancy laws when Orazio was of school age—he and his two brothers were not interested in their studies. He stopped going to school after third grade. By his preteen years, Orazio was apprenticing in a carpentry shop that made fine furniture. He found that he loved working with his hands. Although he earned very little money, Antonia came to rely on the extra income he brought in. Unfortunately, he was the only one of her children that contributed to household expenses. Orazio resented his brothers, who were more interested in chasing girls than finding a job.

Antonia's four Italian children were nearly adults by the time she was finally able to travel to New York to join Francesco. By that time, Carlo could not join her because, at twenty years of age, he was serving his required Italian military service. After fulfilling his two years, he was no longer a minor and would not be allowed to join his parents. He put his name into the quota system and waited to be called.

Younger than Carlo, Orazio was of an age required by law to begin his service in the military. He lamented the timing of his mother's departure but planned to join her later. Orazio reported for his physical, but they told him that while he was in perfect shape, he was too short to be conscripted. He was elated and assumed that he'd join his mother for the journey across the ocean. However, the paperwork took another five months to process, so he waited anxiously for his official document of release.

The postwar expansion in the United States brought unprecedented wealth to the economy. Factory jobs were plentiful and provided security to the working class. Consumerism began in earnest when the forty-hour workweek was established, giving time for leisure activities. The booming middle class garnered enough extra money to further fuel the economy, and homeownership was at an all-time high. New York experienced unparalleled prosperity—it was the largest manufacturing center in the world. Emerging as a financial capital, it traded millions of dollars a day. New York was a shining modern city in whose wealth immigrants from around the world wanted to share.

Antonia's two youngest children couldn't wait to get to America. It was April 1947 when Antonia, Sal, and Francesca arrived in New York

City. The city skyline rose as they neared land. They were the tallest buildings they had ever seen. The thriving city lay gleaming before them. In 1947, New York was just beginning to establish itself as a leading America's city. They joined the thousands of immigrants from around the world who sought to share in its prosperity. As their grand ship pulled into the harbor, fifteen-year-old Francesca sang with delight.

"I can't believe that we are finally here!"

"Look at all those tall buildings. It looks like they're living in the sky!" Sal said. "There is nothing like this in Italy."

Down on the dock, Francesco stood sporting a felt Fedora hat and a double-breasted suit and tie. Lost in a sea of Italian immigrants waving white handkerchiefs and calling out their names, Francesco tried desperately to see above the throngs. The crowd buzzed with excitement at seeing their loved ones. Nonetheless, Antonia spotted him and her three older girls waving at them as the ship pulled into port.

"Look, look, there's your father with your sisters," Antonia exclaimed.

The young women were elegantly dressed, each with long black hair and heels. There was no mistaking them for Biscegliese peasants. New York had given them an air of sophistication.

"They're so pretty. I can't believe how old they look," Frances said.

After their heartfelt reunion, the newly united family fell into an ordinary routine. Frances attended school and learned English. Sal found a job at a factory that made artificial flowers. The work was mind-numbing, but he didn't care. He was nineteen years old and living in New York City—he took full advantage of his good looks and city living.

Five months later, the military paperwork had finally been approved, and Orazio could finally join his family. The ship pulled into port early one morning. The auburn glow of sunrise was rivaled only by the magnificent Manhattan skyline. Slowly, the skyscrapers came into focus as the ship approached the harbor. By the time they reached the dock, the brilliant autumn sun had warmed the day. At last, his dream had come true. Orazio was in New York City. His sisters waited eagerly on the dock. When Frances saw him, she smothered him with kisses.

"Oh, how I missed you, Orazio!" she said.

"What kind of name is that?" Rosie said. "He's in America now. He needs an American name."

"But that's my name, Rosie! What else are they going to call me?" Orazio asked.

"They'll butcher that name. We'll call you Larry," Rosie proclaimed. "That's the American translation."

And although she was completely incorrect in her translation, the entire family in America called him Larry. An entire generation of Dell'Olios had no clue that Larry wasn't his actual name. But he didn't much care; he was starting a new life in New York City, so why not use an American name?

In the years that followed, Orazio worked hard to establish himself in New York City. He lived with his parents in a five-story walk-up on Worth Street in Little Italy. Orazio struggled to learn English by going to night school after a full day at the shop. Having trained as a furniture maker in Bisceglie, he was accustomed to delicate workmanship. He had hopes of finding employment making fine furniture where he could use his artistic skills.

However, his job was a significant step down. The woodworking he did required no artistry or finishing work. The manufacturer was in Brooklyn, where he was making library ladders with rollers. Brooklyn had been one of the central industrial hubs for the country during World War II, and although the postwar years saw many factories move to cheaper locations, it provided many jobs for laborers from the five boroughs of New York.

Although he was utterly bored with the work, it was a job and he was in New York City. He had dreamed of living in America ever since he was a little boy. As challenging as his daily routine was in New York, it far surpassed his life in a small town in Southern Italy. In Bisceglie, the prospect of steady employment in his field was nearly impossible to find. His older siblings had a distinct advantage over Orazio. Lily, Antionette, and Rosie were born in New York and spoke English, while his oldest brother, Gianni, had been living there since he was very young. But Orazio was a hard worker and worked tirelessly doing whatever it took to be successful in America.

Chapter Twelve
Mauro & Despina Return

Mauro remained in Rhodes for two more years before his return to Italy. He knew that people in Bisceglie would be reticent to accept Despina. The people in his hometown were quite provincial. Since they were starting their lives anew, they decided she would take the name Maria to downplay the fact that she was Greek. However, her name change never took. Throughout the rest of her life in Bisceglie, they called her *La Greca,* the Greek.

Rumors about Mauro's life in Rhodes reached Bisceglie before his return. If there was anything the locals despised, it was foreigners. That Mauro had been sleeping with a Greek girl with a Turkish father was bad enough, but the fact that she had been married before and had a son was a shocking scandal. Italian ex-pats who lived in Rhodes told of his common-law marriage to Despina and that she had never divorced her first husband. Nicoletta didn't believe all the talk. Her big brother would never dream of living in sin. Images of Mauro from her childhood loomed large in her memory. He was always the handsome man who brought her treats and treated her like a princess. She looked forward to his return with excited anticipation.

In April 1945, the family gathered to welcome Mauro back to Bisceglie. Antonietta and Nicoletta cooked and cleaned all day. There was an excited buzz throughout the house. Mauro had not been there since before his parents died, and so much had changed. Antonietta had married; she and her husband had taken over the master bedroom, and Nicoletta was a teenager—a young woman with a mind of her own.

Mauro's telegram alerting them of his return was brief. There were no details, just the date. He had given no indication that he would bring Despina and her son. Relatives packed the principal room of the apartment, chatting animatedly. The door opened, and in walked an exotic-looking woman with dark hair and eyes. A beautiful little boy with jet-black hair held her hand in fear. The room went silent. Mauro followed just behind her, but there were no cries of joy. No one said a word, nor did they run up to greet them. Mauro's expression, at first smiling, turned to one of bewilderment. *What was the reason for this cold greeting?* he wondered. Then he looked at the faces staring at Despina and her son. His face grew red with rage. *How dare they greet Despina and me like this? I am the head of this family. They should show me the respect I deserve.* Mauro would never forget how cold his family was, and the chasm that opened between them would remain for many years to come.

After the initial shock passed, Piero and Nicoletta moved in to hug and kiss him. Without explaining their relationship, Mauro introduced them to Despina and her son. There was a cordial kiss on each cheek, a forced smile, and then a scramble to take care of practical matters. How were they all going to fit in their tiny house? Where were they going to sleep? They expected one person, and now there were three to consider. There was already a married couple sleeping in his parents' bedroom. The family owned two other small homes, but they rented them. It was inappropriate for brother and sister to sleep in the same bed, especially at their age, but that was the only option. Nicoletta gave up her bed and shared with her brother Piero. The awkward sleeping arrangement added more ill feelings to an already uncomfortable situation.

From that day forward, Mauro clung to Despina as her most ardent ally. Anyone who dared to treat her with a lack of respect would bear his wrath. He insisted that they call her *La Signora* and required everyone to greet her with deference. Most of the townsfolk thought it amusing, and tongues wagged behind her back. It wasn't just the family who didn't accept her—everyone in Bisceglie called her *La Greca*. It was an awful environment for her, but she was used to adversity. Despina could take care of herself. In public, townspeople understood that to get anything from Mauro, they had to fawn over her. Mauro worked in the medical benefits office for the government, and people continually came to him to push their applications to the top. Anyone who didn't address his wife with honor or respect understood that their cases would be relegated to the bottom of the pile.

"*Buon giorno*, Mauro. How is *La Signora* today?"

If they met while on a stroll in the piazza, the fawning was often exaggerated.

"*Buona sera, Signora.* You look absolutely stunning tonight."

He knew they were disingenuous, but he watched Despina's face light up with each passing compliment. As long as she was happy, he didn't care if it was only an act.

However, Mauro expected more from his relatives. He believed Despina should be on equal footing as he asserted himself as the head of the family. Yet none of them accepted his authority. It was even more challenging for his siblings to witness Despina's rise in status within the family. Nicoletta resented her disruption of their intimate dynamic. Antonietta, Piero, and Nicoletta had to fend for themselves throughout the war and had worked to put their lives back together in its wake. Mauro and Despina couldn't compete with the affectionate relationships that were cemented during the years he was away. The harmonious Di Bitetto clan found themselves in unfamiliar territory.

Not long after their move to Bisceglie, Despina became pregnant again, and she was beside herself.

"How can this be? We were careful."

"Despina," Mauro pleaded. "It will be all right; you'll see. You will love this child just as you love Franco and our little Lucia."

"No, no one will ever come before Franco. You never loved him. See, that's what you really desire. You want to father your own child. Then you'll pay no attention to us. As soon as Lucia was born, no one else mattered. Franco and I could have dropped dead, and you wouldn't have cared as long as you had Lucia."

"Despina, that is just nonsense. Nothing could ever cause me to love you or Franco less. I would do anything for you."

"Anything?" she asked.

"Anything. I mean that, my love," he said as he reached for her hand.

"Then help me get an abortion. You know where to get the drugs. I don't want this baby."

Mauro was shocked, but he promised he would do anything for her. There was no way he could go back on his word. Even though it wasn't legal in Italy, there were always remedies that were sold on the black market. Against his better judgment, he assured Despina that he'd take care of it. It broke his heart—he genuinely wanted another child.

"You have to promise me one thing, Despina," he pleaded. "You can tell no one about this. I couldn't bear the shame."

"Oh, Mauro, you worry too much about what people think of you. Just be a man and do what you promised."

Mauro acquired the drugs that would cause a miscarriage and gave them to her. The poison made her violently ill, and in the end, she lost the baby.

Despina was in bed sick for days afterward. Mauro asked his sister to go take care of her. Nicoletta did not know why she was so ill. They needed her—she would swallow her pride and tend to her sister-in-law. Nicoletta waited on her every need, cleaning their apartment, making tea, and cooking. Despina complained and criticized everything she did for her. Nicoletta bit her lip and kept her anger at bay. But then Despina's ire turned to Mauro. That's when she confessed it to her.

"That brother of yours would have left Franco and me on the side of the road after his child was born. Who knows, he might have sent me back to Greece. There was no way I was going to have his child."

"What do you mean, Despina? What are you talking about?"

"Can't you tell? I was pregnant."

"Oh, my God. Did you have a miscarriage?"

"You really are naïve, Nicoletta. No, I had an abortion."

Then she told her what drugs she took and went into specific detail about the miscarriage itself. The entire conversation nauseated Nicoletta. She was devastated by the fact that Mauro not only knew what she had done, but helped her. It was all born of Despina's jealousy. Nicoletta had always looked up to Mauro, but he was not the man she believed him to be.

Having Nicoletta tending to her every need delighted Despina. She was animated and telling her stories all day long, even about the abortion. Despina was so bold; she confessed to Nicoletta that she had spoken ill of her many times.

"Your brother said you had a beautiful face. But I told him he was mistaken, especially when you smile—that space between your front teeth—ugly."

Nicoletta knew she was trying to get a rise out of her. She wasn't going to give her the satisfaction of seeing her hurt feelings. It was nothing new to Nicoletta. She had heard many of her nasty comments from friends and family. *At least she has the courage to say them directly to my face,* she thought.

But as soon as Mauro returned after a long day of work, Despina put on her helpless-wife act. Tina could see the weariness in Mauro's face and his gait. He rested his hat on the hook and went directly to Despina.

"How are you, my love? Are you feeling any better this evening?"

"Oh, the pain, the pain. Mauro, I suffered all day long, everything hurts."

"Do you want me to get the doctor? Should we go to the hospital?"

"No, no, I just can't stand the pain."

"Ok, let me go to the pharmacy, I'm sure he can give you something to help you sleep."

"Yes, yes, please, I can't take it anymore."

Nicoletta was in the kitchen, boiling the water for pasta. Hearing Despina deceive Mauro just to gain his sympathy was too much. She was angry and slammed the lid down on the pot of water. They didn't even notice. Spending that day with Despina was the final nail in the coffin of their relationship. Nicoletta would never trust her. It was amid this atmosphere of distrust and family struggle that Orazio's first letter arrived.

Nicoletta at 16 years old.

Chapter Thirteen
Nicoletta As a Teenager

Bisceglie, Province of Bari, Italy 1940s

Nicoletta's late teens brought several suitors, but none seemed to keep her interest. Her aunt, Zia Nunzia, would always try to talk to her about boys. She loved seeing people's reactions when making slightly bawdy remarks about marriage or sex. Zia Nunzia would laugh wickedly as she watched Nicoletta's face flush red. She tried desperately to fix her up with eligible young men. Zia Nunzia enjoyed playfully teasing her beloved niece—a giggle or smile from Nicoletta was priceless. Then she would pull her in for an all-consuming hug.

Nunzia's daughter, Lucrezia, was a few years older than Nicoletta and looked upon her as a little sister. With an amused grin on her face, she watched the playful banter between her mother and Nicoletta. Lucrezia learned to sew a few years earlier than Nicoletta. A traveling fabric salesman stopped at their house regularly to exhibit all the new fabric each season. He was a good-looking man with beautiful thick hair. Nicoletta, whose hair was very fine, always noted people with a full, shiny head of hair, especially the young men. Zia Nunzia knew this and concocted a plan.

On one of the salesman's visits, Nunzia invited Nicoletta to her house. She had met him before, and Nunzia believed that there was a spark between them. As he unfolded several bolts of fabric, Nunzia saw that she was riveted. He was waxing eloquent about the beautiful dresses that Nicoletta could sew from them. He exuded charm.

"This one is particularly beautiful, don't you think?" he said as he held it up against her. "The color brings out your golden eyes."

"It is gorgeous. But wouldn't it be difficult to work with?" Nicoletta asked, rubbing the fabric between her fingers.

Then Nunzia disappeared from the room, leaving the fates to work their magic.

"Oh, but I have seen your handiwork. You're a skilled artist; your dresses are some of the finest in Bisceglie," he said as he reached out to touch her lace collar. "I am quite sure that you could work wonders with this fabric."

Nicoletta felt her face flush with heat as he moved closer. She was undoubtedly attracted to him but felt uncomfortable. She lowered her head with embarrassment and was about to speak when his fingers gently lifted her chin. He moved his face close to hers.

"You know, you are quite beautiful, Nicoletta."

When his lips grazed hers, she turned her face, so his kiss landed on her cheek. The moment was awkward, and she held up her hand to put some distance between them.

"Thank you, but I think you might have the wrong idea. I'm sure that we don't need any fabric today. Thank you for coming."

"I'm sorry, Nicoletta. I didn't mean to offend you," he said as he packed up the bolts of fabric. "Will I see you at my next visit?"

"I don't think so. Have a lovely day," she said as he showed him to the door.

After he left, she looked at her aunt with annoyance.

"Zia, why did you leave us alone like that?"

"What do you mean, *figlia*? I had chores to do. Besides, you were getting along so well. He's cute, isn't he?"

"Yes, Zia, he is cute. But I don't like being caught off guard. He tried to kiss me."

"I knew it. So how was it? Did you like it?" she asked teasingly.

"Zia! That's not the point. I don't want you to be my matchmaker. I can do that on my own."

Her niece's spark delighted Nunzia. She was beginning to assert herself—showing her independence. Orphaned at such a young age, Nicoletta had a heartbreaking childhood, and it comforted Nunzia to see her strength.

A year or so later, there was another young man who expressed an interest in Nicoletta.

Tony was a handsome young man with a head of thick brown hair. Once again, Nicoletta was drawn to his beautiful hair. Her cousin worked with Tony at his father's shop, making barrels for wine. The factory was just down the street from her home, on the way to La Misericordia, Nicoletta's parish church. Each day, as she walked to daily Mass, Tony stood at the door and waved. He was totally infatuated with her—it was the worst-kept secret in their circle of friends.

One day, he finally worked up the courage to speak with her. Tony had a beautiful magazine called *The Grand Hotel,* which showed panoramic photographs of travel destinations and worldwide adventures. He waited for her to walk home after Mass and approached her with the magazine in hand. Tony knew she dreamed of traveling away from Bisceglie someday. He just had to chat with her, and he had the perfect opening.

"Hello, Nicoletta. Have you seen the Grand Hotel this month?"

"Ciao, Tony, let me see."

That was how it began. With each new issue, he would stop by to show Nicoletta the feature article and read parts to her, saying, "It's *fantastico,* isn't it?" He made sure to show off his intelligence and knowledge of the world beyond Bisceglie. This went on for several months until he decided she might be more receptive to his advances. He gave Nicoletta's cousin the newest issue of the magazine and a chocolate treat for Tina.

"Please, tell her it's from me. She trusts you."

"Okay, Tony, but you know how independent she is. I can't make any promises."

Her cousin enjoyed being the messenger, but couldn't resist the chocolate. He gobbled it down before he got to her house. He showed up with the gift from Tony and gave it to her.

"Tony sent this for you. I think he likes you."

"Well, that's obvious. Did he say anything further?"

His guilt got the better of him, and he confessed.

"Well, yes. He sent you a chocolate to tell you how sweet you are, but I ate it. I'm sorry, Nicoletta."

"You're such an adolescent," she said as he playfully slapped his arm. "Don't worry about it. But tell Tony I'm too young to get involved with boys."

Nicoletta thought Tony was handsome, but there was no spark between them. Her sister-in-law, Despina, got wind of the budding romance and pulled Tony aside.

"You like Nicoletta, don't you? I see you looking at her when she walks by."

"Yes, Signora, she is lovely."

"You know, Tony, that match is impossible," Despina said firmly.

"Why do you say that? She seems to like me too. I'm a good-looking man and come from a well-respected family."

"You think because you are handsome that you are in her league? Tony, you may be handsome, but you are much too short. Nicoletta likes tall men."

Then Despina turned on her heels and walked away. Poor Tony's jaw dropped as she turned from him. She didn't give a damn about his wounded ego. She was never one to consider anyone's feelings. Even so, her dig seemed unnecessarily cruel, especially because it wasn't true.

The Dress

Given her training as a dressmaker, Nicoletta always had a keen sense of fashion. She knew how to dress in a manner that accentuated her figure without breaking the bank. Nicoletta prided herself on her creations, and people took note of her outfits. One year at Easter time, she lamented to Antonietta that she didn't have enough saved to buy fabric for a new dress.

"I can see it now: cousin Nina will be there prancing around in her expensive new dress. I'm sure she'll have a new bonnet and shoes to match. Then I'll hear Zio Tonino make a rude comment about the poor relations. I am so sick of them and their nasty ways."

"Now, Nicoletta, be grateful for what we have. What does it matter? So she dons a new outfit. You always look better than she does," Antonietta replied.

"I know you're just trying to make me feel better, and I appreciate that. But Nina is beautiful, and she rubs my nose in it every chance she gets."

"Well then, why don't you ask your brother? Mauro can certainly afford it, and you have always been the apple of his eye."

"That was a long time ago, Antonietta. Ever since he returned from Rhodes with Despina, things have changed."

"True, but you will always be his baby sister. How could he resist?"

It was worth a try, she thought. She had never asked Mauro for anything, and perhaps it would be a matter of pride, seeing his sister dressed better than anyone in the family. Resolute in her decision to approach him, Nicoletta searched for a moment when Mauro was alone and in a good mood. When the opportunity finally came, she gathered her courage and swallowed her pride.

"Mauro, it'll be Easter soon, and all the young women will wear their new dresses. It's been years since I had something nice to wear. I'm sure you heard the story about what happened with Zio Tonino and Nina a few years back."

"Tina, that was years ago. You have to get beyond that," he chided her gently. "You're nearly an adult now."

"Of course, but I still want to look pretty on Easter Sunday, and I've outgrown most of my nice clothes. Could you find it in your heart to buy some fabric for me? It's much less costly than a dress. Then I can design and sew it for myself," she reasoned.

"Well, that is a marvelous idea, and I would love to help you, but you should ask Despina. If it's okay with her, I will buy you some fabric."

Nicoletta was startled by his response. It offended her that he wouldn't decide on his own. Mauro knew of the tension between the two women. Despina never treated Nicoletta with respect. She was always making comments about her wispy hair. Nicoletta was self-conscious about the space between her two front teeth, and Despina was sure to point it out whenever Tina laughed or smiled broadly. *How could Mauro not understand how degrading it would be to beg her for money?* Nicoletta thought. She said nothing further to her brother as she walked away disappointed. When Mauro returned home to Despina that evening, he asked about his sister.

"Did Nicoletta come by to see you today?" he asked his wife as he kissed her on the cheek.

"Nicoletta? No, why would she come to visit me? You know she hates me," Despina said with a pout.

"She doesn't hate you, Despina. That's just silly," he said. "She's a teenager. They're all moody."

"Not her. She's sweet and kind to everyone but me."

"Be that as it may, I told her to ask you for a little money for fabric. She wants to sew herself a new dress for Easter."

"Ha! So, she needs something from me after all," Despina said with a self-satisfied grin. Any opportunity to lord her power over the little princess thrilled her. She wanted no competition for Mauro's affections— in her mind, Nicoletta was the greatest of threats. Despina waited in excited anticipation for her sister-in-law to ask for her help. But Nicoletta never visited Despina after the conversation she had with Mauro.

Piero, on the other hand, doted on his little sister. His heart broke for her after the death of their parents. Nicoletta was so young to be orphaned, and he did his best to fill his father's shoes. She, in turn, looked up to him with admiration and respect. There was a natural affection between the siblings, and they always looked out for one another. Holy Week was upon them and it was already Holy Thursday. Piero could see that Tina was feeling down.

"What's going on with Nicoletta? She's usually so excited about the holidays. This is not like her," he asked Antonietta.

"You haven't heard? Your big brother and that witch he's married to are playing a terrible game at Nicoletta's expense."

"*Dio!* What is it this time, Antonietta?"

After she explained the situation to him, he just shook his head. He, too, was disappointed with Mauro's behavior since his return to Bisceglie. He wouldn't have thought twice about buying anything for Nicoletta in the past. His relationship with Despina had turned him away from anyone but her. Fool that he was, Mauro was blind to it.

Piero searched for a solution to his little sister's dilemma. He had finally gotten paid for an extra electrical job he had done a few weeks back and realize the timing was perfect. He decided not to add the extra money into the household account—he had a better idea.

"Nicolettina," he said, using her endearing nickname. It was how he addressed her when she was a child. The name oozed affection. "Shouldn't you be working on a project right now?"

"What? I don't think so. Did I forget something?"

"Why did you spend all those months learning to design and sew dresses? You know Easter is only a few days away," he teased.

"Very funny, Piero. Obviously, Antonietta told you what our big brother said to me. The last thing I'll do is beg Despina for money—no matter how desperately I want something."

"But you don't have to, my dear sister! Look what I have here," he said with a twinkle in his eye as he held out an envelope of cash.

Nicoletta's eyes grew wide. She ran and jumped into his arms with a delighted squeal.

"Go, my dear Nicoletta. Go now before the store closes, and while you're at it, buy yourself a new pair of shoes. Those *ciabattas* you're wearing have had it."

She spent the next two days on her new creation. Every free moment, she sewed. When she wasn't cleaning and cooking to prepare for the holiday, she was at the sewing machine. The sun rose on Easter Sunday just as she put the last stitches on the hem.

"Are you still at it, Nicoletta? Didn't you sleep at all last night?" Antonietta asked as she came from her bedroom, wiping the sleep from her eyes.

"Yes, yes, got a few hours, but I got up early to put on the finishing touches. What do you think?" Nicoletta said as she held up her creation.

Lilac crepe shimmered in the early morning light filtering through the window. It was as if she were holding a freshly cut bouquet of flowers. The crepe fabric was a challenge to sew, and it would often gather at seams ruining the line. Being as fashion conscious as she was, Nicoletta had chosen an intricate design, working tirelessly on the pattern. Fabric is woven at a 45-degree angle and when it is cut on the bias (diagonally), it accentuates the lines and curves of a woman's figure. She knew the crepe would drape softly on her body. The skirt had a little flare, and a fitted top with a rounded collar reached just above her breasts. In her determination, it had taken her less than three days to sew her dress.

"Oh, Nicoletta," Antonietta sighed. "It is your best work ever. How on earth did you come up with such a design? Quick, try it on. I must see what it looks like on you."

Antonietta helped her zip up the back, and Nicoletta turned to face her. Antonietta put her hands on either side of her face as tears streamed down her face.

"Nicoletta, you will be the best-dressed woman at Mass today. I am so proud of you."

"Now, don't cry, Antonietta. You're going to get me started, and after all this work, I don't want to appear with puffy eyes!"

They chuckled at their emotional display, then Nicoletta took both of Antonietta's hands in hers and looked into her eyes.

"Thank you for all your support. I know it was you who told Piero about all of this. You always look out for me. I honestly don't know what I'd do without you, Antonietta."

A few hours later, Piero and Nicoletta walked to church arm in arm. Their smiles were radiant, and Piero could not have been prouder. He nodded at his friends as they glanced appreciatively at his beautiful younger sister. That and her genuine happiness were all the thanks he needed.

"Nicoletta, there's Despina. You should greet her before Mass," he advised.

"You're right. I shouldn't hold a grudge on Easter Sunday."

As she approached, Despina looked her up and down with disdain. She didn't even try to hide her displeasure.

"Where did you get that dress, Nicoletta?"

"I made it. Do you like it?"

"Yes, of course. But how did you pay for the fabric? I thought you were broke."

"Piero worked an extra job and gave me the money. He's the best big brother ever, isn't he?"

"Ha," she scoffed as she looked her up and down. That's when Despina noticed her shoes. "I've never seen those shoes before. Are those Zia Giovanna's shoes?"

"No, these aren't old women's shoes! Piero bought these for me as well."

At that, Despina bristled and scurried away. Those were the only words they exchanged for the rest of the day. Not only was Despina unable to put Nicoletta down, but she and Mauro came out looking bad. Seeing her sister-in-law looking like a new blossom that turned everyone's head made her simmer with resentment, and Nicoletta knew it. She did nothing but smile at Despina the entire day, rubbing it in with every look. She knew she had won this battle, and it was delicious.

Nicoletta's relationship with Despina continued to have its trials. But they had come to a relative truce for the sake of family unity. In her own way, Despina wanted Nicoletta to have a successful marriage and a good life—just as long as it wasn't as good as hers. Nicoletta tired of the conflict between them. Holding on to her resentment weighed heavily on her heart and mind. It cast a dark shadow on her otherwise optimistic outlook. Nicoletta bore a great deal of guilt over her ill feelings toward Despina, and she needed to lift that burden from her shoulders.

One day, after Mass, Nicoletta sought out Don Michelino. She had always had a friendly rapport with him—he had been a great friend of her father and had comforted Nicoletta after his death.

"Excuse me, Father. Do you have a moment to talk?"

"Of course, Nicoletta, anything for you. What's on your mind?" he said, taking her hand.

"I am struggling, Father. I have a heavy heart."

"Do you have something to confess, Nicoletta?"

As she nodded her head, Don Michelino led her to the confessional.

"Father, I'm so exhausted by this feud between Despina and me. The anger lives in my heart and I can't bear it any longer. I don't hate her—she's Mauro's wife, my sister-in-law. Even so, the sparring between us continues."

"I know this has been a very challenging relationship for you. You idolized your big brother, and now his first priority is his wife."

"That's right. I had dreams of his return from the war. I longed for him to treat me as he did when I was a child. I miss his adoring smile."

"Why do you think that changed, Nicoletta? Why does he treat you differently?"

"I'm sure it's because the family treated Despina like an intruder when they first arrived. It must have been heartbreaking to witness the disrespect shown to his wife, especially by his closest family. And I am genuinely sorry for that. She is a part of my family now. I have to let go of this foolish battle."

"You are very wise for such a young girl, Nicoletta. If you are truly sorry for your actions and try to heal your relationship, you have nothing to fear. God forgives our human frailty. He knows how we struggle to stay on the right path."

"Thank you, Father. I was so worried. I don't want to carry this sin with me any longer."

"Don't worry, my little rose. Many of us wrestle with our demons. But you must understand that although you resolve to forgive Despina and yourself, the relationship you have will not miraculously transform. I have a feeling that there will always be tension there. Can you live with that?"

"*Sì*, Father, I understand. But I'm willing to try. I feel so much better now. *Grazie.*"

"Ah, Nicoletta, you always have an friend in me. I made a promise to your father, and I will not let either of you down. Go, and rest in the knowledge that God forgives you and lives in your heart."

As much as she loved being with her family during those years, Nicoletta knew she had to get out of Bisceglie. It was backward-thinking and old-fashioned. She hated the fact that people were into everyone's business but their own. She couldn't make a move without hearing something from her cousin and aunts. But Despina's meddling bothered her the most. She didn't like anyone to tell her who she should like or marry. That was her private business, and it shouldn't concern anyone else.

Her daily household routines of cooking and cleaning were boring, and as she grew older, Antonietta gave her more responsibilities around the house. While she took care of the children, Nicoletta would cook for Antonietta's husband when he returned from the farm. She wanted more out of life—she had always dreamed of a more adventurous future. Looking at all the women in her life, she couldn't imagine being a housewife in her little town.

Nicoletta began to lose interest in sewing as well. After she finished with her chores at home, she hurried to her sewing class. But there was little left to do by that time but sew hems. The more exciting and skillful tasks had been completed by girls who had come earlier. She finally stopped going because she wasn't learning anything new. Instead, she enrolled in a certificate program that trained girls to take measurements and create patterns for dresses. And although it was much more interesting, she couldn't imagine making dresses for the women in Bisceglie for the rest of her life. They had no imagination—there would be little opportunity for her to express her creativity.

Her cousin Rosa, Nina's older sister, lived in Milano with her husband. Knowing that she wanted to get out of her small town, Rosa offered her a place to live. Nicoletta seriously considered moving to Milano. But she couldn't imagine abandoning Piero just yet. His eleven-year relationship with Carmela was fraught with trouble. Both families were against their union, and Nicoletta planned to stay in Bisceglie until things with them were settled. After that, there would be no stopping her move to Milano. She planned to take Rosa up on her offer as soon as possible.

Chapter Fourteen
Looking for Love

New York City 1950

L arry's first years in the states were exciting and new. Though he worked long hours, at twenty-one years old, he had plenty of energy to go out with friends at the end of his workday. Living in Little Italy, he made friends quickly—the immigrant community was tight-knit. Many people from Bisceglie lived in his neighborhood, and there were several that he knew from back home. One of his best friends had brilliant red hair—as did his entire family. They were known as the *Reds*. Together, Larry and Nick frequented clubs and danced the night away.

Through his older sister, Lily, he met a couple of interesting girls. Her godchild lived in Bridgeport, Connecticut. At that time, Bridgeport was considered the country, with trees and a beautiful seashore. Many New Yorkers moved there looking for a place where they could buy a house with a yard for their budding families. Bridgeport offered affordable housing and a great job market. But for single folks it was a desert. There were few places for young people to gather or go out on dates. Bridgeport could never compare to the nightlife of New York City.

Nevertheless, Larry and Nick took the hour and a half drive to Bridgeport for a double date with Lily's goddaughter and friend. Both men looked forward to the evening with great anticipation. The four of them hit it off immediately. Their Italian heritage and culture made their initial interaction familiar and comfortable. The evening had gotten off to a marvelous start. Larry then asked if they had a favorite restaurant.

"Okay then, we're all hungry. Where should we go for dinner?"

"Well, to New York, of course," his date responded.

"New York? But we just drove an hour and a half to get here!" Larry responded with exasperation. "Surely, there's a good Italian restaurant in Bridgeport."

"Well, that's no fun," she pouted.

"Don't you worry, my beautiful ladies. New York City, it is," Nick said, trying to salvage the date. "We'll show you a night on the town."

The women squealed in delight while Larry rolled his eyes and mumbled under his breath. *This is the last time I go out with her*, he thought. *We've only just met, and she's demanding that we go all the way back to the city? Then what? We have to drive all the way back here again!* After the long drive back to the city, they ended up at a cheap Chinese restaurant that Nick knew. Larry was not an adventurous eater, but that night he made his mind up. He hated Chinese food. He just didn't get it; the noodles were mushy, and everything was mixed into one dish. He didn't enjoy the date and never saw the girl again.

On another occasion, Lily tried to fix him up with her husband's niece. She was born in New York and Larry wanted to impress her. He went shopping in search of a gift to offer her on their first date. But when he went to give it to her, he discovered that his brother Sal had taken it. There he was, looking like Don Juan, giving his date the expensive perfume that Larry bought. He was furious but could do nothing about it. Sal had been playing pranks on him for his entire life. He couldn't believe that he was being upstaged by his little brother once again. Not long

Larry Dell'Olio at 22-years-old in New York City.

after, Larry decided American girls were not for him. He hoped to find a girl that had just come to America. That's when his brother Carlo's letter arrived, and this beautiful girl was reaching out from the photo to steal his heart.

Gazing at the picture of five young people strolling in the piazza of his hometown, his mind flooded with memories. The piazza was the central gathering place for young singles as well as married and elderly folks looking to catch up on the latest gossip. The girl from the photo looked awfully familiar, but he couldn't place her. He tried to picture her several years younger when he realized this was the young girl from the balcony that he pined for.

After all these years, his mystery girl reappeared in the photograph Carlo just sent. It had to be a sign. He immediately grabbed paper and pen to write to his future sister-in-law. Larry had to find out who was this beautiful young woman. A hopeless romantic, Larry believed in love at first sight, and his heart was bursting.

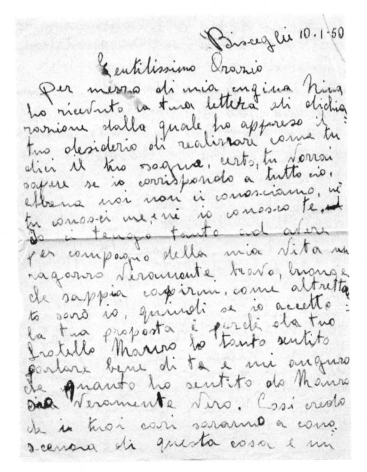

Nicoletta's first letter to Orazio (Larry).

Letter Six

Bisceglie, Province of Bari, Italy
January 10, 1950
Gentilissimo Orazio,

Through my cousin Nina, I received your letter declaring your interest in me. From your message, I understand that your desire is to realize, as you say, your greatest dream. I am sure you would like to know if I would be kind enough to correspond. You must understand that we are strangers to one another. You don't know me, and I don't know you. My hope is to meet a young man who will accompany me throughout my life—a truly good man who is trustworthy and kind-hearted, and who knows how to understand me. I hope to be the same in return. If I accept your request, it is only because your brother Carlo has told me so many good things about you. He never ceases to sing your praises. I hope his words are true. I am confident that those who are dear to you know you best. But before we begin our correspondence, I ask that your parents give their consent.

Now, let me tell you a few things about me. I am a woman whose father and mother were taken from her at an early age. I have two brothers; one is engaged, the other is married. The brother who is pictured in the photograph is everything to me, father and brother. It is with him I live, and now that you have heard my words, you know it is him to whom the request for my hand must be made. Piero is my guardian.

I enclose a little gift. It's a photo of me with my cousin, Nina. In conclusion, please give my love to everyone in New York, especially your parents. Love from Carlo, Nina, and the family.

Cordially,
Nicoletta (18 years old)

Felicia, Nina, and Nicoletta

Letter Seven

New York City
January 18, 1950
Dearest Nicoletta,
Please forgive me for writing so often. It's because I am so in love with you. Perhaps you don't believe me, but I always see you in photos, and I really love seeing your face. I hope you are happy with me, dearest. I can't wait to receive your letters to hear all your news, dear Nicoletta. I showed your photo to my sisters and brothers, and even to my mother and father. They are very happy for me and think you are beautiful. They wished me well as they do in America: Good Luck, Larry! Can you imagine, dear Nicoletta, how happy I am?

I have enclosed a photo of me in this letter, even though it's not that good, but when Papá comes to Italy, I will send you an enlargement in full color done in oils. With that, I will send a crystal frame. Anyway, I have also enclosed a little note to your brother.

Dear Nicoletta, see that I am sending you a dollar. I hope you receive it and that you use it to buy postage stamps so that you will write more often. I hope this doesn't offend you. Next time you write, please send me your measurements because I will send a surprise when my father comes.

Give my regards to your family. I say goodbye with a big kiss,
Your dear.
Orazio

Please write soon.

Nicoletta Di Bitetto

Letter Eight

Bisceglie, Province of Bari, Italy
January 25, 1950
Orazio Carissimo,
On the same day that I received your letter of the 16th, I also received the one you wrote on the 18th. And as soon as I received it, I sat and wrote my response. Oh, how happy I was to receive the photograph that you included. But you know that the dedication you wrote is written in English, and I don't understand it. Would you kindly translate it for me? If you've forgotten what you wrote, I'll write it here.
"I love you, Nicoletta. Remember me always because I love you very, very much."
I was eagerly awaiting your letter because I knew it would be a balm to my heart and give me great joy.
I was with your brother, Carlo, and my cousin, Nina, last evening, and we spoke of you. It made me feel so close to you—together in mind and spirit. It was as if you were right beside me. And perhaps, at that moment, you were thinking of me. I hope so very much that you feel the same for me because it seems that I now live with our love. With the fusion of our thoughts, we pass each day thinking of one another. Everything reminds me of you—when I work, I am surprised by a thought of you, and I imagine you are with me. I would have loved to meet you here in Bisceglie, but alas, it was not possible. Perhaps this way, we will desire each other more. The anticipation reinforces our unshakable sentiment, born between us, a destiny that I hope will always be favorable. I pray to our good Lord that he grants us our true desires.
You wouldn't believe how happy I was to hear that Mamma and Papá will allow me to call them as such and that they are pleased with me. I had always hoped to find the sincere love and affection that I lost when my dear parents passed. They wished for my well-being and happiness, and I have found it. Please tell them not to consider me their daughter-in-law, but rather, their daughter, if they so desire, because I wish them all good things.

Orazio dearest, regarding the photograph you sent with Papá, you wouldn't believe how much I enjoy it. It is a most beautiful gift, and everyone who sees it remarks upon how handsome you are.

I will close now. Please give my regards to your brothers and sisters. To Papá and Mamma, affectionate hugs.

Sending you sweet kisses,

Nicoletta

Orazio Dell'Olio

Chapter Fifteen
The Courtship

Bisceglie, Italy • New York City • 1950-51

The letters began as formal communication between two young people seeking a connection. Nicoletta was wary of writing to a stranger across the ocean. However, with assurance from her cousin, Nina, she felt safe enough to take the risk. Orazio's brother, Carlo, told Nicoletta many sweet stories about his little brother, emphasizing that Orazio was even kinder than he. Carlo was gregarious and handsome—he was a suitable match for her cousin, who loved that people noticed them while strolling in the *piazza*. Carlo chatted with everyone and fawned over his fiancée. Watching how well he treated Nina, Nicoletta could imagine what kind of man Orazio might be.

Yet, even with Nicoletta's willingness, Orazio had to get permission from her family. The two most significant figures in her life were her brother, Piero, and her cousin, Antonietta. He wrote both letters stating his desire to write to Nicoletta. Orazio understood that if his hopes of developing a relationship were to come to fruition, Piero and Antonietta would have to approve. Orazio's sense of duty to family impressed Nicoletta. Not needing to explain her obligations gave her more insight into his values—a further glimpse into the kind of man he was.

The beauty of the written word allowed both Orazio and Nicoletta to express themselves in ways that dove deeper into their hearts. Orazio was never one to speak of his feelings. One never quite knew what he was thinking. If given a gift, he'd smile and say thank you. If pressed, he'd concede that he liked it. Never displaying a look of surprise or emitting a joyful exclamation, Orazio was reserved in his reactions. However, when he put pen to paper, Orazio's genuine feelings came to life and he revealed his heart. What he was reticent to share in conversation came pouring out on the page. He was possessed by romance—he took care to find stationery decorated with roses and other flowers. His phrases were dotted with the words *dearest* and *my love*, and he always closed with a heartfelt expression of love.

Nicoletta was only eighteen years old when they started writing. Although her parents' death forced her to grow up quickly, carrying on a relationship with a man was entirely new to her. Navigating her first romance was even more complicated given the thousands of miles and the ocean between them. In many ways, the letters served as a diary. Nicoletta reflected upon her life and put those thoughts into her words. She wrote about her mother's death and her father's absence during the war. She described her family members in animated detail so that Orazio could come to know the significant people in her life. Her brother, Piero, she wrote, was father, mother, brother, and friend to her. Antonietta was not merely a cousin; she was her older sister, guiding her and raising her from the age of seven.

The letters from Italy told Orazio all he needed to know about this beautiful young girl. Those pages embodied Nicoletta's family history. He vividly pictured who she was and the role she played within her family. Her words illustrated relationships in full color, revealing doubt, insecurity, and conflict. Her fierce loyalty and passion were on full display as she painted the portrait of each of her loved ones.

From New York City came letters filled with dreams of a bright future. Orazio's idealism manifested in his hopes for a life far from the poverty of southern Italy. He painted scenes of elegant storefronts and high fashion—strolls along Fifth Avenue and through Central Park. As the months passed and their feelings grew deeper, Orazio shared his dreams of having a home of their own.

For two years, Nicoletta and Orazio wrote. Never having met, they fell in love. Anyone who knew them could not miss their unique romance. Leading their separate lives in two very different countries, their minds and hearts were consumed with the growing bond they shared. Even the postman in Bisceglie understood the importance of the letters he delivered. Nicoletta's eyes grew wide with anticipation as he walked toward her home. If she was not in sight, he created a distinctive knock when a letter from Orazio arrived. The postman could hear her running to open the door—her grin was wider than the ocean that kept them apart.

Letter Nine

New York City
March 4, 1950
Mia Adorabile Nicoletta,
With great joy, I write to tell you that I am well. I suffered from a cold for a few days,
but I am feeling much better. I meant to write you sooner but was not feeling well. You
would not believe how much I love you. The days pass, and I think of you even more.

Let me explain what I sent in the care package. There are some handkerchiefs, a
veil that you can wear in church, toothpaste, and toothbrushes. I also sent bracelets and
brooches, a ring and a clock. And just this morning, I bought you a beautiful dress.
Just wait and see how lovely you look when you try it on. I don't know how to say this,
but that dress cost a bundle, but it's so beautiful. The cost is not important! I only want
you to be the beautiful doll that I imagine you to be. I'm not sure what else I'll send
you because I adore you so much and I want to make you happy.

I think of you night and day, imagining that you are beside me—your lovely hands
held in mine as I gently caress them. That gives me courage. Now, I am planning to
put money into a bank account for our nuptials. We will have a grand party. You will
see, my love, it will be magnificent.

I won't rest until I send you my most affectionate kisses—kisses of love from your
amore.

Orazio

Letter Ten

New York City
April 24, 1950
Dearest Nicoletta,

As you see, I write to you today because my dear brothers are now married. At this moment, it is 6:00 in the evening, while in Italy, it is already midnight. Who knows how much they are enjoying themselves at this hour with their new wives, dancing and laughing. I hope that you are having fun too. I know that it's difficult to enjoy yourself since we are far apart, my charming and lovely girl.

Don't you worry, my love, because our day will undoubtedly come. I imagine that you are dressed elegantly, and I wish to be near you just for a moment to gaze upon my dear, beautiful Nicoletta. Unfortunately, we have to wait a bit longer, my dearest.

I received a lovely letter from your brother, Mauro, as well as one from your cousin Nina. She told me that you were upset that you hadn't received a letter from me. Don't worry, I will always write to you.

Your dearest,
Orazio

Chapter Sixteen
The Ring

Bisceglie, Province of Bari 1950

As the months passed, the letters became more frequent. The level of intimacy between Orazio and Nicoletta grew increasingly more profound. Back in Bisceglie, Orazio's brother introduced Nicoletta to the rest of the family, and new friendships were formed. Before long, Carlo and his fiancée, Nina, as well as Sal and his fiancée, Felicia, were inseparable. The five young people strolled the piazza or the seawall arm in arm. They laughed as if they hadn't a care in the world. Lives filled with hope and promise lay ahead of them.

Nicoletta and Felicia soon became the best of friends. They were both eighteen years old and had come from similar families. There was no family rivalry as there was with her cousin, Nina. Each discovered they were kindred spirits talking about fashion and the dream of living in New York. In reality, however, Nicoletta was the odd person out. A single woman spending time with two couples left her missing Orazio even more. The Dell'Olio brothers bore a strong resemblance to each other, and she could almost picture the words Orazio wrote coming from their lips. Many evenings, she'd return home and steal away to her room with pen and paper. There, in the silence of the night, she poured her heart into a letter to Orazio. Those were sacred moments when they felt closest to one another—when writing or when reading a letter received. In those private and solitary moments, there was no ocean separating their hearts or minds. On those occasions, they were already united.

Four months after they had begun their correspondence, Orazio and Nicoletta were already writing about their future together. In such a short time, they had genuinely fallen in love. Orazio's father, Francesco, traveled back to Bisceglie for Carlo's wedding. Although Sal was still young, the family had arranged his marriage to Felicia. They were already dating and hoped that the union would be a suitable match that might calm their Casanova of a son. The two brothers had a double wedding so that their father could be there for both of them. Antonia, unable to travel, stayed back in New York with Orazio and his sisters.

Nicoletta was excited to meet Francesco. If all proceeded according to plan, he would be her future father-in-law. Carlo, Sal, and their fiancées accompanied Francesco to Nicoletta's house shortly after he arrived. The evening was festive and filled with anticipation of the impending nuptials. Amidst the celebration, Francesco and Nicoletta found a relatively private corner to chat. He was a quiet man—in this regard, Orazio was most like his father. However, on this occasion, Francesco found his words. He quietly reached into his pocket and pulled out a little velvet box and handed it to Nicoletta.

"My child, this is from your love, Orazio."

"It's a ring!" she exclaimed as she placed it on her finger.

"Nicoletta, he loves you very much," he said. Then, looking out at his sons gathered that evening, he continued.

"Orazio is a good and kind man. He is the best one of the bunch."

Nicoletta rose to hug him.

"He will take good care of you," he said with watery eyes.

She turned to her family and showed off her ring. Tears of happiness and joyous laughter filled the room. Then the teasing began. Orazio's brothers were known for their merciless joking.

"So, Nicoletta, how does it feel to be engaged to my father?" Carlo asked.

"Will you marry him in my brother's place?" Sal chimed in. "My poor mother will be heartbroken."

It was official. What started as a bold request from a stranger in America had now become a proposal of marriage. *How could I have possibly imagined this four short months ago?* Nicoletta thought as she gazed upon the ring.

Many letters hence, they agreed that if their feelings of love were as profound upon meeting as they were in their prose, they would marry. If the magic wasn't there when they met, they would part as friends. Sadly, that encounter would have to wait. In order for Orazio to bring Nicoletta back to New York with him, it was necessary to become a U.S. citizen. He needed to be a resident of the United States for five years before he was eligible—Orazio had two years to go before he could apply.

Once she agreed to marry him, Orazio was desperate to bring her to New York.

Letter Eleven

New York City
May 6, 1950
My dear love,
I write this letter to send you good news. I went to see an attorney regarding how to get you to America, and he informed me it can be done. You would have to state that my sister, Rosa, is your cousin. Then she'll take care of everything. She'll make a deposit at the bank and say that you are her cousin. My love, I hope this makes you happy. You'd be here within the year—imagine what a beautiful day it will be when you finally disembark on the shores of New York. I will be waiting on the dock with a beautiful bouquet of flowers.

I hope you won't refuse this opportunity to be united with your love. Rest assured that after a few years, I promise that we will return to Italy together, as husband and wife. I think that you will be pleased with my idea.

All right then, when you next write, please enclose your birth certificate and the name of your dear father. This way, as soon as I receive it, we can prepare the documents for your arrival. I am so sure that you will accept the great surprise that is presented to you! All I can say is that I anxiously await your response of YES!

Sending big kisses,
Your love,
Orazio

Chapter Seventeen
The Anticipation

New York City 1951

I t had been almost two years since Orazio and Nicoletta began their correspondence. Who knew that his brother Carlo's engagement photo would permanently change his life? Nicoletta's smile shone more brightly than any of the others. It was as if she were calling out to him from his hometown. He couldn't get her out of his thoughts—he felt compelled to write to her immediately. But how do you write to someone you've never met before? Could he tell her she had stolen his heart—that would certainly scare her off. Their initial communication was cordial, but he hoped to relate his enthusiasm, telling her it was love at first sight. Her letters, in contrast, were formal, bordering on cold. But Orazio didn't let that deter him, and Nicoletta finally gave him her heart.

As the months passed by, the letters he received from Nicoletta were his lifeline. He was living with his parents in a tiny apartment, a five-floor walk-up in Little Italy. It had only one bedroom, so Orazio slept on the couch in the living room. His work building wooden ladders, a major step down from the craftsmanship he was used to in Italy, was mind-numbing. He missed the artistry and craft of making fine furniture—the sheen of the final coat of lacquer, and the soft edges of the design. But a job was a job, and he was grateful to be in the United States. Despite all his dreams, his new life in America was far from what he had imagined.

The drudgery of the daily grind steadily ate away at his self-image, and he wondered if he'd ever have a home of his own. His doubts notwithstanding, hope came to him through Nicoletta's letters, letters from Italy. Her heartfelt prose motivated him to work hard and to dream bigger. He devoured each page even as she described the mundane machinations of her family drama. He would close his eyes and try to imagine her going about her daily routine—walking by the fish market on her way to the piazza, stopping for Mass at La Misericordia. Orazio could picture each neighborhood of his former home with Nicoletta brightening every alley of their downtrodden city. How he longed to be with her.

Orazio intended to win Nicoletta's affections and make her his wife. He planned to work as many hours as they offered—saving enough money to bring her to New York. Overtime pay added up quickly. Every Friday was payday, and at the end of each arduous week, he climbed the five-story walk-up to his parent's apartment on Worth Street. When he entered the apartment, he'd see his mother, Antonia, standing at the stove waiting to throw the pasta into the boiling water. His dad was in his usual seat at the head of the table smiling at him. Always the dutiful son, he handed over his pay to Francesco, who would then give him a small allowance. Orazio took his share and tucked it away in his savings. If his dream of marrying Nicoletta were to come true someday, they would need a home in which to raise a family.

"*Papà?* If I'm ever going to get married, I need to start saving more money."

"*Si, caro, si,*" his father said, anticipating his next thought.

"I am so grateful to be living here with you and *Mamma*. I am happy to contribute to our household expenses. But now that I'm working overtime, I would like to put the extra into my savings."

"Of course, Orazio. You have always helped to support your mother in Italy and now again in New York. Here, take whatever you think is fair," Francesco said, holding out the pay Orazio had just given him.

"*Grazie, Papà!* I can't tell you how much this means to me."

"Soon you'll be able to send for Nicoletta, *caro*," his mother interjected. "That will be a day for celebration. Now sit; the pasta is ready. You must be hungry."

It was settled, and Orazio worked as many extra hours as the shop offered to him. With each passing month, his dream drew ever closer to reality. After a year of letter writing, he decided to act. Friends in Little Italy were generous with their advice. They sent him to visit an attorney who helped many Italian immigrants acquire their documents. Orazio was not a citizen yet, so the marriage would not get her to the U.S. any sooner. But if he could arrange for someone to sponsor her, she'd be able to come to New York immediately. However, what the attorney suggested was not legal, even still, he got Orazio's hopes up.

"One way she can become a legal alien is to have a relative sponsor her."

"Unfortunately, all of Nicoletta's family is in Italy. There is no one here for her but me," Orazio said. "And I have to wait until I'm a citizen to bring her to America."

"But you have many people here. One of your sisters could claim that she's a cousin. I could draw up the papers, and she'd be here in no time," the attorney suggested.

"Would that work?"

"I've done it many times. It's just paperwork. Say the word, and I'll take care of it for you."

Orazio wrote immediately to share his good news with Nicoletta. Weeks went by as he waited in eager anticipation for her reply.

Orazio's offer took Nicoletta by surprise. It was an exciting possibility, and there was something terribly attractive about being whisked away from her ordinary life in southern Italy to live in New York City. She tried to imagine what it would be like to arrive in the port of New York with her handsome fiancé to greet her. When she shared the letter with Antonietta and Piero, reality set in. Nicoletta's family was shocked and wouldn't hear of such an idea. When Antonietta read the letter, she was aghast.

"What is he thinking, Nicoletta? Does he think he could just take you away from everyone you know here in Bisceglie?"

"No, no, we are just so eager to meet in person. It has been so long since we started writing to each other. The anticipation is becoming excruciating."

"How could we let you go so far from home to marry a man we've never met?" her brother Piero chimed in. "I'm sorry, Nicoletta, but that's just not proper."

"You'd be going to a foreign country all by yourself. You don't speak the language, and you won't know anybody there, not even your future husband. How could you even consider that?" Antonietta continued.

"I know you're right. My heart aches at the thought of leaving all of you behind. And although we love each other, we won't really know if we are compatible until we meet."

"It's too great a risk, little sister," Piero added. "We may know his family, but we don't know him. If this is true love, then it's worth waiting until he can come to Bisceglie."

It was imperative that they meet this young man who had stolen her heart. And how could she have a wedding ceremony to marry a man thousands of miles from home? She would have none of her family in attendance. No, that was not an option.

Deep in her heart, Nicoletta knew they were right. They hadn't even met in person. How could she leave her country and everyone she loved for a man she'd only met through letters? Although their correspondence had developed and become romantic and intimate, nothing could compare to spending time together. No matter what they decided to do in the future, they needed to get to know each other in person before making a commitment. Orazio would simply have to wait until he saved enough money to return to Italy.

Nicoletta dreaded writing to tell him the news. She knew he'd be sorely disappointed. Somehow, she had to explain to him that her family was everything to her. Losing both her parents at such a young age, her brothers, Piero and Mauro, became her fathers, and Antonietta her mother. They not only filled the cavernous grief Nicoletta experienced, but through their shared grief, they became pillars of strength for one another. Any decision she made concerning her future necessarily included them. Should they decide to marry, and she certainly hoped they would, she needed her family to be a part of her most special day.

The news fell like a lead brick. Orazio was beside himself when he read her response. He thought he had found the perfect solution to their problem. The time until they could be together seemed to grow even longer after that moment. He stared at her words in disbelief. He had only saved enough money for a one-way trip from Italy to New York. There wasn't nearly enough for the round trip to Italy and back. He felt hopeless. How could he possibly wait any longer? His heart broke in two. From that moment on, Orazio worked even more overtime—each night and every

Saturday. He asked his father if he could keep a bit more of his pay plus all his overtime to save for his voyage to Italy. Francesco delighted in seeing his son's determination and agreed immediately. He wanted nothing more than to see Orazio settled and happy.

Another year passed—Orazio had been in America for four years. His plan was to get his citizenship before getting married. Then they could return to New York together as husband and wife. Sadly, it would be another year before he'd qualify to take the test. He didn't know how he could wait that long. They had already been writing to each other for nearly two years, and he had put away enough money for passage to Italy. His childhood friend, Gino, planned to travel back to Bisceglie the following month. His parents had arranged a marriage for him, and he was excited to meet her. Gino encouraged Orazio to go along with him.

"We can have a double wedding!" he suggested.

"A double wedding? Don't talk nonsense. I'm not an American citizen yet, so it wouldn't be possible to bring her back with me."

"So what? When you get your citizenship next year, you can just send for her. At least you'd be married. You never know if someone else will come along and steal her away from you. What do you say?"

The idea grew on him, and he liked knowing that he'd have a travel companion for part of the journey. After nearly two years of correspondence, he and Nicoletta decided it was time to meet in person. By October of the same year, Orazio could wait no longer—he had to meet the love of his life. He bought a ticket on a ship heading for France. From there, he would take the train to his small town of Bisceglie.

Letter Twelve

Bisceglie, Province of Bari, Italy 1951
February 7, 1950
Orazio, My Dear One,

It is to no avail to tell you how much joy I get from receiving your letters. I never tire of receiving them or writing to you. And I must express this, as you read my words describing the love that unites us spiritually. I say that this love is a proven fact with regard to me. I never reply when I receive mail from anyone else. Now, that is no longer the case. I am constrained to write because my thoughts don't give me peace. And this, my dear one, I note with pleasure, because it helps me understand that I love you even more and believe that it is true.

My Orazio, in other people's eyes, love must be arranged; they say that it is not possible to love the way we do. They say that love consists of kisses and caresses. They make me so angry because I say I love you even without the kisses. Tell me that it's the same for you, isn't that true? Maybe it is a mistake to write this. Perhaps you are tormented just as I am. I feel that it's impossible to wait for two years. I just can't bear it; I must express what I feel. Forgive me if I am too forward. In the meantime, I am preparing my trousseau. Rest assured that I will be ready when you get here.

And then, caro, when you come, I will explain my situation. At the moment, I have nothing, but when I turn twenty-one years of age, I will come into my inheritance from my good and dear parents. They left a house for each of my brothers and me. And I may sell mine so that you and I can have a beautiful home of our own in New York. This way, you won't have to sacrifice a great deal. Are you happy with my idea, my adored love? I hope so. I just wanted to let you know.

The most beautiful love is when one feels love in return. Every now and then, I think of our reality—I can't pass judgment on this strange love that we share. I feel as if we are living a dream. A beautiful story begins now, and another will start when we are finally united, and we are married and happy. Orazio, what great joy there will be when we finally meet.

Orazio, you don't know me, and maybe you can't understand how fine and delicate my love is for you. To have you near me would be something divine and sweet. When I torment myself with these thoughts, the only thing that dampens my joy is the question of whether the love we share will be as real when I see you in person. It would be extraordinary to have you with me for even one day.

In my last letter, I wrote a note to your mother. I am completely sincere in the thoughts that I expressed.

I end today, sending my love to your parents and, of course, to you.

Nicoletta

Nicoletta's engagement photo

Chapter Eighteen
The Encounter

Bisceglie, Province of Bari, Italy 1951

Given their long-anticipated encounter, Orazio and Nicoletta decided that if their feelings were as strong upon meeting as they were in their letters, they would marry; if not, they would part friends. There was a great deal resting on their first meeting. Orazio, though confident in his love for Nicoletta, was extremely anxious. With a chiseled jawline and a thick mane of black hair, Orazio was a handsome man but didn't realize it. All he could see was a man, short in stature, who had always endured his brother's jokes. He had worked hard, and his determination had brought some measure of success. He hoped Nicoletta would see how deeply he wanted to take care of her and provide her with the best life he possibly could. Through their letters, he could tell she was more educated than he, and although Orazio felt intimidated after reading those first letters, he opened his heart to her. In return, Nicoletta expressed her profound desire to be with him. The photo that had brought them together showed her beauty, but those letters from Italy revealed her heart. He was confident that they were meant to be together forever.

The train ride from Paris seemed to take forever, but he was on his way to Bisceglie. Orazio had traveled by ship from New York to France, and he had been on the train for over twenty-one hours. Thankfully, he was finally in the province of Bari. The train had passed Foggia and Barletta over an hour before, and he realized he was almost there. Orazio was getting antsy as the train reduced its speed; he knew Bisceglie was the next station. When the train slowed to a stop, he left Gino sound asleep, grabbed his suitcase, and jumped off. There had been no announcement, but he didn't think twice about it. Orazio was in Bisceglie at last!

Orazio gathered his luggage alongside the train and looked around. It was a chilly November morning, and the sun had not yet risen. He had been away from Bisceglie for four years and was trying to get his bearings. As the train pulled away, he realized they had not reached the train station. He was at least a mile outside the city center. Olive groves flanked both sides of the street, and there was no one in sight at that hour. What could he do now? How was he going to get to Bisceglie with all his luggage in tow? He gathered all his bags and hobbled down the road toward the city. It was slow going, and his arms ached from the weight of his burden. Piercing the silence, he heard the clip-clop of a horse-drawn cart in the distance. It was carrying milk from the farms and heading into town. He turned and waved as it approached him.

The driver slowed down to a crawl. "What are you doing out here by yourself at this hour?" he asked.

"I have been traveling for days from America. I was so excited to see my fiancée that I hopped off the train too early."

"Poor young lover! Then you must get to her as quickly as you can. I can drive you as far as the *Palazzolo* (the main square of the town)."

"That is perfect! My brother Carlo lives right near there."

The driver stepped down and helped Orazio hoist his luggage onto the back of the cart. Orazio could not have been more grateful as he climbed aboard and told his love story. By the time they arrived at the piazza, his new friend had bid him farewell with a warm embrace. *"Buona fortuna*, Orazio!" he exclaimed with a big smile.

He looked around to gain his bearings. Finding his way, he lugged his bags to Carlo's apartment. Although he wanted to go directly to Niocoletta's house, he knew Carlo should accompany him on his first visit with her family. It would have been improper to show up alone, especially at this hour.

Carlo opened the door with a broad smile on his face. "Orazio, *finalmente sei arrivato!*" he exclaimed. Orazio had finally arrived, and with one arm holding a baby, Carlo grabbed him by the back of his head and pulled him in for a hearty embrace. In moments, Orazio had little Francesca in his arms. Carlo's firstborn was less than a year old and giggled with glee as he bounced her up and down.

"We have to go now, Carlo. Please come with me to Nicoletta's house. I can't wait to see her!"

"Are you crazy, Orazio? It's much too early. You can't show up at this hour; you'll wake the whole house up!"

Carlo tried to reason with him, but Orazio was like a schoolboy. He couldn't wait one more minute to meet the love of his life.

"Carlo, please, I have been waiting for two years already. What does it matter if I wake them all up? I need to meet my fiancée now," he pleaded.

"Okay, okay, Orazio. Who am I to stand in the way of true love?" Carlo said sarcastically. "Just give me a minute to get dressed. Do you want an espresso before we go?"

"No, no, I just want to be on our way as quickly as we can, Carlo. Please hurry."

It was only 6:00 a.m. when they arrived. With Francesca still in his arms, he knocked gently on the door, but no one seemed to stir.

Maybe Carlo was right. What will they think of him waking them all up at this hour? he thought.

But his excitement won out over his hesitation. He knocked again with more authority, and he heard a woman's voice, cautiously asked, *"Chi é?"* Who is it? He was sure that he had woken her up. How could he be so foolish? He should have waited at his brother's house until it was a reasonable hour. He could have had breakfast and washed up a bit before coming to see Nicoletta. But he was so excited that he wasn't thinking straight. He just knew that he had to see her as soon as possible.

"Sono Orazio *dal'America."* It's Orazio from America. "I just arrived moments ago," he replied.

"Si, si, Orazio. Just a moment, I will be right there," Antonietta yelled out as she grabbed her house dress, slipped it on and headed to the door. She poked her head into Nicoletta's bedroom and said, "Nicoletta, wake up! Orazio is here."

"What? He can't be. It's much too early," she said with a combination of fear and excitement.

"Quickly, Nicoletta! Fix your hair while I let him in," Antonietta instructed.

"I look terrible! I can't let him see me like this."

"You've been waiting for two years, *cara*. What does it matter that you have sleep in your eyes? You have love in your heart! Hurry, now."

Piero opened the door before Antonietta got there. He greeted Orazio and Carlo with a warm embrace. Orazio was still carrying Francesca. Everything was happening so quickly, and Nicoletta was still trying to shake her mind from her slumber. She would have liked to run a brush through her hair, but there was no time. She could hear him coming her way, so she pinched her cheeks to make them red and ran her fingers through her hair. *I can't believe he's here at last! I hope he thinks I'm pretty,* she thought. As excited as she was, Nicoletta could not bring herself to get out of the bed. She sat up in bed and quietly listened through the door.

"Orazio, I am Antonietta. It is wonderful to meet you; I have heard so much about you from Nicoletta."

He reached out and kissed her on both cheeks and said, "I am so happy to meet you after all this time, Antonietta. Nicoletta always speaks of you with such love and admiration. I am so sorry to have come so early in the morning, but to be honest, I just couldn't wait to meet her. I hope you understand."

Nicoletta blushed at his words as she listened intently.

"Please, no need to apologize. We will be a family soon. Go, go see her. She is still sleeping," she said as she pointed toward her door.

Nicoletta straightened the covers just as the door opened; there he was, in the flesh, carrying a beautiful baby in his arms. The image of him with a baby of their own flashed in her mind. Her heart was bursting. He was more handsome in person than in his photos. He crossed the room in three steps and leaned down. Their first kiss was pure and chaste but full of untapped passion. Antonietta stood at the door and smiled, while Carlo and Piero chatted amiably just beyond. Antonietta placed her hand on her heart, and her eyes filled with tears.

This is what it must feel like to be a mother, she thought as she looked on with joy. She stayed in the room with them since they had not yet married. It would have been improper for them to be alone, especially at their first meeting.

Orazio sat on the bed beside Nicoletta. There was so much he wanted to say, but the words wouldn't come. The eloquence of their letters rendered them mute in person, so they made small talk.

"You look beautiful, Nicoletta. I can't believe that I am actually here with you."

"Oh, Orazio, I look terrible! I didn't even get to fix my hair."

"Not to me, my love. At this moment, you are the most beautiful girl in the world."

She felt herself blush, and was grateful he didn't notice in the darkened room.

"How was your trip? Your train ride from France must have been difficult."

"It was arduous—never-ending, and then I got off the train miles from the station. I had to walk until I found a ride. I felt so foolish, but I just couldn't wait to see you."

"Oh, Orazio," she chuckled, "you must have been a sight walking down the road with all your luggage. I am glad you are finally here."

They chatted for a bit longer and made plans to see each other later in the day. He kissed her again, and little Francesca let out a squeal. They both laughed, and Orazio left her room to let her dress. He handed the baby off to Carlo and extended his hand to Piero, Nicoletta's brother.

"*Buon giorno*, Piero. I am sorry that we arrived so early this morning. I could not wait to see your sister."

"No need to worry, Orazio. Who can argue with true love?" Piero said with a wry smile. "It is nice to meet you finally—Nicoletta has been pining over you for months. Let's spend some time together during your visit. I am eager to get to know this American who stole my little sister's heart!"

"Of course, Piero. Nicoletta wrote how important you are to her, that you are father, mother, and brother to her."

"And she means the world to me as well."

The next few days were a whirlwind. The happy couple couldn't get enough of each other as they made the rounds in their little town of

Bisceglie. Nicoletta brought Orazio to meet everyone in her family, and he did the same for his. One day, Nicoletta was a single young woman writing to a man she had never met; then next, she was indeed in love. It was a dream come true. Every moment spent together buzzed with energy. Neither could hardly believe the intensity of their feelings for each other. When he wrote to tell her he was making the journey to Italy, they had decided that if their love for each other was as profound in person as it was in their written word, they would marry. Given their exuberance during their first week together, they didn't delay. They set a date for their wedding just after Christmas—only four weeks later.

The weeks leading up to their wedding also brought unexpected misunderstandings. As much as they shared during the two years they wrote to each other, Nicoletta and Orazio were just getting to know one another. The prose of their letters was heartfelt and filled with love and dreams for their future. However, tending to the ordinary difficulties of daily life and family dynamics was not nearly as romantic.

Orazio had arrived on December 5, 1952, the day before the feast of St. Nicolas. In Italy, it was customary to celebrate each person's name day just as if it was a birthday. Since they named Nicoletta for St. Nicolas, she couldn't wait for Orazio to surprise her with the traditional bouquet of flowers. Similar to the tradition of Valentine's Day in the U.S., Nicoletta was thrilled to have a man in her life who would celebrate her as his sweetheart. But when Orazio visited her that day, he was empty-handed. There was no mention of her feast day when he kissed her hello. Nicoletta hid her disappointment as best she could. *Perhaps he forgot,* she thought. As the day wore on with many visits to relatives, each of them wished her *Buon Onomastico,* Happy Name Day. And even with these constant reminders, Orazio made no mention of it. Still, Nicoletta remained hopeful. *Surely he would surprise her with something later in the day.*

Orazio knew what the custom was, but thought it was old-fashioned. *We don't celebrate name days in America. What a silly tradition,* he thought. Being new to romantic relationships, his insensitivity to her feelings never occurred to him. He chose not to bring Nicoletta flowers and didn't think twice about it. Unfortunately, he didn't explain that to her, so she wondered why not. *Orazio is so thoughtful and kind.* But the flowers never came. Nicoletta put her hurt feelings aside, though never out of her mind. She was just getting to know him in person. She didn't want to seem needy or insecure, so she said nothing to him.

During his first visit back, Orazio saw his little town with open eyes. The big city sophistication of New York shone brightly in contrast to the old world he left. He had no desire to be drawn back into outdated customs. Although his apartment and job back in the States were not much to brag about, the wealth of postwar New York surrounded him. Broadway, Wall Street, Macy's, and Gimbels overshadowed all he had known in Bisceglie. He was in the land of opportunity where one needed only to work hard to achieve his goal. An ambitious young man, Orazio understood that the world was his oyster in New York City. He would never return to his hometown as anything but a visitor. He was an American now.

Many years later, after many years of marriage, Nicoletta told Orazio of her hurt feelings. A man of very few words, he explained his reasoning. As sensitive as Orazio was, he had no clue that he had hurt her feelings and was astonished that she had not forgotten his transgression. "Nicoletta, I didn't know," he simply said. Then he pulled her in for a kiss.

Chapter Nineteen
Dreams Come True

Bisceglie, Province of Bari, Italy 1951

The weeks leading up to the wedding were exhilarating. Everyone in Nicoletta's family and circle of friends was eager to meet her American boyfriend. They strolled in the piazza, socialized with friends, and spent time with family. Christmas was quickly approaching, and everything they did was colored with the glitter of the joyous season. Every meal was an occasion for people to meet them as a couple. For their Italian families, the most significant moments were spent around the dinner table. Orazio insisted on eating at 1:00 p.m., which was the usual time for *pranzo,* and most days he was over at Nicoletta's home. There was something wonderfully ordinary about those intimate family dinners. After the meal, Orazio helped clear the table, stood beside Nicoletta at the sink and dried the dishes. Antonietta was beside herself—men weren't supposed to help with household chores. That was a woman's responsibility.

"What? Am I doing it wrong, Antonietta?" he teased.

"No, no, give me that towel. Go sit down. I'll dry the dishes."

Orazio laughed and continued helping after each meal. That is what he did for his mother back in New York. He didn't see any reason to change his routine. Besides, he loved doing ordinary tasks with his new family. They had a limited amount of time before his return to New York. He planned to savor every moment.

Orazio also enjoyed going for late afternoon walks with Nicoletta in the mild winter weather. The warm sun in Bisceglie was a welcome friend. The frigid winter in New York was just beginning. With each stroll in the piazza, he met his parents' friends and old buddies. Their walks were unaccompanied—there was no chaperone with them on those evenings. So tongues wagged and heads turned. He smiled at the gossipers, not caring what they thought. Orazio didn't miss their old ways and got a kick out of breaking some less enlightened customs. He was an American now. They would live in New York City soon; he and Nicoletta would soon let go of these old fashioned ways of thinking and embrace life in America.

When the big day finally arrived, Don Michelino, the parish priest, pulled Orazio aside. He had watched Nicoletta grow up. Over the years, he had taken note that Nicoletta spent a great deal of time at the parish. She volunteered to teach catechism; she helped clean and care for the church. Before the major holidays, she would even shine the chandeliers. She dedicated herself to her faith and her church.

In the sacristy before the wedding mass, Don Michelino placed his hand on Orazio's shoulder and said, "Promise me one thing, Orazio. Promise that you will take good care of this young lady. I have kept her under my watchful eye since she was a little girl. She is a gift of incalculable value; she is a treasure."

From then on, Orazio referred to her as *tesoro*, his treasure.

La Madonna della Misericordia, the church of Our Lady of Mercy, was a tiny chapel that held only fifty or sixty people. It was just a few blocks from Nicoletta's home, and most everyone walked to the ceremony. Orazio brought her wedding gown from New York City. It was the dress Orazio's little sister, Francesca, wore, and it fit her perfectly. The headdress was like a crown with a veil that flowed well beyond the train of her gown. Nicoletta felt like a princess. Perhaps she was her father's *Reginella* once again. When she stood in front of the mirror, Antonietta tucked a few of Nicoletta's curls behind her ears and adjusted her headpiece and veil.

"*Madonna*, what a beautiful bride you are, Nicolettina. If your mother could only see you now!"

"That would be my greatest wish, Antonietta. I miss her every day. But thank God I have you right beside me. I love you."

Zia Nunzia came into the room and exclaimed in joy, "Only God can see how my loving sister is looking down on you today—such a beautiful bride. Maria is smiling on her beautiful daughter. Thanks be to God that

I am here today to embrace you in her place. What a magnificent moment."

By the time they arrived at the church, family and friends filled *La Madonna della Misericordia*. It was December 29, 1951, and the weather was just perfect. The sun shone brightly, and the mild southern Italian climate gave them a perfectly crisp winter day. Given that it was a holiday week, most people had taken time off from work. The energy was festive and exciting, but Nicoletta could feel nothing but butterflies in her stomach. She had met Orazio less than a month before. *Am I doing the right thing? But we have been writing to each other for two years. Surely, we know each other better than most couples*, she reasoned with herself. She believed the thoughts and fears that appear in the written word are often more revealing and intimate than casual conversation. Yes, she knew in her heart that she had made the right decision. Orazio was the love of her life.

Antonietta could see her anxiety. She reached out and gently cupped Nicoletta's cheek with her right hand. "*Figlia*." *Child* was all that she said, but her touch and eyes communicated all that Nicoletta needed to hear. Antonietta's love and support gave her the affirmation she needed. Antonietta lifted the veil over her head and covered her face. Then Nicoletta took her place in the back of the tiny church, and when she heard the music begin, she proceeded up the aisle. Nicoletta never took her eyes off Orazio as he stood in front of the altar. He was so handsome, standing there looking at her adoringly. *How did she get so lucky?*

Throughout the Mass, both Nicoletta and Orazio had tears in their eyes. There was so much emotion that each of them held inside. Neither had their parents with them for this momentous occasion. Orazio would have given anything to have his mom and dad there. He was incredibly close to his mother, and he could feel Antonia's love within him as he made his lifelong commitment. And Nicoletta always carried her deceased parents in her heart. She bore the pain of their absence during each meaningful passage of her life. On this day, it was especially acute. Gazing at each other, all their fears melted away. Each letter they wrote over the past two years told the stories of their lives. They shared their fears, their family sagas, and their dreams of the future together. Unspoken, they expressed their love through watery eyes until they exchanged their vows.

After the Mass, they gathered in the sacristy with her brother Piero, who acted as their witness and signed the marriage records. It was now sacramentally and legally binding. Orazio and Nicoletta were husband and wife. They exited the church to sounds of a delighted ovation as the crowd tossed flower petals at them. Making their way through the throngs, they climbed into the hired limo as family and friends continued to cheer them on. Then they rode around the city, blowing horns and making noise as amused onlookers waved and shouted, *"Auguri!"* Congratulations!

They drove by the home of Radames, a man who had previously proposed to Nicoletta. Actually, his father had proposed to her on his behalf. He was always in her thrall, trying to flirt, visiting his aunt when Nicoletta was there learning to sew. He was an affable young man, always friendly and engaging. But she felt nothing more than a mild friendship with him. She always thought that perhaps his fear of rejection was the reason for having his father propose instead of taking the risk himself. She saw him as they drove by his house, and she knew she had made the right choice. She turned and looked at her handsome Orazio right by her side. She couldn't be happier.

After riding throughout the city, the limousine pulled up to Nicoletta's house. They hired a chef to prepare a meal for the immediate family of approximately twenty-five people. The *primo piatto* was the traditional *timballo*, a rich dish of pasta, tomato sauce, prosciutto, and mozzarella baked in a flaky pastry dough. Laughter and warmth filled room. Nicoletta was ebullient as she looked at all the smiling faces from both families as they feasted on the wedding meal. After everyone had had their fill, the party continued with a larger celebration at which they served desserts and liquors.

They held the reception at a small warehouse that was used to store items for gift baskets. Nina's uncle had a business of import-export foods, and it had a sizable area usually filled with crates of produce ready for delivery. It was transformed into a festive party venue. They stored the merchandise in adjacent rooms, and friends moved the work tables against the walls, then set the food upon them. They set up a makeshift stage for the band, and flowers and streamers hung over each window and door frame. Their families completely transformed the warehouse. To the bride and groom, it felt like a grand ballroom.

It was customary for the groom's family to pay for the reception, and Orazio was proud that he had saved enough money during his four years in New York to do it on his own. Although Orazio shunned most of Bisceglie's old customs, he looked forward to the traditional pastries, especially *i sospiri di Bisceglie*. *Sospiri* date back to the fifteenth century when the infamous Lucrezia Borgia, the illegitimate daughter of Pope Alexander VI, married the Count of Conversano.

Legend has it that as the guests at the reception waited for the couple to arrive, they grew agitated. Before their eyes were delectable puffs filled with custard and topped with a sweet, colorful frosting. Of course, the eager crowd could not partake in the delicious sweets until the guests of honor entered the hall. As minutes turned to hours, the guests sighed (*sospira*) with helpless desire as they waited to taste the festive treats.

The region of Puglia was famous for its delicious almonds, and so another traditional sweet for weddings was *pastareale*, which were colorful fruits made from marzipan. *Pastareale* translates to royal or real pastry, so they looked like actual fruit, but were also an expensive commodity fit for royalty. These beautiful cookies are fabled to have been made by nuns who hung them from barren fruit trees to impress a visiting bishop. However, for Nicoletta and Orazio's wedding reception, the town's old maid, *La Pizzoca,* baked the scrumptious treats. She made the best *pastareale* in the city and they were beautiful. Tables adorned with flowers and candles were overflowing with colorful treats for the guests to enjoy.

The reception hall gradually filled up, and the fun was just beginning. It was the week between Christmas and New Year's Day. The celebration of their nuptials made the holiday festivities ever more joyous. One could hear the animated conversations and laughter echoing throughout the hall. When the appointed time arrived, the bride and groom followed the custom of visiting each of the guests to give them a wedding favor of almonds covered in sugar. Wrapped in white tulle, the candied almonds glittered with a silver ribbon tied around them. Orazio carried a silver bowl filled with the sweet confections, while Nicoletta used a ladle to scoop them out to each guest.

After they had visited each of the guests, Nicoletta changed from her wedding gown into a dress Orazio had bought for her in New York City. The fabric was black taffeta with a layer of red taffeta beneath, the top layer gathered with a brooch on the left side to show the brilliant red below. Black tulle sprayed with velvet polka dots covered the shiny taffeta, and spaghetti straps decorated the neckline. Nicoletta loved that dress. It was certainly not a design ever seen in Bisceglie, and she couldn't wait to show it off.

When she entered the hall, every eye turned to her and startled cries of approval rose from the room. Orazio dashed to her and took her hand.

"*Mio tesoro*, my treasure, you are magnificent," he exclaimed as he handed her a note that he had just written in English:

I love you so much, forever and ever! My wife, she is beautiful!

He kissed her gently, then led her to the dance floor. The band intoned the first melody, followed by a baritone soloist who burst into song. The rest of the crowd joined them on the dance floor, where they danced well into the morning's early hours. For as shy as he was, Orazio danced throughout the night. The reception lasted from 7:00 p.m. to 4:30 a.m. Although they were all exhausted by the end of the night, the excitement energized the newlyweds. So, the family went back to Nicoletta's house to eat again.

Antonietta's husband, Pierino, made his own wine, which was plentiful at each meal. Antonietta was so busy preparing the meal and setting the table that she forgot to bring out his wine. Pierino complained to her, "Where's the wine?"

Orazio felt the jug under the table and, using the local dialect, said, "*Saut u tain*," Meaning "below your belt." This was a funny yet vulgar expression that was often used playfully to show that whatever you were looking for was right before your eyes. There was a moment of shock after he said it, followed by an uproarious burst of laughter. There were no more formalities; they were family. The ebullient crew feasted on a delicious home-cooked meal as they were all famished from the activity during the last twenty-four hours. They had danced and visited for hours and hours. As is often the case, the bride and groom had little to eat during the reception. They were so busy visiting with guests and dancing, but they made up for it at the ridiculous hour of 5:00 a.m.

Once they all had their fill, the new bride and groom rushed to catch the 6:30 a.m. train to Foggia to begin their honeymoon. Nicoletta and Orazio said their hasty goodbyes and boarded the train.

Nicoletta with her brother Piero.

Nicoletta with her brother Mauro and Despina.

Chapter Twenty
The Honeymoon

After a brief journey, the train pulled into Foggia. They spent a full day and evening sightseeing. After two years of writing letters and a month of wedding preparations, they were finally alone. Despite the lack of sleep, they relished each moment enjoying their first day apart from curious eyes. It was a magical day filled with anticipation and romance. After such a whirlwind day, the reality of their marriage sank in. There were no family members to visit or friends to watch over them. They wandered through Foggia's city center as husband and wife, completely free of all their responsibilities and worries. Less than a month ago, they had never even met in person, and now they were joined in matrimony.

For dinner that evening, they found a lovely little restaurant tucked into a cozy corner of the main piazza. Puglia's Byzantine architecture was on full display, and the white limestone buildings glowed with the late afternoon sun. The maître d' greeted the couple warmly. He couldn't help noticing how they exuded the excitement of blossoming love.

"*Buona Sera!* A table for two? Might I say that you are a very handsome couple. Are you celebrating anything special this evening?"

"Why, yes! This is my beautiful bride—we are on our honeymoon," Orazio said proudly.

"*Auguri!* Congratulations! We have the perfect table right in this corner—nice and romantic."

Neither of them was accustomed to dining in restaurants. Both families had always preferred home-cooked meals. They perused the menu and ordered the requisite pasta for the first course. When the server placed the bowls before them, Orazio made a face of utter disgust. He was never one to hide his disdain. It was the first plate of pasta not cooked by Nicoletta or a family member, and his first bite said it all. Their forks adeptly twirled the spaghetti, and they could see that the chef had overcooked it. For an Italian, there is nothing worse than soft pasta. It should always be "al dente," which means "to the teeth." It should have a bit of hardness that allows the pasta to keep its shape. Neither of them could stomach more than a mouthful; the pasta was inedible.

Thankfully, the second course of local seafood was palatable. Over the years, Orazio had developed a fundamental distrust of restaurants. He always preferred Nicoletta's cooking over anyone else's. Perhaps that all began on their honeymoon.

Their stay in Foggia was brief. The following morning, they boarded a train once again. Nicoletta had relatives in Milano, and they planned to stay with them for the rest of their honeymoon. Milano was the biggest city she had ever been to, and her eyes were wide with wonder. Nicoletta was elated to be out of her small town of Bisceglie. They disembarked the train with their luggage and walked through the grand station. The astounding architecture and soaring ceilings rose above them as they gazed up in awe. As they made their way to the exit, they could see that the infamous winter fog had coated the city. They had expected to see her cousin's husband waiting for them, but as Orazio walked up and down the line of cars in front of the station, he saw no one fitting his description.

Complicating their plans, Nicoletta's cousin, Nina, had forgotten to tell her brother-in-law Nicola about their travel arrangements. Nicola simply looked at the train schedule for that day and assumed they would be on the early train. He had bought a case of oranges for them to share and hoisted them onto the back of his bicycle. The plan was to take a taxi back to his home on the outskirts of the city. It was 10 a.m. when he arrived at the station, and he paced in front of the track, waiting for their arrival. When all the passengers disembarked, and he was sure the train was empty, he assumed he had gotten the date wrong. He hopped on his bicycle and began the long ride home.

Meanwhile, Orazio and Nicoletta waited for their ride for over thirty minutes. Orazio finally went to the taxi stand and gave the address. He could not believe that none of the drivers would drive them far from the city center because of the dense fog. Orazio was sure that they detected his southern Italian accent and refused service. In northern Italy, there is a great deal of prejudice against the southerners, an attitude that remains ubiquitous in Italy today. With no transport to their eventual destination, Orazio became worried. This was not the way he had hoped to start their honeymoon. The uncooperative taxi drivers left them stranded at the train station in an unfamiliar city. He went back to where Nicoletta was standing with the luggage and let her know of their predicament. She suggested they take their bags and just wait at the taxi stand. Surely, someone would take pity on them.

It was New Year's Eve with many tourists eager to get to their families or get settled in a hotel before the big event. The festive holiday atmosphere prompted strangers to wait in the long line to chat with one another. A couple of women took notice of the newlyweds. They were a beautiful young couple who looked at each other as if no one else existed. Despite their concern, Nicoletta and Orazio could not hide their affection. They were deep in conversation about how they might get to her cousin's house. Overhearing them, one of the women jumped in.

"Pardon me for interrupting. What part of Milano are you going to?" she asked.

"Oh, my cousin lives just beyond the center, but none of the drivers will drive to the suburbs. We are on our honeymoon, and we don't know what to do," Nicoletta said, despair coloring her tone.

"Let me see the address; it may be near our destination," the friendly woman said.

Orazio handed her the small piece of paper on which his sister-in-law scribbled the address. Seconds later, she let out a joyful cry.

"This can't be! This is the same building we live in. What is your cousin's name?"

It turned out that the families knew each other. The women invited them to share a taxi out of the city with them. It was a serendipitous moment, which only reinforced their magical honeymoon journey. Upon their arrival, Rosa and Nicola greeted them with big hugs and kisses as they regaled her cousin with their tale. They laughed at the confusion and the ultimate coincidence that brought them together. From that moment on, their first day in Milano settled into the familiar comfort of time with family.

Later that day, when it came time to prepare dinner, Nicoletta was more than willing to help. They had spaghetti with broccoli rabe. This was one of Orazio's favorite meals. The kitchen filled with a delectable aroma of garlic and hot pepper sautéed in olive oil. After their disappointing meal at the restaurant in Foggia, Orazio's mouth watered in anticipation. Nicoletta offered to clean and cut the broccoli rabe for Rosa. She began clipping each of the leaves and cutting off the stems, leaving only the flower on the top of the broccoli. Upon seeing this, Rosa walked to the kitchen sink and placed her hand gently upon Nicoletta's. "*Cara cugina*, dear cousin, we are not in Bisceglie, where the fruits and vegetables are abundant and fresh. This is Milano, and we pay dearly for our produce. We don't have the luxury of cutting away all the leaves. We eat all of it."

Nicoletta looked at her in dismay. It had never occurred to her that cooking the same southern Italian meals would be so different within the same country. At only twenty years old, she realized she was still so very young and that there was so much yet to learn about life outside of Bisceglie.

The next day they were ready to explore Milano's city center. They took the tram to *il centro* and found themselves in the *Piazza del Duomo*, where Milano's neo-gothic cathedral rose high into the winter sky. The imposing structure dominated the entire area. Grand though it was, its architecture was light and graceful. Hundreds of tiny spires soared into the sky, forming lacy swirls right up to the pinnacles. Crowning the very top of the cathedral was a tall, slender spire topped with a golden statue of the Virgin Mary. She sparkled in the cold winter sun as she gazed over the city she blessed. Triumphantly, she stood atop the spire, looking down upon her faithful. It was the most beautiful cathedral they had ever seen. Snapping photos, they wandered around the piazza and inside the grand cathedral. Next to the Duomo sprawled the Galleria, a huge shopping area covered by arching steel beams that looked as lacy as the cathedral. Covering the beams was frosted glass that allowed the sun to fill the space with light and warmth. They wandered from store to store as they took in the new fashions and elegant boutiques. In the years to come, they would continue to enjoy their weekend strolls and window shopping in New York City.

Honeymoon in Milano, La Galleria

Il Duomo of Milano

The sophisticated city of Milano enchanted them. It was a stark contrast to the relative poverty of the south. Industry was ubiquitous— vendors of all sorts featured prominently in shopping districts. The apartments were elegant edifices with carved lintels and stately entrances. At every turn, they were surrounded by high fashion and luxury.

Their days in wealthy Milan passed all too quickly. When it was time to return to Bisceglie, they said a tearful goodbye to cousins Rosa and Nicola and boarded their train for southern Italy. It had been a romantic and event-filled honeymoon. Their time together was a perfect inauguration of their lives as husband and wife.

On their return, they found Antonietta had moved into Nicoletta's old bedroom, giving the newlyweds the master bedroom.

"No, Antonietta! We can't take your room. It's just not right. We will be happy to sleep in my room," Nicoletta exclaimed.

"Absolutely not. You are husband and wife, and you should have a proper bedroom. Besides, my dear Nicoletta, Orazio will go back to New York all too soon. You must make the best of this time you have together," Antonietta declared.

With that, she took Nicoletta's face into her hands and kissed her on her forehead. It was such a lovingly maternal gesture, and it was not lost on Nicoletta.

Orazio could stay in Bisceglie for two months before he had to return to New York. He was nine months shy of the required five years of residency in the United States. The law didn't allow him to be away for more than three months. Otherwise, he'd lose his opportunity for citizenship. Sadly, he would have to leave his beloved bride in Bisceglie until he completed his five years. It was the only way he could gain his American citizenship. As soon as he took his oath, he could send for his wife to join him in New York.

Heartbroken on the day of departure, Carlo accompanied Orazio and Nicoletta to Rome. After a bit of sightseeing, Orazio took a train to Paris to board the ship to the States. Through tearful eyes, the newlyweds gazed at each other.

"I can't believe that we have to say goodbye so soon," Nicoletta said as they embraced. "We've only just met, and now we will be apart once again."

"Don't worry, *mio tesoro*. The time will fly by, you'll see. I will miss you so much."

They kissed one last time, and Orazio boarded the train.

Nicoletta and Orazio at St. Peter's Basilica in Vatican City
before his departure for NYC.

Letter Thirteen
New York City

February 25, 1952

Amore mia,

As you see, I write to give you good news. Let me say, my love, that I am in good health. I was eager to hear from you, and at that moment, I received your letter. You can't imagine the joy that I felt to read your sweet words. Right now, my love, my sister is writing a telegram to tell you that my travels went well and that I arrived safely.

My dearest, you must believe me when I tell you I do nothing without thinking of you. When I said goodbye to you in Rome, I could barely see you through the tears that filled my eyes. When I boarded the train, people asked me why I was so sad. I told them I had left my wife in Italy, so they tried to cheer me up, told me to have courage. I will do everything in my power to make it possible for you to join me, my love.

Having you so far from me is so very sad. I had gotten used to having you close to me and to my heart, isn't that true? In our true love, we were as happy as teenagers discovering love for the first time. Our bond was so strong, it was as if we had always known each other. But now we have to hold fast and have faith in God.

Tomorrow, I will visit the attorney to begin the papers to bring you here, and before you know it, we will be together again, happier than ever before. You will see, my love, that we will be filled with joy.

So here I am, my dear. The voyage went well. I arrived yesterday at 4:30 and disembarked by 5:30. Waiting for me at home were all my sisters. My love, you wouldn't believe their joy at seeing me again. And so, my love, I gave them all the little gifts we bought for them, and they were so happy. But when I look at your photo on my dresser, I cry. But Mamma and Papá counseled me not to be like my brother Carlo, who cried incessantly because he missed his wife so much. I told them, "No Mamma and Papá, you know very well what it's like to leave your cherished wife or husband behind. And all you wish is that she is well and safe."

Nicoletta, my love, please forgive me for not sending the telegram yesterday when I arrived. I was dead tired after five days at sea, during which I didn't sleep. All I did was think of you. Now, my dear, I hope you are not suffering too much. I send you the courage to forge ahead—I beg of you. My love, in reading your letter, I cried a great deal, but I let no one see my tears. I don't want you to rest your head on the pillow in sadness. You know what I mean to say; let's leave it at that. Rest assured that I will do all that is necessary. You will see that you will be here very soon. Believe me, Nicoletta, when I think of you, I want to do something for you so that you won't be lonely.

Tell me, my dear, what would you like me to do for you? Tomorrow will not pass without my attempts to get you here sooner. We were so happy when we were together in Bisceglie, and we will be once again—so many beautiful memories. I hope that by the time this letter arrives, you will have many happy thoughts of our time together. I can't help but remember how we laughed together and pray you won't cry or dwell on our separation. Concentrate on taking care of yourself and your health so that when you come to New York, you'll be even more beautiful. Let me know, my love, when my notification arrives. I am sending 35,000 lire for the wedding expenses, and a little extra for you. Did you receive the postcard I sent from Paris?

A big hug from your great love,
Orazio

Chapter Twenty-One
Separation

Bisceglie, Province of Bari, Italy 1952

After Orazio left Bisceglie, Nicoletta busied herself with preparations for her eventual relocation to America. Although it would be nine long months before her journey, she applied for her visa and looked with eager anticipation toward her new life in New York. The excitement of the wedding and honeymoon faded into the mundane routines of everyday life. And yet, she and her family enjoyed a comfortable life. Unlike many Biscegliese, her parents exposed their children to art and culture. Although their sudden deaths and the outbreak of the second World War prevented Nicoletta's further education, she continued to read voraciously. Her thirst for knowledge and new experiences would continue throughout her life.

The Di Bitettos had never lived an extravagant life. When her parents were alive, she enjoyed the advantages of the upper-middle class. Townspeople always treated them with deference and greeted them with honorific titles. They always referred to her father as *Dottore* (Doctor). But it was through Maria's family that their wealth came. *Papá Nonno,* as Nicoletta called him, was a dear man who came to live with them. Maria's father, Pietro, had been the vineyard manager and assistant winemaker for a wealthy vintner in Taranto in southern Puglia. Vineyard owners throughout the region sought him because of his skill in tending the vines. He had a particular talent for knowing when the grapes were primed for picking. Besides his knowledge of grapes and winemaking, he was an affable man who had a shrewd business sense.

As a young man at the vineyard, he commanded many less-experienced workers. The vines were hung on tall trellises so that the foliage could catch as much sun as possible while shading the fruit and not allowing it to touch the ground. It was an innovative method that yielded tenfold what the competing vineyards could grow. Pietro understood the land and the climate of Puglia as if it were his own body. Coming from a large family, he also knew how to manage people, resulting in an efficiently run vineyard. However, when it came time to check the vines before the grapes' annual crush, he trusted no one. His men built extensive scaffolding that could move along the long rows of vines. Pietro himself would climb up and test each vine to determine the optimal time to harvest.

Over time, Pietro gained a good deal of wealth, and rather than save it, he invested his money in real estate. By the time he was thirty years old, he owned four houses including the one in which he and his family lived. While garnering a lucrative salary at the vineyard, Pietro made a profitable living through his rental properties.

But his good fortune would only last so long. One year, as harvest time approached, his career ended. It was late September, and his men set up the scaffolding and readied it for use. That year, Puglia had been experiencing unusually strong winds coming off the Mediterranean Sea. The Italians called it the *Scirocco*, a strong wind that whipped up from Northern Africa. Severe weather often accompanied the *Scirocco*. The storms associated with it pick up red sand resulting in "blood rain," which can cause significant damage to the grapes. The grapes were nearing harvest time, and Pietro knew he had to check them before the storms began. The winds were already strong, and his crew advised him not to risk going up the scaffolding, but he was adamant. Timing was everything when it came to the harvest.

"Pietro, be reasonable," his assistant pleaded. "It's much too windy today. Why not wait until tomorrow?"

"If we wait and the storms come, it could ruin the entire crop. It's my job to protect these vines. Come now, help me up."

Reluctantly, his assistant helped him climb high onto the scaffolding as he tried in vain to steady it. The winds continued to blow, and the swaying scaffolding moaned its displeasure. The joints were tethered together and visibly strained from the constant pressure. However, Pietro was unstoppable and climbed up and down, inspecting every row of vines. His face burned from the pelting sand, and he turned away from the gusting wind. He was reaching the end of his task when he heard a sharp crack. In a flash, he tumbled to the ground, shielding his head from the falling wood. He felt a searing pain travel up his leg and spine—he couldn't move.

The fall had permanently damaged his right leg. After months of recovery, he could not walk without the help of a cane. His time at the vineyard had come to an abrupt end. It was a heavy blow to his ego and his grand dreams for the future. However, despite the hardship, he could still give his family a good life. His shrewd planning concerning his real estate investments provided a home for each of his children.

Three Houses

Nicoletta yearned for the day when she and Orazio would be reunited. During those three short months together, her life had been completely transformed. With her new American husband by her side, she felt a thrilling sense of freedom—as if she could do anything without fear of reprisal. However, in his absence, Nicoletta found that navigating the old-fashioned customs and ways of thinking to be burdensome. Even though she was a married woman now, her brother, Mauro, and his wife, Despina, continued to treat her like a child which she fervently resented. During the time Orazio was in Bisceglie, Nicoletta was used to going out whenever she pleased. Orazio did not care about what the neighbors thought or what the customs were; he did what he wanted. After all, he was a New Yorker, and he didn't feel bound by any of the unspoken rules from the *old country*. Having a taste of that freedom, Nicoletta found it challenging to turn back. Now that Orazio had left her on her own, she desired her independence. However, she encountered resistance at every turn.

One such occasion concerned the division of property her parents had willed to her and her two brothers. That they owned property at all placed Nicoletta's family above many others. There were three houses, one for each of them upon their marriage. Maria had always said that the larger of the three homes would go to her only daughter, Nicoletta. It was only right, in her mind, that she should have the larger property, because the boys could find jobs and work to improve their station in life. Maria wanted Nicoletta to have financial security during a time when it was unthinkable for a young woman to have a career or a life beyond caring for her family. Also, Nicoletta would need to have a considerable dowry to attract a suitable man for marriage. There was never any discussion or disagreement regarding the distribution of the houses, so Nicoletta never dreamed there would be an issue. Now that she was married, she was ready to take possession of her inheritance.

When the three siblings were together, she broached the topic, addressing Mauro first, since he was the oldest.

"Mauro, when should we take possession of the houses *Mamma* and *Papá* left us? Now that I'm married, we can move forward with that, right?"

"*Sí*, of course, Nicoletta. That was always the plan. But you are still nine months away from majority. Orazio will have to sign for you."

"But surely that won't be a problem," Pietro interjected. "*Mamma* and *Papá* were always very clear about which properties should go to each of us. Can't we simply get the titles transferred to each of our names?"

"Yes, I suppose it could be that easy," Mauro replied with hesitation.

"Orazio's big brother, Carlo, would be my guardian. He's a part of the family on two fronts—my brother-in-law, and married to our cousin, Nina," Nicoletta offered.

"I don't like that solution, Nicoletta. That would effectively put you under his care until your birthday in November. Orazio will be in America, which puts his brother Carlo as the next of kin and in charge of the property. Who knows what he would do with it?" Mauro said, gruffly.

His insinuation irked Nicoletta. This was her new brother-in-law. *How could he be so rude?* she thought.

"Come on now, Mauro. He's a good guy. Why would he swindle his own brother and sister-in-law? That's just silly," Piero said in his defense.

He could see that Nicoletta was becoming angry and wanted to derail any conflict between his two siblings. Ever since Mauro had come back from Greece with his new wife, there had been a perceptible tension between them. Nicoletta was rightfully wary of Mauro. He had done nothing but his wife's bidding since their arrival in Bisceglie. She could feel that there was always a hidden agenda in their interactions. Despina was a selfish and overbearing woman, and she could live with that. But Nicoletta was less forgiving of Mauro. In her opinion, he showed no backbone concerning any of Despina's wishes. He often acted against his siblings to please his wife. To Nicoletta, that was a far more egregious sin.

Nicoletta was right to suspect there was more to the discussion than appeared. Despina's vendetta against Nicoletta had reached a fever pitch after her marriage to Orazio. When Despina caught wind of the inheritance and the fact that the prized property was to go to Nicoletta, she seethed with anger. Her tirades were incessant.

"Why should she get the larger house? You are the oldest, Mauro. You are entitled to have all three of the houses. They should be grateful to get any at all. At least you should get the pick of them. Nicoletta is a spoiled child. Why should she get the largest one? After all, she's just going to sell it and move to America. That's just not right," Despina argued.

Mauro could not reason with her. After all, they were simply following the wishes of Maria and Francesco. But Despina wore Mauro down, and he just wanted her to stop. He needed peace. She did not mask her displeasure. She shared her anger with anyone who would listen, and she was even more vocal among family. Piero and Nicoletta were beside themselves when they learned of her interference. Nicoletta was even angrier at Mauro for entertaining Despina's solution. *All those years of worshiping her eldest brother, and this is what it has come to. Mauro was showing his true colors. Despina will always come first in his life. His own brother and sister will always suffer at her hands. I blame him!* Nicoletta thought.

Mauro's attempts to speak with Piero and Nicoletta were not going well.

"Where is this coming from, Mauro? Your wife, perhaps? There was never any question of our inheritance before now. Why is that?" Nicoletta challenged.

Piero rolled his eyes and let out a deep sigh. *Here we go,* he thought.

"What are you implying, Nicoletta? How dare you disrespect your older brother like this." Mauro's face reddened in anger and embarrassment.

"Respect? Perhaps you should respect your deceased parents' wishes before you toss around accusations of disrespect. You would have never treated any of us like this before Despina came into your life. Where is your loyalty to our family? Or is everything now about money and power?"

"Nicoletta, I am warning you. You have already gone too far," Mauro said through gritted teeth.

Mauro needed to dial back his anger so he could make them see Despina's perspective.

She will always feel like a stranger in this family. Perhaps this one small compromise might show her your goodwill, he thought.

"Come on, Mauro, you know that is not true. Your wife believes that she's the grand dame of the family now. For some reason, she acts as if she's entitled. If she gets her way now, we'll always be cowing to her wishes," Piero said.

"Piero, watch your tongue! That is my wife. She will always come first in my life," Mauro responded in anger.

"Yes, well, that's the problem, isn't it?" Nicoletta said. "Since you brought her back from Greece, none of us matter. You're not even concerned about disregarding the wishes of our deceased parents. How could you discount them and us so completely?"

"How dare you, Nicoletta! This is a perfect example of your childish behavior. You will show her—and me—some respect."

"Respect goes both ways, Mauro. She has never shown Piero or me any respect, and you just stand idly by and let it happen!" Nicoletta's anger was boiling to the surface.

As angry as Piero was, he knew he couldn't let this argument escalate. "Okay, enough!" He held his hand up to both of them. "Let's stop this now before we say things we can never take back."

Mauro was startled that his brother exercised his authority in this situation. It was apparent that he had acted as the head of the family during the many years after their parents passed. But he had to admit that Piero was right; this discussion was getting out of hand.

"Let's all take a deep breath and look at this rationally," Mauro agreed. "It's obvious that Despina will never relent on this point. That will make *all* of us miserable."

"All right then, why don't we all calm down?" Piero said. "Mauro, what do you suggest we do?"

"Well, since you will move to America in less than a year, you won't need the larger house. And since Despina and I have her son with us, we thought that the most logical solution would be for us to take it," Mauro said cautiously. He braced himself for another outburst.

"Oh, do you now? How convenient!" Nicoletta retorted.

"Come on now, Mauro. How is that fair? This is what *Mamma* promised to her. It is rightfully hers. She will need every penny for her move to New York."

"But we have a family. Despina is right to suggest that we move to the larger house."

"I knew it!" Nicoletta exclaimed. "This is all her idea. Of course she wants the bigger house for you. She'll do anything to take from me. She was always jealous of your affection for me, not that it shows anymore."

"I have to admit, Mauro, I agree with Nicoletta. This is none of her concern, and the decision has already been made. You have no right to alter the will of *Mamma* and *Papá*. Besides, of all of us, you have the greatest means. This is just not right."

"It is not about who has more money. This is simply a more practical solution, especially since Nicoletta is moving away."

The argument went around and around. Nicoletta was wearing down. She saw some logic regarding her own departure for America, but there was still no way she would let Despina get her way. If anyone should get the larger property, it should be Piero. He supported the entire family during the war. His continued sacrifice was unfailing. As the argument dragged on, Piero had finally had enough.

"We are getting nowhere through arguing," he said. "This is a legal matter, so I suggest we go to our attorney. At least we will get counsel from a disinterested party."

They agreed to follow whatever the attorney suggested, but they never dreamed that his method of deciding would be so absurd. After listening to their story from various perspectives, he was confident that no amount of reason would convince any of them to stray from their own opinions. A simple solution was the most efficient.

"All right, since none of you can decide who should get the larger house, you'll draw straws. Whoever picks the longest one gets it," he said with authority.

"But that's ridiculous!" Mauro exclaimed.

"Why, Mauro?" Piero asked. "If we choose not to follow our parents' wishes, then perhaps we let fate decide. This way, there is no favoritism and, therefore, no resentment. *Mamma and Papá* would roll in their graves if they knew we were bickering over money."

"Agreed!" Nicoletta chimed in. "And I promise to let it go, regardless of the results—no hard feelings, no grudges."

Mauro knew that Despina's wrath would be harsh should he not come through with the bigger home, but there was little he could say to counter their argument.

"All right then, let's draw straws. At least it will bring an end to this interminable argument!"

The attorney took charge so that the arguing siblings could not blame one another of cheating. He didn't believe they would stoop so low, but he had witnessed many family conflicts over the years. It was always best to have a neutral party step in. He carefully broke the straws into differing lengths and offered them up for inspection. They all agreed that Piero should draw first, since he was the most reasonable among them. He pulled the straw, and with a sigh, showed the short straw to them. He would get the smallest property.

To quell his sister's fears of favoritism, Mauro prompted her to choose next. Looking from one straw to the other, Nicoletta could feel her face turning red and her forehead bead with sweat. *What if I get the smaller house after all this? Why did I give up so easily?* she thought. When she finally drew her straw, she screamed with joy—she drew the longest straw. The big house was hers, the one her parents originally promised. Mauro did not hide his disappointment—he was a sore loser.

"What a ridiculous way to make such an important decision."

"Hold on there, Mauro," Piero responded. "We all agreed. Besides, I'm the one who got the smallest of the three properties. You should be happy with what you got."

"So it's settled, then? No more arguments over what we chose?" Nicoletta needed to confirm this was the final decision. "And we can do whatever we want with the property?"

"Of course, Nicoletta," Mauro replied with annoyance. "I assume you will put it on the market immediately."

"Actually, I have another idea." She turned to Piero and took his hand. "*Caro fratello,* my dear brother, you took care of me all those years after *Mamma* died. You worked two jobs to support us, and you never complained. You deserve the bigger house. Take it; I want you to have it."

With that, she wrapped her arms around his neck and kissed his cheek. She could feel Mauro's seething anger behind her, but she didn't care. This was the right thing to do. It didn't hurt that Despina did not get her way, but she'd be much less upset knowing that the home did not go to Nicoletta. Sadly, the damage done to their relationship ran deep. The rift between Nicoletta and her brother Mauro would last for decades.

Despina did nothing to dissuade anyone's negative opinions of her. She actively stirred the pot and created conflict at every turn. When she first met Nicoletta, she exclaimed in disbelief, "Why, you are pretty after all! From the moment I met him, Mauro had been bragging about how adorable his little sister was. When he finally showed me your photo, I thought, W*hat is he thinking? She is scrawny with such thin hair.* But look at you! You have quite an ample bosom and beautiful figure. Not like Piero's wife, Carmela. She may have nice thick hair, but she has a flat chest. Poor Piero—there's nothing there to grab on to!" She then let out a wicked laugh.

Nicoletta was appalled, not merely at her backhanded compliment, but also Despina's unabashed vulgarity. *Who is this woman my brother brought back from Greece? How could he have married such a cretin?* She could never accept her. She felt Mauro had betrayed them by bringing such a wicked woman into the family. In Nicoletta's eyes, he was not the same man who had gone off to the military many years before. She looked fondly on her childhood memories. She would run to Mauro as he came through the door after work, and he'd crouch down with his hands held behind his back.

"Give your big brother a kiss hello, Nicoletta."

She would enthusiastically oblige him as she tried to look over his shoulder to see what he was hiding. After her kiss, Mauro held out his hand, which contained some little treat. It was usually a little chocolate or candy. The affection between them had always been abundant. But since his return from Greece, significant emotional distance existed between Mauro and the rest of the family. They seemed to disagree about every little thing. Her relationship with Orazio was no exception.

Her brother, Mauro, was never in favor of her marriage to Orazio. In his mind, Nicoletta was marrying beneath her class. His family was mostly made up of uneducated laborers from the *città vecchia* (the old city). The more affluent looked down upon the residents of the old city, especially the upwardly mobile middle class. Townspeople always regarded her family with reverence and respect. Both Mauro and Piero had attended school, and if not for the war, Nicoletta would have pursued her education as far as she could.

Chapter Twenty-Two
Arrivederci, Italia

Bisceglie, Province of Bari, Italy 1952

The months passed and autumn arrived. Orazio was now an American citizen and could bring his wife to the United States. When word arrived, Nicoletta began preparations in earnest. However, most of the Italian ships were entirely booked from third class to first. Every date in November was unavailable. Orazio, eager for her arrival, visited a travel agency in New York and found the same results. In his desperation, he bought Nicoletta an airline ticket. Transatlantic flights during the 1950s were exorbitant, but Orazio didn't care. He drew from his savings and sent Nicoletta a telegram with his good news.

When Nicoletta read his telegram, her heart pounded in her chest.

"What's wrong?" Antonietta asked.

"Orazio bought a plane ticket. He wants me to fly to America," Nicoletta replied.

"*O Dio*! That is so dangerous!" Antonietta cried.

"I know. I may sound foolish, but my horoscope said that Scorpios should stay away from air travel."

"What are you going to do?" Antonietta asked.

"I am so afraid. But I have to tell him no."

Filled with eager anticipation, Orazio was crushed when he received her telegram.

"How could she do this?" he asked his mother. "She mustn't be as eager to join me as I thought."

"Orazio, I'm sure she is simply nervous. She is only twenty-one years old. She's never traveled out of Italy."

"I just paid for tickets—there is no refund. Now she has to wait until there's room on a ship and pay the full fare plus what I've already spent."

Nicoletta knew he was angry, but she wasn't comfortable flying. Luckily, she found a British ship, *The Constitution*, with room in second class. She booked it immediately.

In early November, Nicoletta was helping Antonietta prepare the evening meal when her second cousin burst into the kitchen.

"I have something juicy to tell you," she said provocatively.

"Oh, is that so? Well then, go ahead," Nicoletta said, humoring her.

"Despina is visiting my mother, and she's talking about you," she replied.

That piqued her interest. She stopped what she was doing and looked directly at her.

"And what, *exactly*, did she say?"

"She told my mother to tell you she doesn't want to see you."

"What do you mean? She's my sister-in-law. I see her all the time." Nicoletta said with annoyance.

"When you leave for America, she said that you shouldn't bother to say goodbye to her. You are nothing to her."

Visibly stunned, Nicoletta stared at her blankly. During the months after Orazio left, she had made significant overtures to Despina. She thought they had made their peace, and that they were on good terms. Obviously, she was mistaken.

"Elisa, when you go back home today, give your mother a message for Despina. Tell her not to worry. If that is how she feels about me, there is no way in hell that I will say goodbye to her."

Nicoletta was beside herself with anger, but beneath it all, she was hurt. *Why would she say that just as I am about to leave Italy for good? Doesn't she realize it may be decades before I can return?* She had to resolve the conflict and planned to speak to Mauro. The night before her departure, she walked all the way to the train station to meet her brother at the end of his workday. The walk took about thirty minutes. Surprised to see her, he furrowed his brow; he knew something was brewing.

"Nicoletta, what are you doing here?" he asked.

"I need to talk with you about Despina. She said something that really wounded me."

"I'm sure you're being too sensitive. What is it this time?"

She explained the entire exchange between her and Elisa and turned to him.

"What do you expect me to do with such a hateful statement?"

"Look, you know how she is. Despina is a woman of great passion. I am sure she didn't mean it."

"So I am to simply ignore her awful words and go say goodbye to her? And what of my feelings? Do they not matter?" Nicoletta asked.

"She is my wife," he responded, even though they could not yet marry. "You will show her the respect she's due."

By this time, they had arrived at his apartment building, and they both looked at the door.

"I'm sorry, Mauro—respect is a two-way street. I can't show her respect if she doesn't respect me."

"Nicoletta, you are not a little girl any longer. You're a married woman now. You should have learned to respect your elders. Where did you learn these manners?" he chided.

"Mauro, all those years you were away, I had to grow up quickly. Without *Mamma* and *Papá*, I learned the hard way, and I believe I am the woman they dreamed I'd become. Piero and Antonietta always taught me to be kind and generous. But they also instructed me to stand up for myself, lest I become a carpet to be trodden upon. I will not allow Despina to walk all over me. She is my elder, so she should know one does not treat family members as poorly as she does me."

"Then we disagree," he said, shaking his head in defeat. "You are not the same sweet girl I left many years ago." His last comment was sharp, and it wounded her.

"No, brother, I am a woman who can speak for herself. Now let us say a proper goodbye before I sail on that ship tomorrow." She went in for a hug, and he pulled away.

"Not unless you come up with me and greet Despina. If you do not say a proper goodbye to her, then neither can I."

They were at a stalemate, and neither would give in. Nicoletta stared at him in disbelief. She had lost her big brother. That evening, they parted with heavy hearts.

Finally, the long-anticipated day arrived. The house was bursting with family and friends. The festive gathering lasted late into the evening as people continued to drop by to wish Nicoletta a safe journey and happy life in New York. Noticeably absent from the party were Mauro and Despina. Amid the festive celebration, the guests questioned why and whispered to one another. Family gossip was like sweet syrup, especially among such prominent citizens of Bisceglie. An old friend came by with a message from Despina to say that she regretted her harsh words and that Nicoletta should have never listened to little Elisa.

"If she truly feels that way, why didn't they come tonight to say goodbye?" Nicoletta asked.

There was no response, but everyone knew it was all about pride. An apology through a messenger was as far as Despina could go. And Nicoletta could not let go of her own feelings of disappointment and anger.

Late that evening, she made her way to the station for the midnight train. Piero and his wife, Carmela, accompanied her on the train to Napoli. Zia Nunzia and a few others waved at them from the platform, sobbing, "*La Rosa*," the rose; she kept repeating it as she cried. Nunzia felt like she was losing her sister, Maria, all over again.

The next morning, the three of them took a taxi to the port of Napoli and said their tearful goodbyes. They didn't know if or when they would ever see each other again. It was a painful moment for all of them. But for Nicoletta, the future was rife with possibilities and unique adventures. Although her heart ached at the thought of leaving her family, her excitement and longing to be with Orazio eased the pain. However, Piero's heart was breaking. His baby sister was leaving Italy for good. They had been each other's most significant support after their parents died, and during the last few years, they had become the best of friends. He knew it would be many years before he would lay eyes on her. He held her in his tight embrace and kissed the top of her head.

"*Mi raccomando,* I beg you, please take care of yourself, my angel. And don't forget how much I love you," Piero said as he let her go.

Tearfully, Nicoletta boarded the ship and waved goodbye. After they set sail, she strolled along the deck then made her way to her cabin. The ship was beautiful, and her roommate turned out to be the daughter of her neighborhood produce seller. They served tea and treats often, and the accommodations were almost luxurious. Nicoletta could hardly believe her eyes. It was the perfect way to begin her grand adventure in America.

Chapter Twenty-Three
Welcome to America

New York City 1952

On the fifteenth of November, Nicoletta boarded the ship in Napoli for the eleven-day voyage. At twenty-one years old, she traveled far from her family and the only home she had ever known. On November 26th, the day before Thanksgiving, the Constitution steamed past the symbol of the new world—Lady Liberty stood proudly atop her pedestal. Slowly, the ship pulled into the New York harbor.

During the voyage, Nicoletta became friendly with Paola, who was traveling with her daughter. They struck up an easy rapport and kept each other company on the long journey. As they disembarked, they got split up. She spotted Paola and her daughter across the room when Nicoletta realized she had Paola's papers. Attempting to bring them to her, she stepped out of line and walked over to her. Noticing her, a guard stopped her abruptly and chided her. When Nicoletta explained her reasons, the guard ripped the documents from her hands.

"I'll take those. Now get back in your line."

His demeanor stung. It was not the friendly welcome to America she had expected. When she got to the immigration desk, the clerk, who had overheard her speak of her friend, said mockingly:

"In America non sono amici, solo dollari." In America, there are no friends, just the almighty dollar.

Her first experience in America was startlingly awful. Nicoletta had never imagined the first American she met would treat her as chattel. A wave of homesickness washed over her. *What have I done?* she wondered, questioning her decisions for the first time.

But all her doubts disappeared when she spotted her husband waiting for her. With his Fedora hat, suit, and tie, he stood with a grand bouquet of red roses. Larry, as Orazio was known in the states, threw his arms around her and kissed her. They embraced so tightly she could hardly breathe. Larry collected her luggage and hailed a taxicab to bring them home to his parents' apartment at 170 Worth Street in Little Italy.

Standing at the door of the apartment was Larry's mother, Antonia. Not one for expressing emotions, she watched as her son and his Italian bride climbed the last flight of stairs. She and Nicoletta had exchanged several letters over the years, and their affection for each other was already clear. Antonia stood with outstretched arms, and Nicoletta fell into her warm embrace.

"*Figlia*, my daughter. At last, my son will be happy!"

Tears wet Nicoletta's cheeks, for she knew God had answered her prayers. Since she was a little girl, she prayed to the Blessed Mother for someone to take her mother's place. In Antonia's warm embrace, she felt the love of her mother. *I am home now,* she thought.

There was nothing elegant about the five-floor walk-up, but she loved every corner. From the bedroom window, she could see the statue of Christopher Columbus, a monument to the Italian immigrants. One block away was a lovely park, and on Mott Street was the church where they would baptize their first three children.

Larry's brother, Carlo, greeted her in his usual joking manner.

"All right, sister-in-law, now that you're finally here, we'll see each other a lot. Actually, I'll see you tomorrow."

"Oh, that is great, Carlo."

"Yeah, I don't have to work tomorrow! It's a holiday in America."

"How wonderful! What holiday is it?"

In his usual mischievous way, he responded, "Eh, in America, they celebrate the day of the chicken!"

"Chicken? What a strange holiday."

On Thanksgiving Day, Antonia's children, Antoinette, Rosie, Carlo, and Sal, came to dinner with their spouses. The tiny apartment was overflowing, and Tina was the center of attention as the new member of the family. For her new "American" relatives, she would no longer be known as Nicoletta. It was much too Italian sounding for New York, and much too long a name. They decided she would use the diminutive that was used in her childhood, Tina. Nicolettina simply translated to little Nicoletta, and to this day, her many nieces and nephews call her Aunt Tina.

Since Orazio's father, Francesco, did not like turkey, Antonia roasted a chicken with potatoes and green beans covered in tomato sauce. It couldn't be further from the traditional American Thanksgiving meal, but the family enjoyed every bite. Everyone was in high spirits, and the festivities lasted well into the evening. It was the perfect holiday during which to celebrate her new life in America.

Tina and Larry in New York City

Tina with Francesco and Antonia Dell'Olio

Feeding the pigeons in New York City

In the months that followed, Antonia took her new daughter-in-law around Little Italy to introduce her to all the business owners. She met the butcher, the baker, and the fruit and vegetable vendors. It was essential to establish relationships with all of them to always get top quality food. Bisceglie is on the southern coast of Italy, and seafood and fish were the main staples of their diets. The fish market buzzed with activity every morning just a block away from Tina's house. Everyone in Bisceglie knew whether the fish was fresh or a day old. As they were browsing through the fish market in Little Italy, Tina exclaimed under her breath, "But *Mamma*, how could they sell this fish? It's not fresh at all. Look, look at how cloudy and sunken their eyes are. Some of these must be days old!"

"Ah, my child, we are not in Bisceglie any longer. Here in America, there is no such thing as fresh from the sea. The fishermen's plentiful catches spoiled us in Bisceglie, but that's not all. We are beginning winter in New York. The flavorful fruits and vegetables of back home will be nowhere to be found. So much in your life will change now that you're in New York. But don't worry, you'll get used to it, just as I did. Soon, you will hardly remember how much better the food tasted in Italy."

Tina did not like that explanation and couldn't imagine eating old fish and tasteless fruit. During those first few days walking by the tenement houses and through the filthy streets of Little Italy, she wondered about the America of her dreams. None of the images that she had conjured up as a young woman had any similarity to what she now saw in New York. She missed her brother, Piero, Antonietta, and Zia Nunzia. The familiar walks to each of the vendors and neighborhoods of her hometown were long gone. She had dreamed of a life in New York with Larry for two years, and in those dreams, she pictured elegant neighborhoods, the latest fashions, and fine restaurants. She never thought that her new community in America would be more impoverished and rundown than Bisceglie.

Although her first year in New York City was challenging, she took comfort in knowing that one of her best friends from Bisceglie, Felicia, was her new sister-in-law. Felicia had married Larry's younger brother, Sal, a few years before. Her second child was born on Christmas day, 1953. Tina expressed her desire to visit with her and help her with the new baby. It would be the perfect antidote to her loneliness, and it would get her out of the apartment. However, Larry worried about her wandering New York City on her own. He was certain she would get lost.

"Tina, that is a very long distance from home, and it's much too cold for you to walk that far."

"I understand, Larry. But I really want to get out of the house and spend some time with Felicia. Perhaps I could take the subway."

His fears showing, Larry tried to convince her not to go.

"Tina, you barely speak any English. How will you navigate the subway system? I'm afraid you will lose your way, and then how will you get home?"

"I can do it, Larry. The subway station is just up the block from here. Just tell me which train to get on. I will be all right. I promise."

"Okay, but you must be very careful. Take the uptown train to Houston Street Station. Tina, please be careful."

The next day, after Larry left for work, Tina gathered herself together and descended the five flights of stairs leading from their flat. Then she walked one block to the subway station. Once inside, she approached the booth and asked the attendant which train to take.

"Hello, which train do I take to go ooptown?" she said with her winning smile.

He cocked his head in confusion and replied, "Do you mean uptown?"

"Yes," she responded with better pronunciation. "Uptown."

He then asked where she was heading. She could understand much better than she could speak, so Tina showed him the address she had copied down. He smiled, exited the booth, and led her to the map that was posted on the wall.

"Go to Houston Street Station. That is only one stop."

"Thank you, thank you for helping."

New Yorkers are so kind, she thought. *I will be just fine.* And then she was on her way. Visiting with Felicia was a godsend. The two young women shared so many of the same experiences and got along famously. In each other, they found the comfort they needed. After all, they had both married into the same family and come from the same hometown.

After the holidays, Tina decided she had to get out of the house and out of the neighborhood. Tina was always tenacious. She had left all that she had known to move to a faraway land with an unfamiliar language. The idea of being trapped in a tiny little apartment with her mother-in-law made her head spin. As loving as she was, Antonia was an old-world woman, and her life in Little Italy was incredibly limited. Tina knew that the elegant City of New York existed somewhere. She just couldn't go on her daily rounds with Antonia in anticipation of Orazio's return from work each day. She longed for the independence she hoped for after leaving Bisceglie.

Tina believed the best way to get out of the apartment was to look for a job. In Italy, she had learned to sew. She was confident in her skills and had a proven track record. Tina knew there was a thriving garment industry in New York and that Larry's little sister, Francesca, worked there. Her husband, John, was a mechanic at the shop. He repaired and maintained all the sewing machines and ironing equipment. One weekend, only two months into her time in New York, she asked Larry if he would inquire about a factory job.

Her brother-in-law, John was of Italian descent through his grandparents, but he didn't speak a word of Italian. Tina had barely two months of conversational phrases under her belt. But somehow, they could communicate well enough. He brought Tina to the Rhine Company and set her up at a machine. In Italy, she was used to sewing with a pedal machine, sewing by hand, and finishing work on dresses and other garments. With a little training on the new electric machines, she was a natural. The factory produced panties and slips for girls and women, with all the frills and lace. It was piecework, which meant that the faster she worked, the more money she would make. Most of the women working in the shop were Italians, and one could hear dialects from many parts of southern Italy.

In 1947, a massive wave of Italian immigrants came into the United States to join their families after World War II. It was at the Rhine Company that Tina gradually learned about her unfamiliar country with the comfort of having workmates that spoke her language. One afternoon, as they were punching out at the end of the day, her friends asked where she lived. When Tina told them how long of a walk she had, they looked at her with worry. She traversed the many blocks from 503 Broadway to Canal Street, and from there to the apartment on Worth Street. In the bitter cold of New York winters, this twenty-one-year-old girl from southern Italy walked each day to and from work on her own. Tina didn't think twice about it. She tried to reassure her new friends using a phrase that she learned from Antonia's sister, Lucia, saying, "No weddies."

They looked at her, and one of them said, "You're going to a wedding?"

Confused, she said nothing. Finally, they figured out that she was trying to say, "No worries." They all had a good laugh, and she began to learn proper pronunciation from her new work buddies. As the months passed, she became more comfortable with her life in New York. She enjoyed the stimulation of work and the playful banter with the other girls in the shop.

Determined to learn her way around the city, Tina ventured into unfamiliar neighborhoods and wandered into shops attempting to speak English by chatting with clerks. There was so much to learn about her new country.

She wandered into a lingerie store to look for stockings. The sales associate asked if he could help. With her limited English, she responded.

"Thank you. I need socks," Tina said as she pointed at her legs.

"Socks… Do you mean stockings?"

"Yes, yes, stockings," she said, slowly articulating the word.

The clerk took pleasure in her eagerness to learn the language and engaged her in conversation.

"Now, be sure to come back if you need anything else. I will help you learn more English."

She resolved to speak proper English and reveled in her first successful shopping experience. Tina had always prided herself on her writing and speaking ability. She read voraciously, and people commonly mistook her for a northern Italian because she spoke proper Italian with no hint of a southern accent. In the Italian ghetto of New York, vendors would often ask where she was from, exclaiming with surprise when they discovered she was from Bisceglie.

Tina's determination to speak English harkened back to discussion she had with her brother Mauro. He believed that she would be treated poorly as an Italian immigrant in America. Family status and education were critical factors for the Di Bitetto family. Although they had lost a great deal after their parents died, Mauro, was determined to maintain and further their place in society. When Nicoletta announced her intentions to marry Orazio, he thought she was crazy. Mauro believed she would sink further down the ladder of success if she left Bisceglie. He had warned of the plight of immigrants in America and advised her not to go.

"How can you marry a man you have never met? Just because he writes romantic letters doesn't mean he's the man of your dreams. What if he turns out to be low class and poorly mannered?"

"His letters are beautiful, and they express his heart. That's how I know. We reveal so much more in the written word than in ordinary conversation," she replied.

"Nicoletta, be reasonable. That may be so, but you don't even know if you are compatible."

"I suppose you're right, but that is why we have an agreement. If, when we meet, we feel the same passion for each other as we did in our letters, then we will marry. If not, we will part as friends."

"It's not that simple, Nicoletta, and you should know better than that," Mauro replied with exasperation.

"Maybe not, but I know what I feel. One of the many things I learned in the absence of both our parents is that I must follow my heart."

"But Nicoletta, here in Italy, you are respected for your family and status. You are *La Signorina*. If you go to New York, you'll be nothing but an immigrant who cannot speak the language. People will assume you are ignorant. You are making a big mistake, Nicoletta."

He was seventeen years older than she, and although he was away at war during most of her childhood, he treated her as his child. It was almost as if they were speaking a different language. Neither seemed to understand where the other was coming from. He was often frustrated because she didn't seem to respect his opinion or his guiding instructions. He was the eldest son. It was his responsibility to look after her now that their parents had passed, whereas she resented him for assuming he could simply reinsert himself into her life after all these years. He didn't really know her as an adult, and she was not about to be treated like the child he left so many years before.

All those feelings of resentment were long behind Tina. She was a married woman living in New York. The family conflicts seemed trivial to her now that she lived thousands of miles away. Her persistence in learning to speak English served her well as she attended classes in the evening and gained a better grasp of the language than Larry. He would come to rely upon her to read contracts and instructions. Despite her lack of formal education, her sharp mind led her to achieve more than she imagined. Heeding her brother's words, Tina made sure that no one would treat her as an ignorant immigrant.

Letter Fourteen
Mending Fences

Dear Mauro,

I write to share with you the most wonderful news. You are now an uncle. Larry and I are filled with joy over the birth of our daughter, Annette.

I couldn't wait to share this with you. Her birth made me realize how important family is, and although we have had our differences over the last few years, I believe that our reconciliation is long overdue. Let us move beyond our squabble and embrace the love we've always shared.

You took care of me when I was a little girl and I will never forget that. Now, I've begun a family of my own and I hope you will meet your new niece before too long. I hope you are well. Please give my love to Despina.

Your loving little sister,
Nicoletta

Chapter Twenty-Four
Starting a Family

New York City 1952-1956

In early spring 1954, two years after they married, their first child was born. Named after Larry's mother, Antonia, they always referred to her as Annette. The already tight one-bedroom apartment shared with Antonia and Francesco became even smaller. But it delighted the proud grandparents to have a little one brightening up their lives. Larry and Tina were as happy as could be and appreciated their help. With the birth of their first child, Tina felt the distance between

Proud parents with Annette in New York

herself and her siblings back in Italy. They would be so proud, and she wanted to share her momentous news with them. Tina hadn't communicated with her oldest brother, Mauro, since leaving Italy over a year before. She knew it was time to heal those old wounds. Tina took a pen to paper and wrote to him.

It was the birth of Annette that prompted the healing in their fractured relationship. From then on, both Tina and Mauro wrote to each other regularly. Although they were thousands of miles apart, they were a family once again. The resentment and guilt that Tina had carried melted away as she cared for her newborn baby. She finally put the petty conflicts with Mauro and Despina to rest. Annette had filled her heart with love.

Annette was just over a year old when Tina discovered she was pregnant again. Not long after Annette's birth, Larry's mother, Antonia, had her first heart episode. Climbing five flights of stairs was no longer workable. She and Francesco moved to Bridgeport, Connecticut, to live with their daughter Lily. Although Tina and Larry had the apartment to themselves, they worried it would be too small for them and the two children. However, they enjoyed living in the city and decided the lack of space was worth the sacrifice. But as the months passed, Tina felt two distinct and separate movements. Tina was positive she was carrying twins. She informed the obstetrician, who summarily dismissed her theory.

"I only hear one heartbeat. Sometimes it feels like separate movements, but it's only vibration."

"Yes, Doctor, but it's happened several times. I am sure I felt two babies."

"Like I said, Mrs. Dell'Olio, I hear only one heartbeat. You will have one very healthy baby."

Tina continued to grow larger as each month passed. Although she had significant doubts, she took heed of the doctor's words and prepared for their second child. During the eighth and ninth months, Tina had grown enormous, bigger than she was with Annette, and she struggled to climb the five flights up to their apartment. Her knees continually hit her belly, and she got winded when she was only halfway up. One night, at the beginning of April, she went to bed around 11 p.m. She rose to go to the bathroom several times during the night—more so than usual. And although she had a few cramps, she figured it was just false labor. She was still several weeks before her due date. However, as the contractions became more intense, she rolled over and shook Larry awake.

"*Amore*, wake up."

"What's wrong? Are you okay?"

"Time to go to the hospital."

They rushed to dress, and Larry went next door to wake the neighbor.

"Caroline, so sorry to wake you up. Tina is in labor. Can you watch Annette?"

"Of course. Do you need help to get down the stairs with Tina?"

"No, thanks. I think I've got it."

It was 4:00 a.m. when they caught a cab to the hospital. The doctor met them in the emergency room and took her directly to the maternity ward. Her labor went smoothly, and two hours later, Franco was born.

"It's a boy! A healthy boy!" the doctor exclaimed. "Wait, wait! We have more work to do here."

"Is everything okay?" Tina asked.

"Yes, yes, but you have another baby to deliver!"

Ten minutes later, a baby girl was born.

"You made a liar out of me, Tina. You were right all along."

After the doctor cleaned up, he ambled out to the waiting room to inform the new father. Larry looked up at him expectantly.

"Such a worried look on your face, Larry. Everything is fine."

"So, what is it, a boy?"

The doctor hesitated, toying with him.

"What? What's wrong?"

"Yes, it's a boy… and a girl!"

In a single night, their family grew from three to five. Larry and Tina were in heaven. As the first boy, they would name him after Larry's father, Francesco, but they always called him Frankie. Since she was the second girl, she was named Maria after Tina's mother. The family called her Marisa.

Marisa, though healthy, was underweight. When it came time for Tina to leave the hospital, Marisa was still in an incubator. She held her one more time before she left the hospital as tears streamed down her cheeks. The nurse looked at her and shook her head.

"Silly girl! You are quite lucky, you know. You have two healthy babies. This little one will be home in no time."

"I know, but leaving her behind breaks my heart."

"Be grateful for the extra time. You have a two-year-old and twin newborn babies. This will give you a chance to adjust to your new reality. Believe me, having three little ones that young will be a challenge."

The nurse's words rang true. Frankie had trouble sleeping from the start. When he cried, he woke up Marisa and then Annette. Three babies crying at once several times a night took a toll on the new parents. With only one bedroom, it was nearly impossible to sleep-train them. Annette slept in the living room, while Tina and Larry plus the two infants slept in the bedroom. But that was only one challenge. Carrying them up and down five flights of stairs with a stroller and diaper bags was nearly impossible. It became obvious that their apartment in New York City would not work. It was heartbreaking to think of leaving the city they loved. But they couldn't afford a bigger apartment and the expense of three children.

Larry's sister, Lily, and his brother, Gianni, lived in Bridgeport, Connecticut. A thriving industrial hub, it was just over an hour train ride from Grand Central Terminal. After Tina arrived in the States, they visited Larry's siblings and loved the calmer lifestyle. It was known as the *Park City,* including Seaside Park, thirty-five acres of shoreline donated by P. T. Barnum. A local farmer named James Beardsley donated over one hundred acres of land. Frederick Olmstead, the same architect that planned New York City's Central Park, designed the beautiful open space. Although it was a city with a thriving industrial center, it offered beautiful neighborhoods and plenty of housing. Tina and Larry admired the yards and vegetable gardens and hoped to have a home of their own someday.

Since they could not afford a larger apartment in New York City, they decided to move to Connecticut to be closer to the family. Gianni and his wife Angelina lived around the corner from a pharmacy with an apartment above it. There was no heat, but they could warm the space with the oven. Gianni had always been assertive, verging on aggressive. He was the older brother, so he often instructed Larry rather than suggesting. In this case, he told them they should move to the cold flat. Tina was rightfully concerned.

"Larry, we have three children under three years old. How are we going to manage without heat during the winter?"

"I know, my love. But Gianni said we should take it. If it gets too cold, we can go around the corner to their house?"

"You know we won't do that. Your sister-in-law would never put up with the children. Isn't there anything else available in Bridgeport?"

"Look, let's just try it. While we are living there, we can actively look for a better home. It'll be much easier than looking from New York City."

"I suppose you're right. But it sounds awful," Tina said with a sigh of resignation.

So, with three-month-old twins and a two-year-old toddler, Tina and Larry moved out of New York City. Their excitement grew as they neared the country and the reality of more room for their growing family set in. The New York apartment was furnished, and since they owned very little, moving day was effortless. Gianni had found Larry a job at Bridgeport Brass. It was factory work, but the pay and health insurance were just what he needed to care for Tina and the children. Tina could not work because she had her hands full with the twins and Annette.

The location was perfect. The apartment was around the corner from Gianni and Angelina, and Larry's sister Lily and her husband Eddie were only four blocks from them. Tina and Larry had a ready-made community that provided much-needed stimulation and support. However, both of them missed the hustle and bustle of the city. Window shopping and walking through the many parks in New York were among their favorite activities. Also, they could travel anywhere in the city by subway. They had easy access to the entire city and all it offered. In contrast, Bridgeport was a quiet suburb with poor public transportation, especially from their north-end neighborhood. Fortunately, there was a city bus that stopped close by on Sylvan Avenue.

While the summer and fall had been comfortable, all their fears came to pass when winter arrived. The apartment felt like a jail cell. Unless they were in the kitchen near the stove, there was no way to keep warm. Winter was still a novel experience for Tina. Bisceglie's Mediterranean climate did not prepare her for the snow and freezing rain that was ubiquitous during the New England winters. Without heat in the apartment, they were all uncomfortable and seemed to catch colds that lasted for weeks. They desperately sought a better place to live.

Meanwhile, Francesco, Larry's father, was eager to get out of his daughter's house. Of course, they loved each other, but they drove each other crazy. Lily was very frugal and particular with her housekeeping. She had five children, and at the dinner table, the one loaf of bread was barely enough once divided among the nine mouths to feed. For Francesco, bread was sacred. He believed there should be an abundance at each meal. After weeks and weeks of frustration because of his meager share of the one loaf, he pulled out a dollar and said, "Lily, here, get another loaf of bread. We need more than one for a family this large."

She looked at him sternly and said, "Put your money away, *Papá*. We are doing just fine with one loaf." She cleared the table without another word and didn't speak for the rest of the evening. She was offended; he was frustrated and angry.

Later that evening, when Antonia and Francesco got into bed, she asked her husband, "Francesco, what's wrong? You haven't spoken since dinner."

"Did you hear what our daughter said when I asked her to buy more bread? What is wrong with her?"

"Francesco, you know how proud she is. Don't let it bother you."

"So we are supposed to go without bread because she's proud? Lily doesn't let us do anything around here. She won't let you cook or clean— it's like she doesn't want us to touch anything. I don't feel at home. She makes me feel as if we are a burden to them."

"You're right. I am always worried that I am doing the wrong thing. Lily always tells me to sit down and relax. I know she means well, but I feel useless and bored."

"Maybe we can live with Tina and Larry again. We got along well when they were living with us in New York."

"Ah, Tina, there's no one with a heart like hers. She treats me as if I am her mother."

Francesco decided they would help Tina and Larry look for a house. They planned to move in with them.

Just as they did in New York City, Tina placed the twins in the double carriage and Larry grabbed Annette's tiny hand. They walked throughout the neighborhood each weekend when the weather permitted. One day, they turned off Sylvan Avenue onto Trumbull Avenue. They noticed several empty lots. Further down the block, three lots had foundations poured. They both got excited. Perhaps they could buy a brand-new home right in the neighborhood. Larry took down the phone number from the for-sale sign and dialed it as soon as they returned to the apartment.

With the money Tina had received from the sale of the house in Bisceglie, and what Larry had saved over the years, they had enough for a down payment on a brand-new house. Their dream of owning their own home was about to come true. There was one wrinkle, however. The house was $16,500, and the bank only allowed for a $10,000 mortgage. Tina planned to start working at a lingerie factory, and given her work experience in New York, they assumed the bank would recognize her earning potential. Sadly, during the late 1950s, the wife's salary could not be included in the mortgage calculation. Thankfully, the builder agreed to give them a second mortgage to make up the difference. That sealed the deal.

Larry asked the builder if he would provide a discount if he left the second-floor bedrooms unfinished. Having been a carpenter, he knew he could put in floors and walls gradually. The builder agreed and took four hundred dollars off the price. Whenever Larry worked overtime, he would buy several sheets of plywood or drywall. By the time the children were old enough to have their own bedrooms, he had completed the second-floor rooms.

Tina with her newborn twins, Frankie and Marisa.

Shortly after their move, Larry's parents moved in, and Tina was able to go back to work full time. The hourly rate was $1.25 an hour or whatever she earned through piecework. Her average take-home pay was approximately $42, all of which went to pay the second mortgage.

Larry brought home $54 a week, plus money from any overtime hours he put in. Their dream of having a family and a home of their own had come true. They had little extra, but they were content.

In their new home in Bridgeport, Connecticut with Marisa, Frankie, and Annette.

Tina and Larry in front of their garden in Bridgeport.

Three Generations

With three generations living under one roof, the Dell'Olio home was a wealth of culture and history. Antonia and Francesco spoke the local dialect of Bisceglie, which bore little resemblance to Italian. A derivative of the Neapolitan dialect, Biscegliese included words and phrases from many languages. Southern Italy was once called the Kingdom of the Two Sicilies. Spanish kings had ruled the region and it was subject to invasions from Saracens. There was a heavy influence from the Greeks whose ruined temples continue to spot the countryside. The many dialects of southern Italy were highly localized, however. From one town to the next, one could detect myriad differences—accents, conjugation of verbs, and words borrowed from other languages. Before the unification of Italy in 1861, there was no official Italian language, since foreign powers ruled many of the separate states. The Tuscan dialect, first recorded in the tenth century, was the language spoken by some of the most famous Italian poets: Alighieri, Boccaccio, and Petrarch. With Italy's unification in 1861, the governments declared the Tuscan dialect as the official Italian language of the newly formed country.

Many regions continued to speak their native dialects at home, but any official business required knowledge of Italian. However, it wasn't until the era of Mussolini that formal schooling was required. Both Tina and Larry learned Italian in school. But since Antonia and Francesco had never attended school, they spoke the Biscegliese dialect while Tina's parents spoke formal Italian. The letters Tina and Larry wrote to and from Italy were in Italian. Tina and Larry continued to use official Italian with each other and spoke the dialect with Antonia and Francesco. Given that they were living in the United States, they made a commitment to speak English as well. Ultimately, three languages were spoken in the Dell'Olio family home.

The trilingual period did not last very long. During the 1950s, Italian immigrants sought assimilation into American culture. Larry's siblings anglicized their names. Having grown up in the U.S. since childhood, Gianni, Lily, Antonette, and Rosie spoke mostly English plus the little dialect they remembered from their younger years. Tina and Larry hoped that their daughter, Annette, would speak all three languages. At age four, she understood and spoke all three. Annette responded in kind in whichever language they addressed her. But her older cousins spoke only English, and she wanted to be just like them. One day, Antonia spoke to her in Biscegliese.

"Annette, *vaw a bosh e pigya una shactua de primidol?*"

A few minutes later, Tina asked her the same thing in Italian.

"Annette, *vai giú a prendere una scatola di pomodori?*"

She placed her hands on her hips and responded in English.

"Make up your minds. Which is it? Why don't you ask me to go downstairs to get some tomatoes?"

After that, Annette spoke only in English. By the time the other children grew older, the adults spoke Italian among themselves. The younger children understood a few words and phrases but could not understand conversations between the adults.

Their home on Trumbull Avenue in Bridgeport was always the center of much commotion and excitement. With Larry's parents living with them, they had constant visitors from New York and Massachusetts. Each weekend would bring carloads of relatives with children in tow. During summer months, the barbecue was always fired up. From the butcher, Larry ordered a quarter of a steer that was supposed to last for six months but barely made it through the summer. Larry's sister, Lily, and his brother, Gianni, lived within walking distance to their house, so they were always dropping by, often unannounced.

In addition to the many visitors they received on behalf of Antonia and Francesco, Larry's brothers from Italy treated it as their family home. They invited themselves to live with them on their frequent trips back and forth from Italy. If they couldn't find work back home, they would come to live with Tina and Larry until they had enough money to send back to Italy. There was never any thought of contributing to the household expenses. After all, in their minds, they were staying with their parents.

However, both Tina and Larry bore the financial and emotional burden of having live-in guests. It was difficult enough to raise three children while caring for aging parents. Having to navigate the constant interference with their family life became a constant burden. There was always a battle regarding child-rearing. Tina tried her best to keep a consistent routine and set of rules. She believed it was important that the children learn proper manners. She sought to provide a solid foundation of values in a home that was subject to frequent visitors that showed little to no respect for their elders or the head of the household. This was made even more difficult when Larry's brothers shared their home.

Carlo had no intention of remaining in the States. When he first started dating Tina's cousin, Nina, she made it perfectly clear that she would never move to America.

"Don't get any big ideas of joining your brothers in New York. If you want to be with me, you'll be staying in Bisceglie. I will never abandon my family like Tina did," she declared, showing the deep resentment she bore for her cousin. The unspoken rivalry between the two girls since childhood continued into adulthood.

Carlo was perfectly content with his life in Bisceglie until he lost his job. That's when he started traveling to the States to make money. While in New York City, he worked as a photographer and sent a considerable amount of money home to Italy. Whenever finances would allow, he returned to Italy to see if he could make a go of it. He never had much luck holding down a job in Bisceglie, and soon enough, he was on the next ship to America. By the time Tina and Larry moved to Connecticut, much of the Dell'Olio family was in the neighborhood

But Carlo tired of the back and forth and began to resent his life in the States. Time and again, he would make disparaging remarks about the United States and how expensive it was to live there. One night, Larry had enough. He was tired of hearing his brother complain.

"Yeah, you hate America so much, but every time you go to Bisceglie, you turn right around. If things are so bad here, why do you keep coming back?" Larry said.

"You shut up. What do you know about anything?" Carlo shouted at him.

Hearing how rude he was to Larry, Tina could not hold back

"Don't you ever talk to my husband that way again. He's no longer your baby brother who you can push around. He is the father of three children, and this is his house. You will speak to him with the respect he deserves."

Silence covered the room. Carlo never raised his voice to his brother again, but he resented Tina for putting him in his place.

Chapter Twenty-Five
Unwelcome Advances

Bridgeport, Connecticut 1960

In Bridgeport, two of Larry's siblings lived within walking distance. Every Saturday night, the three couples would gather at one of their homes for cocktails and dessert. Larry's older brother, Gianni, and Lily's husband, Eddie, were always busting each other's chops. A typical evening would include highballs, cigarettes, and cigars. Larry was the only man in the family who didn't smoke, and they would often make fun of him for it. But he didn't care. The whole idea of smoking sickened him. During the summer months, his sisters, Rosie and Antionette, would take the train from Grand Central Terminal to Bridgeport and stay for a week or two. Their New York City apartments were oppressive during the hot and humid summer.

While many of their neighbors gathered with friends, their main social interaction was with Larry's siblings. Since his parents, Antonia and Francesco lived with them, they received many visitors over the years. After Larry's parents passed, the routine changed very little. The first stop after Sunday Mass was at Saint Michael's cemetery. During spring and summer months, Tina planted seasonal flowers and dutifully watered them and weeded around the gravestone. After a few brief prayers, the family loaded into the car to stop at Lily and Eddie's house for black coffee (espresso) and fresh-baked biscotti. Gianni, and his wife, Angelina were often seated at the kitchen table awaiting their arrival. Shortly before 1:00 p.m., they would all return home for Sunday dinner of pasta with fresh meat sauce.

Larry's brother, Gianni, had always been a terrible flirt. As a young man, he could never keep his eyes or hands off the young women. Gianni's Zia Francesca had arranged his marriage. When Gianni expressed his interest in Angelina's sister, his aunt dismissed his foolish thought.

"Don't be stupid, Gianni. You know she can't marry until her older sister is spoken for."

"But Zia, we don't love each other. We have nothing in common," he whined.

"What does love have to do with anything? This is a suitable match. She will make you happy. You'll see."

That was the end of the discussion. Gianni and Angelina married, and she was soon pregnant. But Gianni never stopped looking at other women, and Angelina knew it. She resented his indiscretions and didn't hide her feelings. Squabbles between the couple were frequent. Gianni busied himself with his buddies, smoking, drinking, and staying out late.

"Do you think I don't know what's going on, Gianni?"

"What are you talking about? I was just out with the guys."

"You think I'm stupid? I hear the rumors," Angelina said.

"You're imagining things. Besides, who do I come home to every night? You should be grateful."

"Grateful? For what? I cook and clean—I take care of the children. And what do you do? You eat our food then carouse with the guys and have your way with loose women."

"And who gives you the money to pay the rent and buy the food? Just drop it, Angelina."

It was a rocky start to their lives together. During the first years of marriage, World War II broke out. Most men of Gianni's age got drafted and shipped overseas. Gianni was lucky—he was a married man with children and therefore exempt from the draft. However, Angelina knew if she signed a release, he could go fight in the war. The tension between them reached a boiling point. So when she found his conscription papers, she signed them and mailed them in. Sadly, she didn't give a second thought to the possibility that he might die in combat. Her only wish was to have him far from home.

"I'll show him. Good luck finding other women in the army," Angelina thought.

Not long after, Gianni received notification from the government regarding the start of his military duty. He looked at them in disbelief. He never sent in his conscription papers. How could they have drafted him? He tore his dresser apart looking for them, but they were nowhere to be found.

"Angelina, have you seen the conscription papers? I can't find them anywhere."

"What do you mean?" she asked innocently. "Why do you need those?"

"Because I just received a letter from the Navy telling me when to report for duty. They can't do that because I have a wife and kids."

"Oh, that. I signed the release and sent them in for you."

"You did what?" He was furious. "How could you have done that? What in God's name were you thinking?"

"Oh, Gianni, don't be so dramatic. Maybe a little time in the Navy will straighten you out. You could use some growing up."

"Are you kidding me? That's what you think? Angelina, I could die out there."

"Well then, be extra careful," she said, turning back to the stove and continuing to cook dinner.

Gianni could see the satisfied grin on her face. He felt his blood boil as his muscles tightened with rage, but there was nothing he could do. Two weeks later, he reported for duty.

Upon returning from the war, they learned to live with each other's quirks and got on with their lives. Angelina was always a dutiful wife, and he the breadwinner. Theirs was a loveless marriage, but they made it work. Once the children had grown and left home, Angelina discovered Gianni was having an affair and threw him out of the house. They separated for a little over a year, but eventually came back together again. After all their years of marriage, they came to a detente and lived as amicably as they could.

Given his history, Tina had always been wary of Gianni. Shortly after they moved to Connecticut, Tina completed the requirements to receive her American citizenship. Since they didn't own a car, Gianni volunteered to drive her to New Haven for her test and swearing-in ceremony. Tina was nervous on the thirty-minute drive from Bridgeport. She ran through the questions over and over in her mind as she tried to remember the answers.

"Relax, Tina. Why are you so nervous? You studied, didn't you?"

"Yes, but what if I forget something? There are so many facts to memorize."

"You're a smart girl and a pretty one at that. Try to calm down, and you'll do fine."

Gianni waited in the car as Tina scaled the steps of the municipal building. Her big day had finally arrived. She had voted in only one election back in Italy, and she was excited to have the right to vote in the United States. It was December 1957, just over five years after she'd arrived in New York. Tina sat nervously in the waiting room, reviewing her notes. When the clerk called her name, she entered the judge's chambers and took a seat.

The judge greeted her with a friendly smile and peppered her with questions about the American system of government. He was impressed with her confidence and the accuracy of her answers. Satisfied, he looked up.

"Have you ever been in the Communist party?"

"No, I have not."

"Do you know anyone who is a Communist?"

"No, I do not."

"All right then, you speak English very well. Let's see how you write." He handed her paper and a pen. "You can write any phrase you like."

She thought for only a moment and put the pen to paper.

"I want to…" She paused and looked up at him. She couldn't remember if "to" had only one "o" in it. She looked up at the judge; he smiled and nodded. Then she completed her sentence.

"I want to go to school."

He gave her a broad smile.

"Congratulations! You can go back to the waiting room until the swearing-in ceremony."

Six others lined up with her facing the judge and the American flag.

"Raise your right hand and repeat after me," the judge instructed.

Proudly, Tina recited the oath of citizenship.

The Oath of Citizenship

"I hereby declare, on oath, that I absolutely and entirely renounce and abjure all allegiance and fidelity to any foreign prince, potentate, state, or sovereignty, of whom or which I have heretofore been a subject or citizen; that I will support and defend the Constitution and laws of the United States of America against all enemies, foreign and domestic; that I will bear true faith and allegiance to the same; that I will bear arms on behalf of the United States when required by the law; that I will perform noncombatant service in the Armed Forces of the United States when required by the law; that I will perform work of national importance under civilian direction when required by the law; and that I take this obligation freely, without any mental reservation or purpose of evasion; so help me God."

Tina skipped joyfully down the steps of the municipal building. Her patter was almost unintelligible, like a giddy schoolgirl. But she didn't care—she had passed and was now a citizen of the United States. Gianni pulled her into a warm hug.

"Congratulations, Tina! You are now an American!"

"Thank you, Gianni! I am so excited I can hardly breathe."

"What do you say we stop for lunch to celebrate?"

"Sure, why not? Let's go somewhere American," Tina said.

"All right, how about a cheeseburger?"

"Sounds good to me!"

And off they went. Stopping at a typical American diner, they ordered burgers and fries. After lunch, they went to Woolworths to shop. Tina wanted to buy little gifts for the kids. This was her day, and Gianni offered to pick up the tab. She was more than happy to let him. They stopped in several clothing stores and wandered through the aisles.

"Tina, look at this leather jacket. It would look great on you," Gianni said as he held it up.

"That feels like Italian leather. It's so supple."

"Try it on."

It hugged her curves like a second skin. She turned in front of the mirror and marveled at the contemporary cut. She looked elegant and youthful.

"You look gorgeous, Tina. Good enough to eat."

She ignored the sexual tension and continued to admire her reflection in the mirror.

"Do you want it?"

"Don't be silly, Gianni," she said as she glanced at the price tag. "We can't afford this kind of extravagance."

"I'll buy it for you."

"Are you crazy? We could never pay you back for this. It's much too expensive."

"Admiring how beautiful you look while wearing it is payment enough," he said as he reached out and caressed the soft leather on her arm. He had taken his playful flirting a step too far. She moved away immediately and promptly took off the jacket.

"You're too kind, Gianni. But Larry and I could never accept a gift such as this."

The mere mention of Larry's name broke the spell. Gianni knew he had crossed the line. They continued shopping, but the mood had changed. Gianni's not-so-subtle advances tarnished Tina's unbridled happiness over her accomplishment. However, Gianni acted as if nothing ever happened. He was used to being rebuffed by women, and he was undaunted. He knew there were plenty of occasions when a pretty woman gave in to his charms.

But Tina never forgot his advance and kept a safe distance from him. She tried never to be caught alone with him.

Several years later, he tried again. One Sunday, while the children were still young, Tina stood at the stove, stirring a pot of sauce. She heard the back door open and looked up to see her brother-in-law walking into the house. This was a regular occurrence. None of them knocked before entering each other's homes, and unannounced visits were commonplace.

"How's my favorite sister-in-law this morning?" he said as he kissed her on the cheek. "Where's Larry?"

"He just took a walk to Lily's house. He should be back in an hour."

"Mmm, that smells delicious. Angelina never fries her meatballs; they don't taste as good as yours," he said, moving behind her to peer over her shoulder.

"It never fails, Gianni. You're just in time for a sample."

Moving his body close to hers, he pressed into her.

"It's not your meatballs I want to sample."

She pushed her backside into him with force, and he fell back. He was not expecting such a violent reaction from her.

"Don't you ever touch me again. Do you hear me? I'm your brother's wife."

"Take it easy, Tina. I was just having a little fun," he said, holding his hands up in surrender.

"Well, it's not fun for me. If Larry ever found out…"

"Hey, there's no reason for him to know. I promise I won't do anything like that again."

"No, you won't. I think it's time for you to leave."

"Don't be like that, Tina. I'll be good. Now let me have a couple of meatballs."

"You heard me. Get out of my house now. Let's never speak of this again. Clear?"

"Yes, yes. I'm sorry, Tina," he said as the door closed behind him.

Tina knew it would be the last time he'd attempt anything with her. Although he'd had many affairs, making a move on his own sister-in-law was too risky. When anger flashed in her eyes, Tina could see that Gianni was afraid. The last thing he wanted was for her to reveal what he had done. His foolishness could have erupted into a drama beyond repair.

Although Tina was affable and easy to get along with, her sisters-in-law looked down on her independence. She was the only woman in the family that worked full time. They believed she was shirking her responsibility as a mother. She let their digs roll off her back, but push her too far, and you'd live to regret it. Tina knew Gianni had learned his lesson—at least as far as she was concerned.

Letter Fifteen

Feb. 20, 1950

Mio Caro Orazio,

I respond to your dear letter and I assure you I am in good health. Today is Monday, but yesterday, Sunday, I could not stop the tears. Something with the family is not going well, and I couldn't hold it in any longer. Your brother, Carlo, has caused so much anxiety regarding your parents not sending him money from New York. Please forgive me for being indiscreet. I am trying to understand. You do not know how much I suffer from this. Carlo received the letter saying that he had to support himself from now on. He has said nothing and blames me in your stead, and we don't know why. He doesn't know I am writing this to you. I want him to be happy, because he's your brother. I know you want that more than I. Now that he is married, he hoped that Mamma and Papá would continue helping him.

Anyway, I am so happy with everything you plan to send. For me, everything is beautiful—everything you send me is lovely because it comes from you—beautiful or ugly! I accept it with great joy. You are my great love, the most wonderful thing in my life.

Your dearest,
Nicoletta

Chapter Twenty-Six
Difficult Days

Bridgeport, Connecticut 1960-1965

Tina and Larry lived frenetic lives. Both worked full time. The overtime Larry worked kept him away from home twelve hours a day. They were raising four children, and Antonia and Francesco needed constant care. With frequent visitors and long-term guests, Tina and Larry had little time for themselves. Amidst this chaos came trauma. Conflict among siblings was to be expected.

One of Larry's brothers was a recurrent tenant. Sal was a challenging houseguest. He was gregarious and opinionated. Although he worked full time, he never missed an opportunity to go out with friends. While he lived with them in Bridgeport, Tina found a letter on his dresser. It was from his wife back in Italy. She and Tina had been close friends during their teens and grew even closer after they married the two brothers. Felicia started the letter expressing her deep love for Sal and how she missed him. Then she went on, acknowledging that as a man, he had needs and that she would understand if he strayed, as long as his heart rested with her.

She knew Sal very well, and she didn't expect him to be faithful while they were apart. Felicia was simply acknowledging what she knew to be true. In her own way, she was maintaining her integrity. She needed him to see that she was not a fool; she knew exactly what he was doing. For Sal, her letter gave him all the permission he needed. His affairs grew more frequent, and his discretion went out of the window.

Sal would often get home at all hours of the morning. Tina always worried he would wake the children. One night, the ringing of the telephone startled her from a deep sleep. She glanced at the clock to see it was just past midnight. Her heart was pounding in her chest as she answered.

"Hello, who's calling?"

"I'm looking for my wife. Who's this?"

"What do you mean, your wife? It's the middle of the night—what business do you have calling at this hour?"

"Never mind the hour. Is this where Sal lives?"

That's when she realized. She stretched the phone cord as far as possible and glanced at the empty living room couch. Sal had not come home yet.

"That is none of your business."

"Well, you tell that son of a bitch that if he ever touches my wife again, I'll wring his neck." Then he hung up on her. When she confronted Sal about the call, he denied the affair.

"Tina, honestly, we're just friends. He's just a jealous husband. You've got to believe me."

"If you say so but let me make one thing perfectly clear to you. If you ever put my family's safety in jeopardy, you will never be welcome in this house again. I mean it, Sal."

What could he say? He knew she had caught him. A few years later, Tina ran into the woman at the grocery store. Tina looked at her son, who was the spitting image of Sal as a child. She knew immediately that Sal was his father. That was the beginning of the end for Sal. Not long after that incident, Tina and Larry discovered something unthinkable.

Tina had just prepared breakfast for the children and was about to head upstairs to wake them when her youngest daughter came down with a look of utter despair on her face.

"Sweetheart, what's wrong, my love? Are you not feeling well?" she asked.

She shook her head and looked down—she wouldn't make eye contact with her mother.

"Tell me, honey. What's bothering you?"

"Mommy, something happened," she said in a whisper.

"Come, come here and tell me. Everything is going to be all right. Why are you so upset? What happened?" Tina asked gently as she held her five-year-old daughter.

"Last night, Uncle Sal came into our room after we had gone to sleep. He put his finger over his mouth and told me to be quiet."

"He did? Tell me, honey, did he do anything else to you?"

Her daughter's eyes filled with tears spilling onto her rosy cheeks.

"Yes. He took out his pee pee and put it on me." Then she began to cry.

Tina's eyes flashed in anger while compassion poured out for her precious one. She hugged her little girl as tightly as she could and reassured her.

"I promise you with all my heart, that will never happen again, ever! We will take care of you, my love."

When her daughter had calmed down, Tina climbed the stairs and walked into the girls' bedroom. Fully dressed, her older daughter sat on the bed waiting. Having witnessed the horror the night before, she knew why her mother was there. Tina sat beside her and looked at her with concern.

"You know what happened to your sister, don't you?"

"Yes, Mommy, I saw him come in," she said in a soft but measured tone.

"Did he ever…"

"No! He came to my side of the bed once, but I kicked my legs and pulled up the covers. He never touched me, Mommy, never."

"Was last night the first time he touched your sister?"

"No, it wasn't."

Tina was beside herself. What kind of animal did she have living in her home? How could she and Larry have subjected their children to such depravity? She doted on them during breakfast, then sent them off to school. Larry and Sal had already left for work, and there was no way to contact her husband at the shop. It would have to wait until dinnertime. She walked to the corner and waited for the bus to arrive. She was nearly catatonic—that day at work was the longest day she had ever experienced.

Once they were home from work, she cooked a quick dinner. Larry had noticed her mood from the moment he walked in the door. Her jaw was tight, and she barely spoke during dinner. Larry knew she was angry. After they cleared the dishes, Tina asked if she could speak to Larry alone.

She closed the door to their bedroom and told him what his brother had done. His head nearly exploded. Larry was a shy and mild-mannered man, never swift to show emotion of any kind, but it all changed that night. He was breathing fire and wanted to wring his brother's neck. After the kids had gone up to bed and Antonia and Francesco retired to their room, he pulled Sal into the bedroom. Tina remained in the kitchen, sitting at the table. Although the door was closed, she could hear everything. Larry spat out his words as he explained what he had just discovered.

"She's lying! I would never do such a thing!"

"My little girl is not a liar. Where would she learn such disgusting things at her age?"

"She must be imagining things. I never touched her!"

"You filthy animal! You're nothing more than a slimy pig wallowing in his own shit. No, you are worse!" Larry was on a roll. He could not hold back, nor did he want to.

"You take your depraved, perverted self and get the hell out of my house."

"You can't do that to me. I'm your brother. What will Mom and Pop say?"

"Do you really want to go there? What will they think of their youngest son when they discover that he's a disgusting child molester? Do you think they will jump to your defense?"

"You wouldn't dare tell them that! You know it's a lie."

"I know my daughters, and they are not liars. They are sweet, innocent girls who could never dream up anything like this. It is you who is the liar—you perverted animal. Get out of my house!"

"You can't do this to me. Where will I go?"

"I don't give a shit where you go. You can sleep in the gutter for all I care! You will never touch my children ever again. Get out!"

Sal had never seen Larry like this. Larry had always been the butt of his jokes and pranks throughout their childhood. Sal knew there was no coming back from this. Though he would never admit what he had done, he understood his brother would never take him back in. It completely broke their relationship. Returning to the kitchen, he saw Tina glaring at him. He lowered his head and climbed the stairs to the room that he shared with Frankie. He packed an overnight bag and slipped out the back door. Never again would he defile the family with his depravity.

Tina and Larry had kept the circumstances of the crisis a secret.

"How could we tell Mom and Pop what he did? It would crush them," Tina said later that evening.

"My God, I can't even imagine how I would speak those words to them. I can't even think about what he did to our baby girl. It is just unthinkable. Who could do such a thing to a child—in his own family?"

"And just think about his poor wife, alone with her children in Italy. If she ever found out, she'd be wrecked."

"What do we do, Tina? What are we going to tell them?"

"Well, I've been seeing the doctor about my exhaustion and weight loss. Maybe we can just tell them I couldn't handle the extra burden of caring for the children, aging parents, and your brothers whenever they decide to move back from Italy."

"That makes sense, Tina. Besides, my sister, Lily, has plenty of room. I'm sure that is where he is sleeping tonight."

When morning came, Tina prepared homemade eggnog for breakfast. This was a breakfast routine she had brought with her from Bisceglie. The protein would strengthen them and sustain the children until lunchtime. She used the electric mixer to beat the eggs as she stared out the window, contemplating all that had happened the day before. She was emotionally drained, but felt sure they had taken the proper action. Lost in her thoughts, she didn't hear her daughter come up behind her. The little girl simply walked to her side, put her arm around her mother's waist, and leaned her head against her. Tina put down the mixer and kneeled down to kiss her precious girl.

"Is he gone, Mommy?"

"Yes, he's gone. He will never live here again," she said as she kissed her daughter on the forehead.

They remained there in a silent embrace until Frankie came bounding down the stairs singing "I've Been Working on the Railroad." Their normal routine was up and running again. Tina prayed their lives would go on with no further trauma.

Many years later, Sal's daughter Anna moved from Italy to America. She and her family were living in another state. She asked if she could visit with Tina alone. It seemed odd, but Tina welcomed some time together to catch up. During the visit, Anna said she always wondered if something seriously wrong happened between Larry and her father. She bluntly asked if Sal had ever made any advances toward her. Over the years, rumors flew, because Larry's brothers always preferred to stay with him and Tina rather than with his sister, Lily. Tina immediately put those rumors to rest.

"No, he would have never dared to approach me. But other unspeakable things happened."

"Tell me, Zia. I need to know," Anna pleaded.

"Anna, it is the most awful thing that has ever happened to our family. Your father molested your cousin when she was only five years old. We had to kick him out of our home. We were all devastated."

Anna bowed her head and said, "I always suspected something of that sort had happened. I can't explain it, but when he looks at my daughters, I become very uncomfortable. There is something unnatural in the way he looks at them or holds them on his lap."

"Oh, Anna. I am so sorry. You should have been told, but we were trying to protect your mother and father. Of course, you know he can't be alone with them, don't you?"

"Yes, but I needed some confirmation. I am so sorry, Zia."

"No, no. It is not your place to apologize for his actions. But all of us must be on our guard so nothing like this can ever happen again."

Another Brother

Although they loved having Larry's parents with them, there were many challenges regarding the children. One evening, Larry was trying to get his son Frankie to eat his green beans. He refused to eat them, but Larry persisted.

"Come on now, Frankie. At least try them. How do you know you don't like them unless you try?" Larry reasoned.

Frankie just pushed his dish away, crossed his arms, and shouted, "NO!"

"Frankie, you must obey your father." Larry put a fork full of green beans up to his mouth and firmly insisted, "Open your mouth and try one bite. If you don't like it, you don't have to eat anymore. But you have to at least try."

With that, Frankie turned to his grandpa, seeking solace, and cried. Francesco picked little Frankie up and placed him on his lap. He wagged his finger accusingly at Larry and said, "You donna make da baby cry!"

He and Tina exchanged looks of exasperation. How could they raise their children as they saw fit with undermining interference from so many fronts? They felt the tremendous strain of their home life and could not see their way out. Larry picked up as much overtime work as he could get, working twelve-hour shifts most days of the week. If the shop offered Saturday work, he jumped at it. Tina's work at the dress shop was grueling. During the summers, it was a sweatshop with noisy fans blowing the humid air around them. Without insulation during the winters, the cold drafts blew through the cracks in the windows and doors.

After a day of sweating or freezing in the noisy shop, she would come home to four energetic children and her aging in-laws. Tina could not take a moment to rest—she had to begin dinner preparations immediately. She would barely get her coat off before she was being tugged at by at least two of her kids complaining about some argument or disagreement that had taken place in her absence. As Antonia and Francesco's health deteriorated, the responsibilities grew even more burdensome.

Tina lost weight and had difficulty sleeping. The family doctor chided her for neglecting herself while playing hostess to extended family besides caring for her family and ailing in-laws. Her health continued to suffer, and their financial security became more tenuous. Amid all the stress, they received a letter from Larry's brother, Carlo, who had returned to Bisceglie the year before.

Once again, he lost his job and announced he would make the trip back to the U.S. to earn more money. Of course, he expected to live with them in Bridgeport. With all they were wrestling with, the burden of housing Larry's brother once again would be the final straw. Tina and Larry were at a breaking point—they had reached their limit. Putting pen to paper, they wrote him a compassionate letter stating that they would be pleased to see him again in the U.S.; however, because of Tina's health, they could not accommodate his request to live with them. Larry knew he would be disappointed, but surely he would understand. Besides, he had two other siblings living in the neighborhood.

Their adult children had moved from their homes.

However, the response they received was unexpected. He wrote a scathing letter to Larry. He denounced him for his lack of commitment to his own brother. How could he leave him without a place to stay?

His spitefulness flared as he wrote:

I now know who wears the pants in your family. You're not even a real man.

Larry was terribly hurt, but Tina was furious. How dare he question their dedication to the family? He had sponged off them for years and never paid a cent of rent. The only contribution he made was $15 a week for the food he ate. Tina would no longer cater to Larry's mooching brothers. This was their home and their family. From then on, they would always come first. They would no longer welcome long-term houseguests. That was the last letter they received from Larry's brother for many, many years to come.

Letter Sixteen

New York City
April 4, 1950
My dearest daughter, Nicoletta,
As you can see, I am responding to your sweet letter to me. I want to let you know I am well and that I am happy to be together with my dear children. But now, my dear, I would love to hear more about you.

My dear, you cannot believe how happy I was to read the beautiful things you wrote to me that my husband reminds you of your dear father. I must tell you the truth: Francesco has been good to me from the first day I met him, and from the day we married. And that is why, my dear daughter, he is a good father who deserves a great deal of respect and admiration.

I hope you enjoy the special wedding of my sons, Carlo and Sal. I wish I could be there with them. But, in my place, I hope you will enjoy yourself, although I know you miss Orazio. But right now, don't think about his absence, because your joyous day, the day that you so desire, will come. Please be happy, because you are there in my place as you celebrate this wedding.

I wish you will always be close to your dear father, and he will make you happy. You tell Orazio that you wish all good things to me, an my dear, that is my wish for you, as well. I know that you two will be good together and you will be happy.

Please know that I have the greatest admiration for you. Never doubt that I love you as a mother.

Sending you hugs and kisses,
Your Mamma

Chapter Twenty-Seven
Cherished Parents

Bridgeport, Connecticut 1961-1967

The 1960s started with another life-changing event. Tina discovered she was pregnant again. While she and Larry loved children, they assumed their family was complete. When she told Antonia, her tears flowed.

"Tina, why you cry? It's happy news, no?"

"Si, *Mamma*, but what if I have twins again? I don't think I can go through that again," she choked out through her tears.

"Silly girl, don't you worry about that. We can help."

"But, *Mamma*, you're not well, and I can't let you take care of two babies."

"Tina, you don't know how many babies. *Piano, piano*, Tina! Slow down, child. Take it one day at a time."

"I know you're right. Larry is so happy—I am, too. Just afraid."Her fears waned as the months passed, and she felt only one child in her womb. She was going to be okay. The Christmas festivities were exhausting with her three young children, especially given that she was in her ninth month of pregnancy. She barely slept and was always on the move with the children and caring for Antonia, who seemed to get weaker by the day. She was often short of breath and tired.

Just after Christmas, Tina went into the bedroom to give Antonia her insulin shot. Her eyes grew wide, and her brow furrowed with worry. Antonia lay on her bed, clutching her chest and moaning. Tina ran to the phone and called the ambulance. They rushed her to St. Vincent's Hospital, which was only a few miles away. The heart attack was so strong that Antonia spent two weeks there.

During that time, on a snowy morning in early January, Tina felt her contractions intensify. There was a young family living in the house next door. Joe was from Poland, and although English was a challenge for both couples, the two families had a friendly rapport. Joe was kind and generous, always willing to lend a hand. He and his wife, Dorothy, had their first child a year before. He was shoveling the driveway when Larry came out in a panic.

"Larry, what's wrong? Where you go?"

"I need to walk to my sister's house. My brother-in-law, Eddie, has a car. Tina is having the baby," he said over his shoulder as he turned to walk. It was only two blocks away, but Larry panicked.

"Larry, no, no. Bring her here. I will drive you," Joe said as he ran into the house.

Moments later, Dorothy stood at the door with her daughter in her arms, watching Larry help Tina into the car. Joe brought a warm blanket and wrapped it around her.

"Here, Tina, it's freezing today. This will keep you warm."

A few hours later, Tina gave birth to her fourth child. When the doctor came out to tell Larry he had another son, an enormous smile spread across his face. It would be awhile before they would let him see Tina and the baby. Since his mother was just a few floors away from the maternity ward, he ran up to tell her. She could use a bit of cheerful news. Their family was complete with two girls and two boys.

Later that morning, Larry held his son for the first time. Not one to show emotions, there was only a hint of a smile on his face. They had not settled on his name since they had exhausted the naming traditions. The custom was to name the first boy after the father's father and the second after the mother's father. Since both fathers were named Francesco, they were free to pick any name.

"So, should we name him Orazio?" Tina asked.

"No, the Americans will butcher that name. I can hear it now. It would be awful."

"How about Lorenzo? We can call him Larry."

"No, that's not even my name."

"I've always loved the name Roberto. It's so strong and beautiful," Tina offered.

"Then they'd shorten that to Bob. Can't you just hear Mom and Pop call him Bub?" He laughed as he imagined their Italian accent. "Let's name him after your brother, Mauro."

"Larry, he would love that. But that's another name that sounds awful in English. It would sound like 'Mawro.'"

"How about Mario? There's very little they can do to ruin that name! Who knows, maybe he'll be a singer like Mario Lanza," Larry said.

Three days later, they brought baby Mario home. They had hoped the doctor would have released Antonia from the hospital by then. A week later, when Antonia finally came home, she could not get enough of the chubby little infant that was just starting his life. They could see her light up each time they brought him to her.

The crib was in Tina and Larry's bedroom, and they worried the crying would keep Antonia up at night. They didn't close both bedroom doors for fear that they wouldn't hear her should she have another attack. But Antonia didn't mind the crying. In fact, she had another idea.

"Tina, put the crib in my room. I want to be closer to Mario."

"*Mamma*," she said, "how will you rest with his constant crying?"

"*Figlia*, my child, it will heal my heart to hear the baby's cry. Please bring him here."

How could she say no? Antonia became little Mario's second mother, and he clung to her as tightly as he did to Tina.

Baby Mario

A happy visit with Santa?

The dining room became the fourth bedroom for Francesco and Antonia. Antonia battled diabetes, and Tina administered her daily insulin shots. Her heart attack had severely weakened her and in the following years she suffered several more episodes. Francesco, always seen with an unfiltered Camel cigarette hanging from his lips, suffered from a chronic cough deep in his chest. Larry and Tina could see that they were growing older, and both required more and more care. Tina loved them as if they were her own parents. The bond she formed with her mother-in-law during the early days of their marriage only grew stronger. Although they were from entirely different worlds, they bonded in their love of family. Antonia loved her four grandchildren with her entire heart, and because they lived together, she had a guiding hand in their upbringing. The nuclear family on Trumbull Avenue consisted not only of the mother, father, and four children but also of the grandmother and grandfather. Every evening, Antonia put the pot of water on the stove and stood by the front door watching for the city bus. In each hand was a box of pastina or pasta. As soon as she spotted Tina walking into the driveway, she'd call out.

"Which one tonight, the stars or the alphabet?"

As exhausted as she was from a day at the sweatshop, Tina smiled. It really didn't matter, but she chose one just to make her happy. Grandma and Grandpa, as the children called them, watched over them after school each day until Tina and Larry returned from work. Frankie, who was always hungry, asked before the door closed behind him, "Is there anything to eat, Grandma? I'm starving!" Antonia was always ready with a snack and something to quench their thirst. She sat at the kitchen table with them and asked about their day. She and Francesco were always happiest when the noisy children were in the house.

1965: Tina, Larry, Marisa, Annette, Frankie, Mario

1969: Frankie, Mario, Annette, Marisa.

1973: Annette, Tina, Mario, Larry, Marisa, Frankie.

During the early 60s, their home seemed to have a revolving door. Larry's brothers had come and gone many times. Having had twelve children, Antonia and Francesco had frequent visits from their children. Relatives would arrive from New York or Massachusetts with a carload of children. They would often come unannounced, and it left Tina and Larry scrambling to prepare dinners and serve drinks. For their four children, those were some of the best years of their childhood. There were always cousins to play with, and the house was filled with food and family.

For Tina and Larry, however, it was a constant burden on their health and budget. Throughout the United States, civil unrest marked the latter part of the decade. The military action in Vietnam raged with unending reports of casualties. Many cities experienced growing crime rates and economic decline. In the northeast, a massive departure into the suburbs took place. Their lovely neighborhood in the north end of Bridgeport deteriorated. Local stores in the nearby housing projects closed due to continued robberies and an overall increase in crime.

Directly across the street from their house was a liquor store that brought drunken customers each evening. Many were desperate for a drink before the 8:00 p.m. closing time. They left a trail of broken bottles in their wake. Tina and Larry became progressively more concerned with the safety of their family.

However, their greatest worry focused on Larry's parents. By 1967, Francesco's and Antonia's health had seriously deteriorated. Even so, Francesco was out shoveling the driveway after a late winter snowstorm. He coughed incessantly and ended up in bed with a nasty cold. Days later, it developed into pneumonia, and they brought him to the hospital. The doctors took X-rays and discovered he had advanced lung cancer.

Six months later, bedridden, he struggled to breathe. The doctor made house calls regularly but had no additional information to share with the anxious family. After tending to him and getting the children off to school, Tina waited for Larry's sister, Lily, to arrive. Lily spent the day caring for her father, keeping a close watch on his diminishing strength.

One day in early November, Tina went off to catch the bus for work. Francesco's health had reached a stasis. The doctor gave no indication of dire concern, but by eleven in the morning, Tina's boss called her into the office and handed her the phone. Lily was on the line telling her that Francesco had died.

She was distraught and immediately gathered her things. Rather than wait for the bus, Tina called a taxi to get home as quickly as possible. Her already challenging day got worse when she discovered that the taxi company was on strike. With no other options, she walked to the bus stop filled with worry over Antonia. She could only imagine the extent of her grief. Anxiously, she checked her watch and craned her neck to look down the block. The buses came infrequently except for rush hour. She ended up waiting for nearly thirty minutes for the next bus to arrive.

Tina was right by Antonia's side throughout the funeral events and took some extra time off to be with her in the days that followed. She and Larry were very concerned about her health as well. Her grief was all-consuming. She ate very little and spoke even less. They watched as Antonia sat in her chair by the window, fingering her rosary beads as she silently prayed. She was wasting away right before their eyes. Five weeks later, on December 11, Antonia had a massive heart attack and died. To this day, they believe she died of a broken heart.

Francesco and Antonia Dell'Olio celebrate their last Christmas in 1966.

Chapter Twenty-Eight
Beloved Brother

Bisceglie, Province of Bari, Italy

Tina planned to travel back to Italy for the first time during the summer of 1969. Her brother, Piero, had been ill for many months. He had been in the hospital several times due to stomach pain, so she planned to take her youngest son for a visit once school was out. She would have loved to travel with the entire family, but they simply couldn't afford it. However, in February of that year, Tina received a letter from her cousin, Antonietta, telling her that Piero's condition had deteriorated significantly; he was gravely ill. The gravity of his condition changed her travel plans. They called a family friend who owned a travel agency and told him about the situation. The next evening, he arrived at their house just after dinner. Tina was just drying her hands with the dish towel, and Larry had just finished sweeping the kitchen floor. Mr. Galluzzo walked in the door, plane tickets in hand as well as a passport application. Since Tina had become an American citizen, she could no longer use her Italian passport.

"Fill this out now. There is a passport office near Rockefeller Center in New York City. As soon as you enter the building, you will see a photo store to take your passport photos. Bring them with you, show them your plane tickets, and explain why this is so urgent."

The next day, Larry took the day off from work, and the two of them took the train from Bridgeport to Grand Central Station. Having lived in the city for so many years, they had no trouble finding their way. Tina presented the forms to the agent in the passport office, but he was reticent.

"This is all well and good. But it hardly meets the criteria for an emergency," the clerk said, sliding the forms back to her.

"Please, I have to be there for him. He's dying, and I'm his only sister."

"Look, I sympathize. But we normally grant emergency status for a sick parent or child. He's only your brother."

"But he was more than a brother to me. He was like a father to me. At seven years old, I lost both my parents. Orphaned, it was Piero who raised me. He was my father, mother, brother, and best friend. Now he's dying, and he needs me at his side," Tina explained with tears running down her cheeks.

"I... I'm so sorry. I didn't mean to dredge all that up. Let me have the forms. Come back in two hours. I'll have the passport waiting for you."

"Thank you. You do not know what this means to me," Tina choked out through her tears.

They left the office and walked outdoors. They were not in the mood to stroll or shop. Walking across Rockefeller Plaza, they looked up at the gothic spires of St. Patrick's Cathedral reaching toward the heavens. Neither of them spoke of their intentions as they crossed Fifth Avenue and climbed the steps to the main entrance. Larry took out a quarter and inserted it into the slot while Tina took the taper to light a candle for her brother. They knelt in silence for the better part of an hour. Afterward, they walked along Fifth Avenue, gazing through the beautifully decorated store windows until the remaining time had passed.

Back in the office, they issued her passport without delay. Tina asked if she could send a telegram to inform her brother that she was coming. The agent looked at her and smiled.

"You know, you'll probably get there before your telegram does."

"Just the same, I'd like to let them know."

Sixteen years earlier, she left her home in Bisceglie. All the family drama, which tortured her all those years before, seemed trivial. Even though her heart wanted nothing more than to stay with the cousin who raised her, she knew Antonietta would understand. Tina chose to stay with Mauro and Despina throughout her visit. She believed it would be a show of good faith in their reconciliation.

Mauro and his stepson, Franco, stood waiting at the gate of the Bari airport. It had been a long day already—an overnight flight to Rome, a layover, then the trip to Bari. Weary, relief washed over her when she spotted Mauro, since she doubted he had received her telegram. He embraced her warmly, with no hint of their old conflicts. When they arrived home, Despina greeted her with open arms as she entered the apartment. She even complimented her figure and clothing, which surprised Tina after fifteen hours of travel. However, warm as her reception was, Despina remained as self-centered and deceptive as always. Despina never informed the rest of the family of Tina's visit. She wanted to show she was first to know, and that Tina had chosen to stay at their home rather than anyone else's. Tina looked out the window, across the street, and spotted Antonietta. Opening the balcony doors, Despina shouted to her.

"Antonietta, look who I found!"

With a grand sweep of her arm, she motioned toward Tina as she appeared at the door. Antonietta trembled as she brought her hands to her face.

"*Madonna Mia, Nicolettina!*" she cried.

The joy of their reunion was short-lived, given the reason for her visit. Tina turned to Mauro once they sat at the table.

"So, how is he?" she asked.

"Not good, my dear sister. Not good."

She entered the hospital with trepidation. Tina didn't know what she would find when she first saw her brother. No one seemed to know much about his condition, just that Piero was in constant pain, and the prognosis was not good. Walking down the corridor to his room, she saw Don Marino, the cathedral's assistant pastor. They had known each other for years, and their greeting was warm and friendly.

"You look wonderful, Tina. You are a woman now," he said. "What brings you here all the way from America?"

"My brother, Piero. He is very sick."

"Oh, our wonderful Piero, I didn't know he was ill. What's wrong?"

"He's been having pain in his stomach for months. They just diagnosed it as cancer," Tina said gravely.

"*Che peccato*, what a shame," he said, shaking his head.

"But he doesn't know I'm here. I'm afraid I'll scare him when I walk in." "No worries, wait here, I'll take care of it," he said and walked right into his room.

"*Buon giorno, Pierino, come stai oggi?*" "How are you today?" Don Marino asked him cheerfully.

"Eh, so, so. I have my good days—but more bad days," Piero responded honestly.

Tina listened intently as she waited just outside the door for Don Marino's signal.

"Well, what news could I give you that would make you feel better?" he asked.

"Oh, it's only a dream, but I would love to see my sister, Nicoletta."

Don Marino raised his eyes to the heavens, making a great show of asking God to grant his wish.

"*Dio, ti prega.* God, I pray to you, help soothe Piero's pain. Bring Tina across the ocean to visit her big brother."

Piero rolled his eyes thinking, this guy is quite the actor, but he has a wonderful sense of humor. No sooner did the priest finish the prayer when his baby sister walked through the door. His eyes grew wide as he gasped with delight.

"Tina, what are you doing here?"

"What? A sister can't visit her big brother?"

She ran over to his bedside, and the two embraced and kissed. The tears of joy were mingled with sadness. How often do people gather during times of pain and death? There are always epithets of "We should get together more often," or "We should see each other on joyous occasions, not just when we're ill." But here they were, brother and sister, grateful for their unexpected reunion.

"Beh, where's Mario? Didn't you tell me you would bring him?"

"Oh, Piero, it's the middle of the school year. I couldn't pull him out of classes for so long."

"Then why didn't you wait until the summer? Why come now?"

Tina didn't want to tell him the truth. How could she say, "Because I was afraid to take the chance that you might die before then?" She came up with a white lie on the spot.

"Well, there was a group of Biscegliese that organized a trip. I just jumped at the opportunity. Anyway, I'm here now. I promise to come back with him this summer."

That seemed to quell his curiosity. But in his heart, he knew he had little time left. He couldn't have been happier to see his baby sister after so many years. She was only a child when she left, and now she was a woman, a mother with four children. She left Italy with stars in her eyes and a dream of a better life. He marveled at her looks—so elegant and cosmopolitan. Most women her age in Bisceglie dressed in housecoats and slippers. He was so proud of her.

The joy of their reunion was brief. The following two weeks were an emotional rollercoaster for Tina. There were so many people to see, but her top priority was to spend time with Piero—nothing else would take precedence.

"Mauro, please do me a favor."

"Of course, Tina, anything. What is it?"

"The rest of the family is hounding me. They all want to know when I will call on them, have dinner with them. As much as I want to see everyone, I just can't leave Piero's side. Honestly, Mauro, I don't think he has much time left."

Her composure all but gone, her tears spilled onto her cheeks. She didn't fight her grief. Mauro pulled her into his embrace. Without a word, he stroked her head as he had when she was a child.

Each day, Tina boarded the bus and traveled to the hospital. She and Piero found there was no end to the stories they shared. They filled the hours spent together with tales of their children and the ordinary trials of life. He peppered her with questions about life in America. He wanted her to describe every detail of their home in Bridgeport. They had written often over the years, but there was nothing like being together and talking.

"And what about the children? What do they like to do?"

"Well, they certainly keep me and Orazio busy."

"Tell me about each of them. Don't leave any details out. Start with Annette. Is she shy or boisterous? Does she like to cook and clean?"

Tina chuckled.

"Annette is definitely not shy. She is gregarious and clever, always quick with a joke. But no, she does not like to cook or clean."

"Neither did you when you were a little girl. Remember how you used to make little balls from the white of the bread? You were so picky. You only ate the crusty parts, then hid the white balls under the furniture."

They laughed with abandon at the memories. Tina described each of her children and how different they were from one another. She asked about his boys, Franco and Pino, then about his wife.

Carmela and Tina had been fast friends during their teen years. Their friendship only deepened through the many letters they wrote to each other after Tina moved to the U.S. Sadly, Carmela suffered with mental illness and had had several breakdowns. Piero's extended suffering and eventual cancer diagnosis sent her over the edge. She didn't believe it was real and couldn't conceive of a life without her true love. Carmela concocted a lavish story to explain what was happening around her. She believed that *Cinecittá*, the Italian version of Hollywood, was filming a movie in which she and Piero were the stars. He was playing the part of a sick man. The scenes they were shooting took place in the hospital.

When Tina came back to town, Carmela was elated to see her again. They broke into their familiar patter, laughing and telling stories. But as the days passed and Tina spent more time in the hospital with Piero, she grew jealous. She couldn't understand why Tina was visiting Piero every day. Noticing that Tina was always well-dressed compared to her own everyday clothing, Carmela grew suspicious, believing Tina had gotten a bigger part in the movie. If anyone should be the supporting actress in the film, it should be his wife. Preparing for her next visit, Carmela dressed in a stylish dress with stockings and high heels. To top it off, she put on a full-length coat with fur trim and a silk scarf, then made her way to the hospital.

She burst into the room as if she were walking on stage for her big scene.

"Piero, my love, how are you today?" she sang as she strolled over to his bed.

She placed her hands on either side of his face and leaned in for a lingering kiss. She lifted her head, staring into the distance with a broad smile on her face as if she were looking into a camera lens. Piero turned red and shifted uncomfortably at her inappropriate display of affection. He was having a tough day, wincing as spasms racked his body. Carmela was oblivious to his pain as she continued to act her part.

"My, what beautiful flowers," she said as she bent to smell their fragrance. "Who gave these to you?" she asked with a twinge of jealousy.

"Tina did. You know she's visiting from America, don't you?"

As if seeing her for the first time, she glanced at her sister-in-law and gave her a weak smile.

"How nice to see you again, Tina," she said, kissing her on each cheek.

Carmela turned her attention back to Piero and began caressing his face and straightening out the hair above his temples. She murmured loving words to him as if they were alone in their own bedroom. Piero, having enough of her erratic behavior, spoke out.

"Carmela, stop that now! Why are you all dressed up? This is not the opera."

"What do you mean? I can't make myself pretty for my beloved husband?"

She was still playing her role for the movie in her head.

"That's enough. I'm worn out today. Please," Piero pleaded.

Tina took her cue and took Carmela's arm.

"Carmela, you look ravishing today. What do you say we take a walk to show off your beautiful outfit?"

"Oh, yes, thank you. But what about Piero?"

"He's exhausted, Carmela. Let's leave him to rest a bit. You can come back tomorrow when he's feeling better."

Carmela made a big show of kissing him goodbye, and they left the room. As they exited the hospital door, Carmela continued to play to the imaginary cameras. She smiled broadly and strolled provocatively down the boulevard, leaning down to caress the flowers and bringing them to her face. Each time, she would look up for her shot, then continue as if they were simply on an afternoon stroll. Tina grew impatient. She needed to get her home as quickly as possible and then return to the hospital before visiting hours ended. A five-minute walk to the bus took over fifteen minutes, and they nearly missed it. Once on board, Carmela did not break character. She sang a song as she waved goodbye to Tina. Carmela's mental health continued to deteriorate throughout Piero's illness.

The precious weeks she spent with Piero flew by, but Tina relished each moment with her brother. The silly banter, the quiet reflection, and the sharing of their fears. All too soon, Tina was back in her routine in Connecticut. The memories of her last days with him were balm to her grieving soul. When she received word that Piero had died, she felt like a part of her heart had died as well. The love her big brother expressed throughout her life would always remain with her. She was grateful for the time they spent together in his final days. She took comfort in her belief that he was reunited with their mother and father.

Letter Seventeen

Bisceglie, Province of Bari, Italy
Feb. 26, 1950
Mio adorato Orazio,
The most beautiful moment of my day is when I sit to write you a letter. It's as if we are together, talking about our profound love (immenso amore) that, with passage of time, grows stronger and more robust. I live only by waiting, but it is even more sweet to wonder who we will become. It is even more beautiful, as each day passes and I await your letter—it's a surprise each time I receive one.

You know Antonietta, my dear cousin, is in effect my sister, since we have lived together from the day I was born. Do you know, my love, that at the sound of the mail carrier's voice, she asks me, "Have you seen the postman? Aren't you expecting a letter?" I say, "Yes, of course, but the postal worker usually comes in the afternoon."

Then, while we are chatting, I hear a loud knock on the door. I know that he's come with a letter for me, not my brother, because he knocks in bursts of four. That's his signal that there's a letter from you. But then he delivered not one, but two letters. As you can imagine, I didn't know which to open first. So, I opened them both and discovered that you wrote them on the same day. I read them quickly, knowing that I would take the time later to read through them thoroughly. But I was eager to read your dear news. And I won't hide the fact that I sighed in relief and joy at the news that your father is coming to Bisceglie to help Carlo and Nina with their wedding. Both he and Nina were anxious about finances. The great surprise is that Sal will come with him. How exciting that your two brothers will celebrate a double wedding. Given all your splendid news, my joy is complete. I am so happy to meet your dear father and that he will be with us. It will be such joy for all of us who await him. Please tell me the exact date of his arrival.

Oh, my dear Orazio, I am so happy for the love you have for me. The gifts that you send are, for me, signs that you are with me always. I wear your ring as a symbol of our love. It is the bond that will never divide us. Isn't that true, my love? You see,

Orazio, when I touch these things that you held in your hands, it's as if I am touching yours and gripping those very same hands as tightly as lovers do.

I must ask you to thank your dear sisters, Rosa and Francesca, for helping you to pick out the beautiful dress you bought for me. And please thank them for all that they've done for me. Please give my love to your dear mother. I will write a few lines to her before I close. Give Papà and Mamma a big hug for me. And for you, I send a thousand big kisses.

Your dearest,

Nicoletta

Chapter Twenty-Nine
Italian Vacation

Trumbull, Connecticut • Milano & Bisceglie, Italy

For Tina and Larry's twenty-fifth wedding anniversary, Annette, Frankie, Marisa and Mario wanted to do something special. A party was not really their style, so they put their heads together to come up with something unique. Since they were adults and working, they began to save their money. Throughout their childhood, they witnessed their parents' joy each time a green and red-bordered envelope would appear in the mailbox. Letters from Italy brought tales of the faraway land from which they hailed. Photos of aunts, uncles, and numerous cousins were passed around. Tina and Larry told stories about how each was related and what they were like. Having Italian relatives they had never met was a world they could only imagine. Photos by the seashore, or in front of ancient buildings, were always a part of their lives. The four of them watched their cousins grow up through the many photographs sent throughout the years.

Tina regaled them with stories of her deceased parents and of growing up as an orphan. The Di Bitetto grandparents grew to legendary figures as she described each tale in vivid detail. Of course, always included in Tina's stories were Antonietta and Piero. Photos of his two boys, Francesco and Pino, brought tears to her eyes, and she dreamed of seeing them again.

"Has Dad ever been back to Italy?" Mario asked.

"No, just me. I went when you were in the third grade to see your Zio Piero for the last time," Tina said.

"It must be weird to have a whole family over there that you haven't seen in years."

"It is. At this point, I've lived in America longer than I was in Italy. It was a lifetime ago, but I can picture every corner of Bisceglie."

"You miss them a lot, don't you?"

"Of course, *caro*. A piece of my heart will always be with our family there."

Annette's eyes grew wide—the gears started spinning. They wouldn't buy them some gift that would sit on a shelf or have a dinner that would be over in one evening. No, they would save as much money as possible to send them on an Italian vacation, a second honeymoon. She couldn't wait to tell her siblings.

"That's a great idea," Frankie exclaimed.

"They'll be shocked. There's no way they'd expect anything like that," Marisa chimed in.

"Wow! But I only have a part-time job; there's no way I can give as much as all of you," Mario said.

"Mario, don't worry about that," Annette reassured him. "We all give what we can. Besides, you're still in high school. No one expects you to do more than you can."

"Annette, do you really think we can save enough money for both plane tickets?" Marisa asked.

"Probably not. But even if we can only buy one, it will be that much less they have to spend."

The month passed with Annette collecting the money from each of them. Their parents' milestone anniversary was only four days after Christmas on December 29, 1976. Since it was a Wednesday night, there was no grand celebration as the family gathered after work that day and had a simple dinner. Afterward, Annette brought out a cake she had picked up from the local bakery. Mario was beside himself with anxious anticipation.

"When are we going to give it to them? Why do we have to wait until after the cake?"

"We don't want them to expect anything, Mario," Marisa explained. "If we wait until they clear the table, they'll think we didn't buy a gift. It'll be perfect."

The four of them cleared the table, then washed and dried the dishes, while Larry and Tina sat in the kitchen.

"We have something for you," Annette said as she handed them an envelope.

Tina and Larry smiled and opened the anniversary card while their grown children waited with gleeful anticipation. Inside was a check and an inscription that read:

25 years of marriage calls for a special celebration.
A second honeymoon awaits you in your homeland.
This is to be used toward your first trip back to Italy.
Love,
Annette, Frankie, Marisa, and Mario

Rarely speechless, Tina looked up at them with tears in her eyes while Larry looked confused. *What does this mean?* he thought. *How could they save so much money?* Although he didn't speak those words, they could tell he was worried about the money. The check didn't cover the entire cost of two airline tickets, but it put a significant dent in it. The kids hoped they would be able to go the following summer, but Tina and Larry decided to wait a bit. 1976 had been an expensive year. Their firstborn got married, and they pulled out all the stops for Annette and Wayne's wedding. There was a grand reception with over two hundred guests. It was a wonderful family reunion with people coming from New York, Massachusetts, and Connecticut. They decided to wait a year, so they could replenish their savings. Their youngest child, Mario, was the only one who had the opportunity to study Italian throughout high school. Since he was graduating in June of 1978, they decided they would take him along. Tina and Larry hoped he'd be able to communicate with his cousins and get to know them.

The summer of 1978 finally rolled around—their trip to Italy was scheduled for August. Before that, however, was Mario's graduation from Trumbull High School. It was an oppressively hot day for late June, and the ceremony was held on the football field. Under the glaring sun, over seven hundred students in his graduating class endured the interminable ceremony. Tina and Larry couldn't have been prouder. This was their fourth and final child to graduate high school, an achievement neither of them had the good fortune to attain back in Italy. Tina spent days preparing for Mario's big party. The guests included aunts, uncles, and cousins, as well as many of his friends. They set up the backyard with picnic tables and lawn chairs. Larry was at the barbecue grilling hamburgers, hot dogs, and Italian sausages, and Tina baked pizzas and desserts. Everyone was in a festive mood, despite the heat.

Although Tina was in her element as she entertained the yard full of guests, she battled a nagging headache all day. She had taken aspirin several times throughout the day, but it just seemed to get worse. By mid-afternoon, she could no longer take the pain. Larry was concerned and told her to lie down.

"Tina, you can barely keep your eyes open. Go to bed."

"What, with a house full of people? I can't, Larry."

"Mom, we've got this," Marisa said. "Listen to Dad; go lie down,"

"I can't ruin Mario's party. It's his big day," Tina argued weakly.

"Mom, he'll never know. He's too busy hanging out with his friends."

The party lasted through the evening, with high school kids laughing and carrying on. Mario hadn't even noticed that his Mom wasn't there. But Tina's headache grew worse overnight. By morning, she realized she needed to see a doctor. Dr. Pasquarello had been the family doctor for decades. He had delivered Mario seventeen years earlier and knew of all the family drama during the 1960s. He was laid back, slow to panic, but perhaps not as medically aggressive as necessary.

"Tina, you've been pushing yourself too hard. You think you're Wonder Woman, but even *she* needs to rest every now and again," he gently chided.

"But Doctor, this feels different. I've never had such a painful headache. I couldn't even keep my eyes open. Aspirin had no effect, and it's worse today than yesterday."

"You've always put yourself under a great deal of stress. Your home had a revolving door, you housed your in-laws, and now you are busy launching your children into adulthood."

"We're leaving for Italy in a couple of weeks. Is there nothing you can do?"

"Okay, I'll write you a prescription for the pain, but don't push it if you feel one coming on. Go directly to bed. What you need to do most is relax. Go have fun in Italy and stop worrying so much."

Larry, Tina, and Mario boarded an Alitalia flight to Milano in the first week of August. Mario was filled with excitement for a trip of a lifetime. He never dreamed that he'd be joining his parents on their second honeymoon to Italy. Tina and Larry were so proud to show him all the places described in countless stories of their childhood. They sat three across on the flight, and, of course, they gave Mario the window seat. By the time the meal was served, they reached the cruising altitude.

Strangely, as the plane climbed higher, Tina felt pressure building behind her left eye. *No, not again. Not now,* she thought. Throughout July, her headaches came and went, but none were as debilitating as the day of the party. She came to agree with the doctor that they were due to stress. As the pain began to build once again, Tina reminded herself of the doctor's counsel. *Stress is causing your headaches. Try to relax and enjoy the vacation.*

Throughout the night, her headache worsened. After eight and a half hours of flight, her head was pounding. They landed at Malpensa airport in Milano, and Mario could hardly stay still. His excited chatter felt like a thousand needles piercing her temple. Passing through customs, Larry and Mario gathered the luggage and exited the controlled area. Waiting for them with a huge smile on his face was Massimo, their niece's husband. Tina put on a happy face as he kissed her on either cheek and led them to the parking lot. The four of them squeezed into the smallest car Mario had ever seen. The Fiat 500 was heavy with four passengers and three large suitcases packed into the little trunk. Massimo weaved through the morning traffic with fits and starts. Each time he applied the brakes, they'd lunge forward. In the back seat, Tina began to feel nauseated.

"*Massimo, per cortesia*, please pull over. I'm feeling ill."

"*Certo, Zia.* Certainly, right away," he said with concern.

Tina opened the car door and vomited. Her head pounded mercilessly.

As soon as they got to the apartment, she briefly greeted the family and went to lie down. She spent their entire first day in bed, only rising for a dinner she could not bring herself to eat. That night, she found no relief to the increasing pain. She went to the restroom to splash cool water on her face. When she looked in the mirror, she was startled at what she saw. Her left eyelid had closed entirely. Try as she might, she could not get it to open. She took her finger and lifted it up; the light looked extraordinarily bright and caused her even more pain. She tried to focus, but everything was blurry. She felt nausea building and became dizzy. She steadied herself on the sink and sat down. *What was going on?* Now she was worried.

The following morning, Larry was startled. Her left eye remained closed, and she looked awful. The first few days in Milano were spent going to medical professionals who were baffled by her symptoms. No one seemed to know what was wrong. To keep Mario from worrying, his cousins toured him around the city and took him out with their friends. Larry joined Mario for a tour every now and again while Tina rested back in the apartment. He knew his mother was ill but had no idea how serious it was.

To make matters even worse, the doctors were on strike—the only people she could see were medical technicians. None of them had the training to diagnose her correctly.

"*Signora*, I am very sorry, but there is just so much we can do without the doctors," a technician said.

"But you must know something?" Larry pressed.

"Our best guess is that she has a problem with her veins. In any case, her condition is severe. She will surely need surgery, but who knows when the strike will end?"

Returning to the apartment, Larry immediately contacted the Alitalia travel agency to book a flight back to New York. It was the first week of August, *ferragosoto*, the vacation month in Italy. Italians flee the cities and travel throughout Europe, and many head to the US. There was not a seat to be found—all flights were booked. They had no choice but to stay in Italy. The original plan was to spend the first week in Milano, then head south to Bisceglie. But the relatives in Milano advised against it.

"Zia, even with the strike, the hospitals are better in Milano than in Bisceglie," Rosa said.

"But there is nothing they can do for me here. They've told me so."

"That may be so, but if your condition should change, you've got the best facilities in Italy right here."

"Look, I appreciate your concern," Tina said, "but I didn't travel this far to sit in an apartment in Milano. I just have to see my family, especially given that I am ill."

Massimo shook his head. He was born and raised in northern Italy. His prejudice toward the south was deeply ingrained.

"Zia, please. The doctors in Bisceglie are all hacks. Whatever you do, don't let them touch you. They're likely to make you worse."

"I understand, Massimo. Larry has not been back to Bisceglie since we were married, and I want Mario to meet his Italian family. But most of all, I need to see my brother and Antonietta. I have lived in America with Larry's family for all these years. This will only be the second time I will have seen mine in over twenty-six years. I must go to Bisceglie."

Her resolve was clear. No one spoke for a few minutes. They understood her reasons, but their worry was profound. The following day, with a patch over her left eye, she boarded the train to Rome and then to Bisceglie. Her pain continued, but she made a point to visit with each of her family members. She downplayed her illness and hid it as best she could when she was with Mario. She knew he was enthralled with Italian culture and their family history. Watching him speak Italian with his cousins filled her with great pride. He was the only one of their children who studied it, and because of that, he was becoming friends with his cousins. It gave her great satisfaction that he was forming a bond with his Di Bitetto cousins. She watched as he met Antonietta, his Zio Mauro, and all the relatives he had only heard of throughout his life. All the stories Tina and Larry had told came to life as he walked the very streets where they grew up. Seeing Mario's wonder was one of Tina's few joys throughout the grueling three weeks in Italy.

Tina did the best she could during the time they spent in Bisceglie. The demands of each faction of their families weighed heavily upon her and Larry. While they were concerned for her health, each was offended if an invitation to *pranzo* or *cena,* lunch or dinner, was declined. Tina genuinely wanted to see everyone. It had been nearly ten years since she had been in Italy while her brother was dying. Spending time with Carmela and Piero's boys gave her much needed comfort. Franco and Pino were no longer children; they were young men with fiancées. Despite their mother's battle with mental illness, they grew into kind and generous young men. Larry took the time to heal old wounds with his two brothers. He walked the *città vecchia,* the historic old town, with Mario, pointing to their old apartment and the water pump from which they got their drinking water. He was reliving his history through Mario's eyes. But at every turn, Larry worried that Tina was pushing herself too hard.

One day, her nephews, Franco and Pino planned a visit to *Le Grotte di Castellana*. Though Tina had heard of the caves throughout her childhood, she had never visited. Formed ninety million years earlier, the caves featured three kilometers of stalactites and stalagmites. The prehistoric natural museum was not to be missed, and Tina insisted on going along. Arm in arm, she and Larry slowly descended into the caves. The cool air was immediate relief from the heavy August weather. For a moment, Tina was transported from her pain into a world of natural beauty. They were in awe of the brilliant colors and great size of the columns that loomed before them at every turn. As they descended deeper into the caves, the ground became wet and slippery. Without warning, Tina lost her footing and slid onto her backside. The impact rattled her already aching body, and her head felt as if it were to explode. Larry was beside himself.

"Tina, are you hurt? Don't move, stay seated—the tourists can go around us."

"I'm okay, Larry. I need a moment to catch my breath."

When she was able, she took Larry's arm as he helped her up. The rest of the tour was a blur, but she was tenacious and made it to the end. The final days in Bisceglie, Tina stayed close to home, taking naps often and counting down the days until their return flight to New York.

The Aneurysm

The flight home seemed endless. They arrived at JFK at midnight. Their flight had been delayed in Rome, and by the time they waited for their bags to appear on the carousel, they almost missed the shuttle back to Connecticut. After the constant pressure changes of flight, Tina was in a great deal of pain. The altitude seemed to make everything worse. By the time they walked into the house, it was nearly 3:00 a.m. Annette had trained in X-ray at St. Vincent's Hospital, and Marisa worked there as well. Tina had kept them apprised of her condition throughout the stay in Italy. Marisa made an appointment at 11:00 a.m. the following day. Tina tried to get some sleep, but the pounding in her head continued to intensify. As soon as the sun rose, they were on their way to the emergency room.

There was a flurry of activity in the ER. Since many of the staff knew both Annette and Marisa, they were more attentive than usual. Within minutes, Tina heard the doctors mention an aneurysm. She was an avid watcher of *Ben Casey*, a popular medical show, and recalled an episode where the patient was diagnosed with an aneurysm and died. Her mind went blank, and she pulled her rosary beads from her purse and began to pray. The doctors said it was a miracle that it hadn't burst from the altitude changes on the plane to and from Italy.

The neurologist scheduled her for surgery the very next day; there was no time to waste. Larry went through it all with stoic silence. But it was easy to see the weight bearing down on his shoulders. He couldn't believe this was happening. Their long-awaited trip to Italy was supposed to be a second honeymoon. Instead, it turned into a nightmare from which he couldn't awake. None of the medical information made much sense to him. He relied on his daughters to explain what was happening and left the medical decisions to them. He literally wrung his hands at the thought of losing Tina.

That night, he sat at her bedside, holding her hand. Larry had always hated hospitals. He would often get nauseated and lightheaded when he had to visit. But he hadn't left her side that day, and nothing could tear him away. Tina, in all her pain, could see the worry on his face. Lines of exhaustion creased his smooth olive skin.

"Orazio," she said, using his Italian name, "go home. Get some sleep. I'm safe now, and they're going to take good care of me."

"It's okay, Tina. I don't want to leave you." His response was almost inaudible.

"Larry, you look terrible. Go, please, you're making me worry."

At that, his eyes grew wide. The last thing he wanted was to make it worse through stress.

"Okay, *tesoro.*" He hadn't called her treasure since they were young. "But I will see you in the morning before surgery," he said as he kissed her fingers.

"No, Larry. I don't want you standing around all day worrying. Go to work; it will make the hours pass more quickly."

"Are you crazy? I can't do that. You need to know I'm right here"

"Listen to me. There is nothing you can do. By the time you get out of work, I'll be coming out of surgery. I know you; you'll make yourself sick pacing in the waiting room." She placed her hand over his heart and said, "I know that I'm right here, my love. I don't need you to suffer more than you already are."

It was an unreasonable request; she knew that. But she also knew Larry was barely holding it together. The best thing for him was distraction. Marisa and Annette would be at the hospital all day. They'd be able to give him the news in a way he'd understand. Tina had a strong will. He knew better than to fight her on this. But he wasn't happy about it.

The next morning, Annette and Marisa waited as they prepped Tina for surgery. She was placed on the gurney and wheeled out of her room. They knew she would have to be shaved for the operation, but seeing her for the first time without hair startled them. That's when Annette spotted a bag full of Tina's hair beside her on the gurney.

"What is this doing here?" she asked the orderly.

"We thought you might want to keep it."

She looked at Marisa and shook her head.

"Please throw it away. That's the last thing Dad needs to see."

"Yeah, it'll make him sick to his stomach," Marisa agreed.

Entering the operating room, the bright lights made Tina squeeze her eye shut. She could feel her heart beating rapidly in her chest. She fingered her rosary beads tightly and continued the Hail Mary.

"Ave Maria, piena di gracia, il signore e con te," she prayed in her native tongue.

"I'm sorry, Mrs. Dell'Olio, but I need to take those from you now," the nurse said, pointing to the rosary.

"Let her be," the doctor said. Turning to the nurse, he quietly said, "We can take them once the anesthesia sets in."

The surgery lasted over eight hours. The aneurysm's proximity to the occipital nerve made its removal extremely dangerous. Precision was everything. When it was all over, they had saved her life. By time the neurologist came out to give them the news, Larry had joined the girls in the waiting area.

"She made it. The aneurysm was a ticking time-bomb. The weeks leading up to her trip to Italy and the pressure changes of flight could have easily caused it to burst. Your wife is a strong lady. She's lucky to be alive."

Larry's relief was palpable, and he anxiously waited for her to come out of recovery. He paced in the waiting room, just as Tina said he would. When he finally saw her, a wave of nausea came over him. They had shaved her head and drilled into her skull. The swelling made her head look like a basketball. Her left eyelid remained closed and was a deep purple color. Seeing her disfiguration, the fear welled up within him once again—he had come so close to losing her. A single tear rolled down his cheek as he sat beside her waiting for her to awaken. *She's alive; that's what is most important*, he reminded himself.

Tina's recovery was gradual and frustratingly slow. Her rosary beads never left her hands in the weeks that followed her surgery. Lying in her hospital bed, her anxious thoughts swam through her mind. *What happens next? Why are both my eyes swollen shut? Will they ever open?* She understood that she was lucky to be alive, but the way her body ached, it seemed she would never feel better.

They allowed Mario to visit the next day. Hearing his voice, she perked up. Using her fingers, she took hold of her swollen eyelid and lifted it up. Although his voice was even and loving, she could see the alarm in his eyes.

"Hi, Mom. How are you feeling?" he asked perfunctorily. He couldn't get beyond the sight of her bruised face and enlarged head. He was frightened, and tears built behind his eyes.

"Thank God I am alive. I'm sore, but the headache is gone," she said. "Come, come sit by me."

She patted the mattress, and he gingerly sat beside her. He took her hand, brought it to his face, and kissed it. Although she couldn't see him, she could feel his distress. She cupped her hand under his chin, trying to comfort him.

"I'm going to be okay, Mario. I made it this far; I'm not going to give up now."

He could not hold back the tears any longer and remained silent for a moment while he composed himself.

"So, have you finished packing for college?" she asked, trying to distract him.

"No, I haven't even started. I'll get to it soon."

"I'm sorry I'm not home to help you."

"Don't be silly, mom. I'm seventeen years old. I can pack for myself. But before that, I'm going on the Muscular Dystrophy telethon to present a check."

"Oh, my God. I completely forgot about that. You're going to be on TV!"

"Yeah, I can't believe it. We raised $2,500 this year," he said proudly.

A few days later, she asked the nurse to put on the TV but it was not working, so the staff helped Tina into the next room.

"My son will be on the Labor Day telethon. I can't miss him on TV," she said with pride.

"Don't worry, Mrs. Dell'Olio, we'll make sure you don't miss it."

She was in the hospital for weeks, and lamented that she was not there to help Mario prepare for college. She worried he wouldn't bring the right clothes and school materials. Everyone in the family was necessarily focused on her, so she was even more concerned that they would forget things. Annette, her oldest daughter, volunteered to drive him to Hartford and get him settled in the dorm. But Tina couldn't let go of the idea that she should be there with her son. After all, he was the first in the family to go to college.

When she was finally released from the hospital, Larry carefully led her up the stairs to the front door of their home. Their dog, Sargent, startled by Tina's disfigured look, started barking furiously. She glanced at the mirror hanging in the foyer and saw why he was agitated. *No wonder*, she thought *I look like a monster.* She knew he was just a dog, but her feelings were hurt, which only reinforced her negative self-image. *Will I ever be pretty again?* she wondered.

With her head swollen and shaved, Tina never took off her turban, not even in bed. She refused to let anyone see her without it, not even her husband. If she was horrified by her looks, how much worse would he feel? Not only was she recovering from physical trauma, but the emotional strain took its toll as well. Fear and anxiety invaded her consciousness. Self-doubt and frustration, along with the slow pace of recovery, tortured her each day.

One night, as they laid in bed, Tina struggled to get comfortable. No matter how she placed her head on the pillow, she felt pressure on her incision. She continually adjusted her turban so that the seams would not irritate the scar. Seeing her discomfort, Larry rolled over to face her. With both hands, he carefully removed the turban.

"No, Larry, leave it be," she protested. "I look terrible."

He kissed her tenderly on her forehead and looked in her eyes.

"You don't have to wear this for me. You are beautiful, and I love you more than I ever have."

"Oh, Larry, I love you too."

"I was so afraid I'd lose you," he said as she rested her head on his chest. "I don't know what I'd ever do without you." They both started to cry, and she fell asleep, lying in his arms.

Letter Eighteen

New York City
March 23, 1950
My Dear Nicoletta,

As you know by now, I think of you always, and I rush to write to tell you that I love you so much, and I can do nothing but hold you in my thoughts. I can't help but love you more after receiving a photo of you from our sister-in-law, Nina. I am so happy, because it is a beautiful photo of you, and you look so beautiful. As I gaze upon it, I can't help but think that you are trying to say something to me—I just can't look away.

My sister, Rosa, was thrilled when I received it. She came right over to our apartment to see it. Rosa told me that she is so happy I have found a woman as precious and beautiful as you. When my mother saw your beautiful face, she remarked on how lovely you are, and wishes you many good things, just as she does for me. She said, "I love that your Nicoletta is willing to come to live in America to be with you." Mamma always says lovely things about you and hopes you will be happy. I tell her that I am sure that my Nicoletta wishes the same for her—that you are the sweetest creature in our entire family.

So, this weekend, I will send another package. I'll include cigarette lighters for your brothers, Mauro and Piero. I'll send something for you as well, but it will be a surprise!

I send my love to everybody, but especially to you,
Orazio

Chapter Thirty
Empty Nest

Trumbull, Connecticut 1970-2001

One by one, the four Dell'Olio children married and left home. Annette and Wayne built a home in Oxford, Connecticut. There was an empty lot next door, and they encouraged Marisa to buy it. At the time, she had only recently been dating David, but Tina and Larry were content that she made the investment. After she and David married, they built a home of their own right next door to Annette's. They had two children, Cristina and Matthew. Together, they formed their own little community, while Frankie and his wife, Kathleen, settled in Norwalk.

Over the years, and many hours of overtime, they saved enough money to launch each of their children from the nest. Just as it had been for them, they dreamed of homeownership for the children. With meager means, they were always there to lift them up should the need arise. Their generosity knew no bounds. One of Larry's most common phrases was, "Eh, you like? Take it."

Tina and Larry stood by their children through their struggles and joys of life, regardless of whether they understood. No questions asked—they were there to support and love.

Eventually, both Tina and Larry retired, which brought a new rhythm to their lives. When Marisa's children were young, Tina and Larry reveled in spending time with them. Some of the family's most treasured photographs are of Larry feeding them spaghetti for the very first time. Marisa dropped them off on her way to work, and they spent the day together. Cristina and Matthew were engaged in each and every activity. *Nonna* (grandmother) involved them in her cooking and cleaning. Matthew had a particular affinity for vacuuming and still does. When the weather permitted, Grandpa had them raking leaves or picking up branches in the yard. Both Cristina and Matthew laugh at how they made tedious chores into games. The time they spent with their grandparents is imprinted on their hearts.

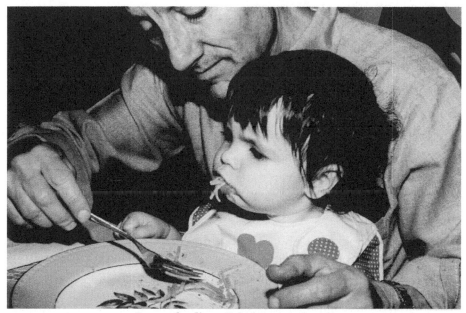

Larry feeding Cristina spaghetti.

Matthew helping Tina frost a cake.

As they grew older, Larry and Tina found the winter months difficult and traveled to San Francisco. Arriving just after Christmas, they stayed for several months with Mario and his husband, Jim.

Never would they have dreamed they'd be living with their gay son and his husband. Many years before, in 1989, Mario moved away from friends and family to live in San Francisco. Tina and Larry could not understand why he would choose to be so far from them. Just before the move, Mario sat at the kitchen table with Tina. They had always had an especially close relationship, but he dreaded having this conversation.

"Mom, sit down," he said. "There's something I need to tell you."

"What is it, Mario? Is everything okay?"

"Yeah, it's just...the reason I need to move to San Francisco is that I'm gay."

He barely took a breath as he continued to explain how he felt and how lonely he had been. He barely gave her a chance to respond.

"I need to find a community of people like me, Mom. Does that make sense?" He finally paused.

"Yes, I wondered why you'd leave us. But are you okay? I mean, do you have AIDS?" she asked with a furrowed brow. It was the height of the crisis.

"No, Mom, thank God. I am healthy."

The conversation continued with her asking about the well-being of his friends. They hugged, then went on with their day. But little was said over the following days, so Mario stopped her one morning and asked, "How are you doing with all of this?"

She stopped what she was doing, took his hands in hers and looked at him with watery eyes.

"It just makes me so sad."

"Why, mom? I'm okay."

"I know you are. But we call ourselves a close family—we support each other through all our difficulties, but you've been carrying this burden all by yourself. All these years, you were alone in your struggle. You shouldn't have had to do that without your family. I'm so sorry that you were afraid to tell me."

Then she pulled him into her warm embrace, and together they cried. It struck Mario that her only concern was for him, for his loneliness, for his hardship. It took Larry much longer to come to terms with the idea of a gay son, but once he met Jim, his attitude changed. When he saw the two of them together, all that mattered was that his son was happy.

Just a few years later, Larry and Tina were wintering in San Francisco. It was the first time they had lived in a city since their time in New York, and the two of them took full advantage. Walking down Castro Street, they hopped on the streetcar and explored downtown San Francisco, North Beach, and the Marina district. Each evening they would tell of the many new neighborhoods visited and foods that they discovered.

On one of the visits, Cristina and Matthew came along. The kids were twelve and ten years old, respectively, and they were wide-eyed as they discovered a whole new world. Coming from a tiny town in rural Connecticut, they were not used to seeing so much diversity. There were few people of color in their little town of Oxford, whereas in San Francisco, every shade of the rainbow passed them by. They heard people speaking Spanish, Tagalong, Mandarin, Cantonese, and more. With wonder in their eyes, the two Connecticut Yankees soaked up all the diversity like sponges.

When Mario and Jim were working, Tina took the lead and toured them around. One day she took them on the streetcar to visit North Beach. They walked down to Castro and Market Streets, and just before the trolley arrived, they spotted a very tall drag queen. Auburn locks of hair framed her brightly made-up face. Her dress sparkled with multicolored sequins, and her heels made her already impressive height an overpowering presence. She looked over at Tina with the two young children, handed her a flyer, and said, "Oh, honey, look at you with those beautiful kids. My name is Donna Sachet, and I'm running for empress. I would die if you'd vote for me."

Cristina and Matthew stood there looking up at her with mouths wide open, not knowing how they should react. Not fazed at all, Tina didn't skip a beat and took the flier.

"Oh, well, I'm sure you'll win," Tina responded.

"You rock, girl!" Donna said and winked at the kids.

When they got home that evening, neither of them could stop talking about their encounter with Donna Sachet.

"You should have seen Nonna. She was so cool!" Cristina said.

"Yeah, the woman said Nonna rocks! She just laughed and thanked her," Matthew chimed in.

"You know that wasn't a real woman, right?" Mario asked.

"Yeah, she had a beard!" Matt said, and they all laughed.

For almost ten years, Tina and Larry spent the winter months in San Francisco—the City by the Bay became their second home. Together with Mario and Jim, the four became not only parents and sons, but friends. Mario and Jim hosted many dinner parties, always with a colorful cast of characters—none of whom curbed themselves because of Tina and Larry's presence. Discussions wandered the gamut of cultural events from legalizing prostitution to burlesque shows to relationship drama. They were fully immersed in the lives of a new community of friends.

Mario was the director of music at the historic Mission Dolores Basilica. Jim sang in the choir he directed while Tina and Larry sat in a pew right near them. They were treated like royalty by the parishioners and like family by the choir members. Tina kept touch with a number of singers throughout the years and visited with them while Jim and Mario were at work. They formed lasting friendships with many members of the choir.

During that time, Mario traveled extensively with his choirs. Oftentimes, he invited his parents to join them. The students at Sacred Heart Cathedral Prep came to know Tina and Larry as surrogate grandparents. They continually pressed them for childhood stories of their teacher and director. For Tina and Larry, those were some of the most endearing memories.

Tina was adventurous—she loved to travel to new places and eat different foods. When it came to food, Larry was the opposite. Tina's cooking was the best—why take a chance on strange cuisines? He and Jim had a playful relationship. Jim was able to make him laugh and loved to tease him.

"We're going to torture you for dinner tonight, Larry," Jim said.

"Whatta you sayin'?"

"Mom's been cooking all week," Mario responded. "We're going to give her a break."

"How about some Mexican food?" Jim asked mischievously. "I know that's your favorite."

"Nah, those beans, so mushy," he responded with a look of disgust. "That's okay. Tina will cook some spaghetti."

On one of their first visits to San Francisco, Mario wanted to do something special for them. Fior d'Italia was a well-known Italian restaurant in North Beach—a quaint Italian neighborhood with many cafés and shops. Fior d'Italia was frequented by many notable San Franciscans. Wille Brown, the speaker for the California State Assembly at the time (and later mayor), was a regular. Not used to fine dining, Larry was uncomfortable from the moment they entered. Mario was oblivious to his discomfort as he watched Tina enjoying every detail. The presentation of the appetizers was elegant—served on extra-large plates with green and red sauces decorating the edges. Larry scoffed.

"What is dis? They give dis tiny antipasto on a big plate? It's only one bite."

"That's so you don't get fat, Larry," Jim said, getting him to laugh.

For his entree, Larry ordered the traditional *zuppa di pesce*—linguini smothered in seafood and a rich red sauce. The waiter laid the bowl in front of him, followed by an empty plate to place the discarded shells. No sooner did he leave the table when Larry exclaimed, "What is a dis shit? They give dis huge dish with nothing in it. What *zuppa di pesce*? There's only two clams, two mussels—what do we need this big plate for?"

Mario was hurt, but Jim burst out laughing. "Don't worry, Larry. Tina will cook some spaghetti for you when we get home."

"Sure," Tina said. "You treat me to a fancy dinner then put me to work when we get home?"

They all laughed, even Larry.

Those years visiting San Francisco created some of their happiest memories. It was such a contrast to their quiet lives in Connecticut. They attended concerts and shows. There were dinner parties every weekend, and they traveled extensively with Mario and Jim. When the boys decided to leave San Francisco to sail to the Virgin Islands, Tina and Larry felt that they, too, were leaving their beloved community behind.

50th Wedding Anniversary front row: Larry, Tina, Marisa, Frankie back row: Jim, Mario, Matthew, Annette, David, Cristina, Wayne

On December 29, 2001, Tina and Larry celebrated their fiftieth wedding anniversary. Mario, then living in St. Thomas, Virgin Islands, arranged for a special Mass at their parish church. He and Jim flew up for Christmas, and together with Annette, Marisa, and Frankie, they planned the entire event.

A Mass was held at St. Stephen's Church in Trumbull, Connecticut, during which the couple renewed their wedding vows. Marisa and Annette brought up the gifts during the offertory procession, and Frankie read from scripture. Mario planned the music and gathered several of his best friends to sing. Their Catholic faith had always been a central part of family life. With each of them contributing to the Mass, it was clear that faith continued to blind them together. As a special surprise, Mario presented them with a papal blessing commemorating their fifty years of marriage.

The party that followed was reminiscent of their first wedding reception. It was held in the church basement and featured an abundance of Italian favorites, including pastries from Luigi's Italian bakery, a Bridgeport tradition. Many of Larry's nieces and nephews were in attendance with their children. Tina's relatives had not emigrated from Italy and were obviously absent from the gathering, but the Dell'Olio clan had been her family since she first placed her feet on American soil so many years before. She knew them better than her family in Italy. Tina and Larry could not have been happier to have so many friends and relatives celebrating with them.

Larry's infamous way of approaching food was on full display that evening. If it wasn't Tina's cooking, it wasn't good enough. If asked whether he liked something served at a restaurant or cooked by

Renewal of wedding vows

one of his children, he'd simply respond, "Eh, you gotta eat." A catered

Italian meal was bound to evoke a spirited response, and Larry didn't disappoint. While standing in the buffet line, Mario watched him pass up the eggplant Parmigiana.

"Pop, aren't you going to have some eggplant?"

"Eh, the Sicilians, they leave the skin on. It makes me choke," he said with utter disgust.

Everyone around laughed. It was just Larry being Larry.

Chapter Thirty-One
The Diagnosis

White Plains, New York 2004

The dawn of the new millennium came with unexpected changes. Tina and Larry's routine did not vary much. They cut coupons, searched for sales at various grocery stores, then made the rounds. If Stop & Shop had olive oil on sale, that would be the first stop, then Big Y for San Marzano canned peeled tomatoes, and of course pasta. There were cabinets full of those three staples, and their children carried on the tradition. None of them would ever be caught without pasta, tomatoes, or olive oil.

One day, as they were embarking on the grocery rounds, Larry backed out of the garage. After thirty years in the same house in Trumbull, Connecticut, he misjudged the opening. Startled by the squeal of bending wood and crunching metal, he slammed the brakes. *What happened?* he wondered. Putting the car in park, he got out to inspect the damage. The back passenger door was caved in, and the frame of the garage door had been ripped off. Larry looked at it in disbelief. *How could I have hit the door?* He had backed out thousands of times. This was no different.

Tina could see him spinning out of control. Larry was always anxious about driving. Fender benders had always made him worry about the insurance going up. Each time he had an accident, he became increasingly more anxious. In recent years he had become less confident in his driving.

"Larry, don't worry about this. We'll get it fixed. There is no serious damage."

"Don't you see? We have to fix the garage door too. We can't even close it."

"Can't you do that yourself? It's just the wooden frame. That will take no time."

"Maybe, but look at the dent in the car. That I can't do."

"It's not that bad, Larry. Come on, let's go back inside. You need to calm down."

That was just the beginning of a long journey. It wasn't merely an accident—something about it didn't feel right. Larry's balance seemed to be off. He felt dizzy—off his game. Tina suggested they visit the family doctor. He was like another son, and Larry felt entirely at ease with him. Dr. Gabriel had treated Mario and knew Marisa and Annette through their work at the hospital. After his examination, he gave Larry a prescription.

"Ok, Larry, you can stop worrying. I think you have an ear infection. That can throw off your balance. Don't drive for a few days, and you'll be fine."

However, his balance issues lasted for weeks, during which time he let Tina drive. Unfortunately, Larry was not an easy passenger, especially when his wife or children were in the driver's seat.

"Watch!" he shouted. "There's a car coming. Red light! Slow down!"

He was relentless. Tina hated driving with him in the car, and so did his son. Mario was much less patient with his father.

"Dad, you're driving me crazy. You're going to cause an accident with all your shouting. Just let me drive."

Mario and his husband, Jim, had recently moved in with Tina and Larry after losing everything in a boating accident in the Caribbean. The emotional baggage they brought into their new reality provided more than its share of tension and anxiety. Living together again, they spent a great deal of time with each other. During that time, they detected significant physical changes in Larry. He was dragging his feet more and listing to one side when he walked. Something was off, and it wasn't from an ear infection.

"Mario, I bet you he has Parkinson's," Jim said carefully.

"You think so? It does seem odd that his listing is caused by an inner ear infection. Besides, how could it have lasted all these months?"

"You have to get him to a neurologist."

"Are you kidding? Getting him to his primary care doctor is difficult enough. He'll never agree to a neurologist. It'll just freak him out."

"All right then, let's go with him to Dr. Gabriel. At least we can ask him what he thinks."

Dr. Gabriel examined him and asked if there was any family history. Since there was none, he said Larry's symptoms were just part of growing older. There was nothing to do about it. He didn't believe that he had Parkinson's, so that was that. But neither Jim nor Mario was convinced. A few months later, they persuaded Larry to see a neurologist, and he was immediately diagnosed with Parkinson's and put on prescription medication.

In front of their elementary school in Bisceglie shortly after Larry's
diagnosis.

Living with Parkinson's

Not long after the diagnosis, Tina and Larry moved in with Mario and Jim. They had bought a grand house in White Plains, New York. Mario and Jim always assumed they'd eventually share a home. Together, they looked for a house that might work for all of them. Tina and Larry were very familiar with the city, because one of their childhood friends lived in White Plains. Back when the children were young, they had packed up the car and drove to White Plains to visit their dear friends from Disceglie. Moving with Mario and Jim allowed them to remain somewhat independent with friends nearby.

The house was big enough for them to have a master suite with a full bath and their own sitting room. Although Jim and Tina jockeyed for control of the kitchen on the weekends, she had complete control during the workweek. Jim was often frustrated when Tina would rearrange utensils to make things more convenient.

"Where is the spatula, Tina? It used to be right here."

"Oh, I moved it to the drawer near the stove. It makes more sense to have it there, don't you think?"

"I suppose, but let's leave it there. With you constantly moving things around, I can't find anything."

Conversations like that were a common occurrence, but they settled into a comfortable routine—not without growing pains, however. Both couples were used to maintaining their own homes. For Larry and Tina, leaving their home in Trumbull was a painful necessity. They no longer had the responsibility for maintaining their house and yard, which had become increasingly burdensome. However, the sense of loss was significant. Larry often lamented in his pessimistic way.

"Eh, I got nothing no more. I have no home, no car, nothing."

"Pop, this is your home now. This is our home," Mario said.

"No, this is your home. Ours is gone."

In a way, Larry was right. In a shared space, both couples had to negotiate differences of opinion and control of the kitchen or gardens. Little things, like decorating the Christmas tree, became moments when the change in their lives was most evident. Mario and Tina had strong traditions, especially when it came to decorating the tree. They had both collected ornaments over the years, each with special meaning. But there's just so much room on the tree. Leaving some of her precious ornaments off the Christmas tree was one moment when she felt like she was living in someone else's home.

As their time together continued, they adjusted to the inevitable disagreements and idiosyncrasies. Jim and Mario commuted into NYC each day. Tina and Larry had the house to themselves and were within walking distance to the city center. There were many walks to the bakery to get fresh bread, to the pharmacy, and to the market. They lived on a lovely tree-lined street, and Larry paced in front of the house—back and forth. Ever the social neighbor, he met many people as they strolled by. During the warmer weather, Tina weeded, planted a beautiful flower garden, and tended to the vegetable garden with Mario. Although Larry hated yard work, he would help her with more strenuous tasks.

Tina would often cook with Mario when he got home from work. He loved the comfort food that he was raised on and was determined to learn from the best. Jim used to tease Mario that he was "a mess in the kitchen." Together, he and his mother made quite an impact. There were pots and pans used, drops of tomato sauce or sprinkles of flour on the floor, and grease splattered on the cooktop. Jim was incredibly meticulous about cleaning. His briefcase still in hand, he picked up the sponge and began to wipe down the countertops as soon as he entered the house. Tina and Mario learned to clean up their mess before he drove to the train station each night to pick up Jim.

Because Larry and Tina had traveled to San Francisco and St. Thomas for many years, the two couples fell into a comfortable routine. Although Larry grieved the loss of his own home, he enjoyed the many projects that Jim led as they renovated their old house. Tina loved the frequent dinner parties they hosted with new and old friends. She reveled in telling stories, and each gathering offered her a new audience.

Each year, they hosted a Christmas open house. The three of them baked cookies and cakes, fried zucchini patties, prepared eggplant Parmigiana, and baked ziti. There were roasts and mountains of shrimp. The cooking parties lasted days. Both Mario and Tina loved to decorate for Christmas, so the house looked like Santa's wonderland. Once the guests arrived, the day passed in a flash. They refilled food trays and bowls, washed wine glasses, and picked up the trash while entertaining the myriad guests from their places of work, neighbors, and family. Though exhausting, they loved these parties.

Larry and Tina became friendly with the neighbors on their daily walks and soon began to feel at home. However, Tina was feeling the strain. As was their custom, they strolled arm in arm or holding hands. But Larry listed heavily to one side as they walked; he leaned into her so much that she had to push back to straighten his body. Both of them would return home after an outing drained from the physical effort.

One day on their walk, his pace accelerated. It was almost as if he were going to break into a run.

"Larry, slow down. We're almost there."

He didn't respond. She assumed he must have been tired upon their return and was anxious to get into the house. She couldn't keep up with him as he moved quickly up the driveway. He pulled away from her without warning when all at once, he fell, tumbling forward. He crashed onto the asphalt face first, hitting his head and breaking his glasses. Tina ran to him, and as he turned his head to look up at her, she could see the blood trickling down his face.

"Don't worry, Tina. I'm fine," he said as he tried in vain to get back on his feet.

Tina struggled to pick him up—his body was like dead weight. She bent down to put an arm under his and lifted him, only to lose balance herself. They both fell back down. After several attempts, she draped his arm around her shoulder and lifted him. They hobbled up the driveway and into the house. After she cleaned him up, he lay on the couch for hours. He was totally wiped out.

Larry had always been a proud man. Seeing what Parkinson's was doing to his body ate away at him. He was reluctant to accept help from anyone, but it became increasingly clear that he needed it. Tina was by his side at every turn, and although she worried, she understood that she couldn't let Larry know. If he had seen her worry, he would circle the drain more rapidly. She was determined to strengthen his muscles and keep his mind stimulated. Together, they watched exercise DVDs, and she went through the paces with him. Although their walks became shorter, she made sure they continued to get out. Larry was always a pessimist—seeing his world with the glass half empty. It was difficult for her when his negativity prevented him from seeing clearly. Whereas Tina presented a hopeful or positive face. She did everything in her power to emphasize his small victories.

Only three blocks away, St. Bernard Church was a lovely walk. On Good Friday, they walked to the 3 p.m. services. When they arrived, his pride took over. Not wanting to look helpless in front of strangers, Larry climbed the staircase without holding on to Tina. He had only climbed five or six steps when he lost his balance. Larry reached for the handrail, but it was just out of his grasp. He fell back and down. Fortunately, he was leaning to the left, and rather than fall squarely onto the sidewalk, he tumbled into the bushes. That is what saved him from serious injury. With only a few scratches and a bruised ego, Larry was able to get up with the help of some parishioners. From then on, his movement became increasingly more limited.

Caring for him became too much for Tina, so they convinced him to accept a home health aide. She was able to bathe him and run him through exercises. As the disease progressed, he had trouble swallowing liquids and it became necessary to add thickener to prevent him from choking. Eating became more challenging as he developed hiccups that lasted longer and longer.

Tina never left his side, and they continued to do minor chores around the house to keep engaged and active. Keeping busy distracted him from his plight and feeling useful helped his ego. During one of their ordinary tasks, everything changed. They had just finished folding laundry in the kitchen. Tina handed each item to Larry, and he dutifully placed it into the basket. When they were done, she went down to the basement to put the other load into the dryer. Larry, wanting to be helpful, decided to bring the basket of clothes up to the second floor. He bent over and lifted the basket without a struggle, walked carefully to the staircase, and began to ascend one step at a time. But the weight of the basket caused him to lose his balance. He tried desperately to correct himself, but it was of no use. He let go of the clothes and reached out for the banister rail and missed. Larry fell backward down the stairs onto the wooden floor. He barely felt his body hit the floor when his head hit the brass hinges on the closet door, causing him to see stars. A flash of pain shot through his body and knocked him out.

Tina heard the commotion and flew into the foyer to see what had happened. There he was, lying in a pool of bright red blood. She screamed.

"Larry, Larry. Oh, my God! What did you do?"

There was no response. Tina ran to the phone and dialed 911. Kneeling by his side, she patted down his hair and caressed his face.

"It's going to be okay, my love. Help is coming. Don't worry. I've got you, *amore*. I've got you."

Tina couldn't stop her tears as he lay in a pool of blood, unresponsive.

"Please be okay, Larry. I love you. Please, please."

Slowly, he regained consciousness but was disoriented. He wanted to be helped up, so Tina helped him sit upright, leaning against the door. He was sitting in his own blood, and the sight of it made him queasy. Tina knew he was getting more anxious.

"Don't move, Larry. Just stay still. I'll get some rags to clean this up."

She ran into the kitchen, returning with a pile of rags, and mopped up as much as possible.

"The ambulance is on its way, Larry. It won't be long."

The words were barely out of her mouth when they heard the siren and saw the lights. Tina opened the door, and they wheeled a stretcher into the house. The rest of the afternoon was a blur to her.

Mario and Jim took the commuter train home from the city and sat with him in a packed emergency room. It was a Friday, and the place was bustling, which made it difficult for Larry to rest. His speech was labored.

"I…I'm thirsty," he choked out.

"Sorry, sir," the nurse responded. "We can't give you water. You may need surgery."

It was late in the evening; after spending nine hours in the emergency room, they admitted him to the intensive care unit. The swelling of his brain from the impact of the fall caused them to worry. The doctors were unclear about his prognosis but told the family to get his affairs in order. By that time, all his children were by his side. For the following week, Larry drifted in and out of consciousness. They drained the fluid from his brain, which relieved some pressure, but was still in danger.

"Larry is incredibly strong," the doctor told the family. "I have never seen anyone fight as hard as he has."

"Will he recover, Doctor?" Tina asked.

"To be honest, I didn't think he would make it," she responded. "He is stable for now. But I need you to understand he may never be back to what he was before. You need to prepare yourself."

After two weeks, he was moved to a local rehabilitation center. However, his faculties were never the same. He began to hallucinate and could not understand why Tina was abandoning him when visiting hours were over.

"Where you go?" he asked.

"Larry, I have to go home. I'll be back tomorrow."

"I come with you," he insisted as he tried to get out of bed. But he was strapped in to prevent him from falling. When he realized that, his eyes grew wide and his paranoia kicked in. He believed he was being held prisoner.

"Larry, I can't stay. I promise I will be back first thing in the morning."

"No, I come home with you."

It broke Tina's heart. He could not understand where he was and that she could not stay overnight. It was bad enough that he experienced so much physical pain, but the lack of cognition was much worse. Each night, it was the same thing. He was relentless and made her feel as if she was abandoning him. For two months, she suffered the same routine.

Three weeks later, Mario and Jim hosted Thanksgiving, but it was a somber holiday. The frenetic preparations had always been colored with the excitement of a festive family gathering. There were more side dishes than anyone could possibly eat, plus two turkeys—one roasted, the other deep-fried. However, that morning, Tina and Mario made their first visit of the day to Larry at the rehab facility. When it came time to leave, Tina promised she'd be back later in the day with the rest of the family. Larry argued with her once again. He could not understand why he couldn't join them at home.

With everyone around the dinner table, Tina asked Mario to say grace. They held hands as he spoke the words that lay heavy on their hearts.

"Dear God, we thank you for Dad, and we ask that you heal his tortured mind and his frail body. Bring him home to us soon."

After a moment of silence, the family celebrated his life in the way each knew best. The most sacred time for Larry had always been with his children gathered around the dinner table. He sat back and took it all in—the pandemonium of several conversations at once, food being passed around the table, and the laughter of people who were entirely too familiar with one another. As dishes were cleared, he would often catch the ear of whoever sat beside him. That was when he shone, telling stories of his childhood and life back in Bisceglie. His tales were often a bit more fantastic than real, but that's what made them great stories. When Tina came back to the table, she would chime in, and his yarn would become ever longer.

That Thanksgiving, his absence was palpable. Once the table was cleared and dishes washed, Annette and Marisa took their turn visiting Larry with their spouses and children. Later in the evening, Frankie and Tina returned for the final visit. On that Thanksgiving, they were thankful indeed but continued to worry about his recovery.

They all hoped that Larry would be home for Christmas, and their wish came to pass. On December 23, the day before Christmas Eve, 2008, he was released from rehab and came home to White Plains.

It was clear from the moment he entered the house that his life with Mario and Jim would be drastically different. Although he was significantly impaired, Larry's memory led him to follow his routine. The master bedroom was on the second floor, but he could not manage the stairs any longer. A gate had to be placed at the top of the stairs so he wouldn't try to descend on his own. They considered setting up a bed on the first floor, but there was no shower in the tiny powder room off the dining room. And although Tina, Mario, and Jim anticipated that their lives would return to normal upon returning, that was far from reality. Larry had a faraway look in his eyes and had great difficulty speaking. It broke their hearts, but they tried to carry on as they had before the fall.

Mario taught and was the choir director at an all-girls school in Manhattan. On Christmas Eve, six of Mario's singers traveled from the city to welcome his father home. Both Larry and Tina had attended their choral concerts in New York City, and the girls had a great affection for them. They gathered around the piano with Larry and Tina sitting before them. They intoned the first song, and one of the girls said, "Since you couldn't come to our Christmas concert this year, we thought we'd come to you."

Mario and Tina were all overwhelmed by their thoughtfulness. Larry sat in the overstuffed chair with Tina at his side. He was still disoriented since his return home and wore a blank face with a distant look in his eyes. But once the girls began to sing, he perked up and turned his head in their direction. Noticing the change in demeanor, Mario's heart swelled. He was thrilled to have these lovely young women before them. As they began to sing, tears welled in his eyes. It was the most beautiful gift they could have offered.

Letter Nineteen

Bisceglie, Province of Bari, Italy
Feb. 2, 1950
Mio Adorato Orazio,

I responded the moment I received your letter. I couldn't let any time pass before I sat down with pen, inkwell, and paper. Until then, I did not feel peace. It was such a great surprise to come home to your letter. I was out with your brother, Carlo, my cousin, Nina, and your brother Sal's fiancée, Felicia. We were having a wonderful time. I can't tell you how much I care about her. I wish both Sal and her a life of happiness. When we are together, we never want to say goodbye. When I returned home with Carlo and Nina, Antonietta told me of your letter. From that moment on, I could think of nothing else but reading your message. But they continued asking me questions, leading me on and teasing me. They had hidden your letter from me to surprise me. They obviously know how much I look forward to your letters.

As soon as I got a moment alone, I dedicated myself entirely to you, only to you, who is my dearest, my love, my joy. You are the only one to whom I can give myself completely. It is late at night, but I felt a burning need to write to you before I can go to bed. I need to feel that we were talking with each other in person. Writing to you and reading your letters makes me feel like I can actually hear your voice. Please respond to me and tell me many beautiful things. Oh, my dear one, I don't know what to do to hear your voice. I hope to see the beautiful person that you are in person, but for the moment, I must be content to see you only in my dreams. It would be such great satisfaction to have you rock me in your arms. For now, it eludes me. With my arms stretched out to you, I remain your dearest one. Sending you a passionate embrace—as lovers do—as we are.

I have so many more things to say to you, but I don't have the words to express myself. The words escape me, but I need to tell you how much you have changed my life from the moment we began to love each other. The days never seem to end. They are interminable because I am just waiting, waiting to hear from you, to see you.

When your brothers visit me, Carlo is with my cousin, Nina, Sal has his wife, and I am left with your father. What do you think of that, my love? Are you happy that your father takes your place?! I didn't think so.

I hope that your mother is happy with us. I would love to write a few words for her. I feel the necessity that your parents support us in our love. I hope that Mamma loves me like a true daughter, as I have found a true mother in her. It has been too many years that I have not been able to call anyone by that sweet name, Mamma. I can't tell you how happy I am now that I can begin to use that word once again.

Thank you for the photo you sent. I didn't like the original photo you have of me, so I will send you a better one soon. Thank you for the dollar you sent. I don't know how to thank you for all you do. You are so good; there aren't words to praise you enough. Your spirit is gentle and kind, but I don't want you to sacrifice so much for me through your kind gesture. You understand me.

It is midnight, and my brother, Piero, is working at the cinema for the grand opening of Carnival. The students invited us to join this evening, but I declined to go because you would not be with me. Are you happy, caro?

I close with a good night. Give my love to everyone. Sending warm hugs and big kisses.

Your dearest,
Tinuccia (little Tina)

Chapter Thirty-Two
His Last Year

Oxford, Connecticut 2008-2010

Shortly after Christmas, Tina realized living in White Plains was no longer feasible. Their bedroom was on the second floor, and Larry could not navigate the flight of stairs. Mario and Jim discussed installing a stairlift or moving their bedroom to the first floor. Since there wasn't a shower on the first level, moving the bedroom was not the right solution. The stairlift was promising, but Tina worried she would not be able to get Larry in and out of the lift when they were home alone. Mario and Jim were away from home twelve or more hours a day working in New York City. Before Larry's fall, the time apart did not prove to be problematic. But he needed more care than ever, and Tina couldn't do it alone. Life would never return to the way it had been.

Along with all the good memories of living in White Plains were also painful ones. Each time Tina turned to climb up to their bedroom, images of Larry lying in a pool of blood at the foot of the stairs haunted her. Her fear that he would take another tumble consumed her.

Ultimately, they decided to move in with their daughter, Marisa, and her husband David in Oxford, Connecticut. It's in a rural part of Connecticut without stores or services within walking distance. However, Annette and Wayne lived right next door. Having their two daughters close by made all the difference. Both worked in doctor's offices, which made access to medical care much more accessible. Their hours and commutes were significantly shorter than Mario and Jim's daily commute to New York, so they would not be home alone for so many hours.

Mario was heartbroken at their departure. He and Jim had chosen their home in White Plains with his parents in mind. The four of them had discussed living together since their yearly visits to San Francisco ten years earlier. Mario had always been very close to Tina. She was not only his Mom but was undoubtedly one of his best friends. He returned from work the week after the move and opening the door he found his dog, Pete, jumping with anxious excitement. He had rarely been left alone for so many hours.

They had gotten Pete to keep Tina and Larry company during their long days at work, and he had bonded with them—they were with him twenty-four hours a day. As Mario passed through the kitchen, he felt a wave of sadness wash over him, an almost suffocating heaviness. There were no pots of sauce on the stove, no aroma of meatballs or zucchini patties; all were noticeably absent. He walked into the front room that had six windows looking out onto the street. Larry's chair was vacant. He knew that the move was the best solution, but Mario's heart echoed with emptiness.

The transition to Oxford was not smooth. Larry was utterly disoriented in his new environment. He had no sooner returned home from the rehabilitation center when he was whisked away again. At the end of each day, he turned to Tina with questioning eyes as he reached for his coat.

"When are we going home?"

"We are home, Larry."

"No, you know, with Mario."

"We live with Marisa and David now. Put your jacket away."

Although Larry continued to heal and grow stronger, he was not himself—it was as if a part of him was missing. He was not able to speak in full sentences, and it was difficult to understand him. There was a great deal of guesswork involved when conversing with him. In his compromised state, Larry had trouble adjusting to his unfamiliar surroundings. Larry used to walk all around the neighborhood in White Plains, talking to anybody who passed by. He also loved to watch people walk by while sitting in his chair. In Oxford, there were no sidewalks, and houses were far apart, many obscured by trees. There were no neighbors strolling by and no one to chat with.

As the months passed and winter turned to spring and summer, Tina encouraged Larry to walk down the street with her to get a bit of exercise, but Larry became fearful of losing his way. They could walk no further than Annette's house next door before he prompted her to turn back. Tina decided to help Marisa and David build an addition to their home to provide a bedroom and full bath on the ground floor. When construction began, workers came in and out of the house. Larry couldn't understand why so many strange men were interacting with his wife. His paranoia shifted into high gear, and he accused Tina of having an affair.

"Larry, don't be silly. Don't you see that they are building a room for us?"

He eyed her with confusion.

"You remember, right? We'll have our own big bedroom and bathroom."

A glimmer of recognition lit his eyes, and he let go of his anger momentarily. Trying to get him to laugh, Tina continued.

"Besides, what would those men want with an old lady like me?!"

It worked, and he laughed through his confusion. Sadly, as the months passed, his paranoia worsened. He thought people were coming for him or that burglars were trying to break into the house. He ambled to the windows and pulled down the shades. Then he turned on all the lights, hoping to scare them away.

"Larry, what are you doing?"

"Nothing, it's dark out. People can see in. Who knows who's out there?"

"*Tesoro*, we live in the country now, in the middle of the woods. No one is walking by or trying to break in."

But reasoning with him wasn't helpful. He was suspicious of everything. One evening, Larry went to the bathroom, and hearing the voices on the television, he believed that people had come into the house. He was afraid to come out in his pajamas for fear that he wasn't appropriately dressed. The distinction between reality and the world of television blurred. He thought the characters were real and were watching him. He began hallucinating, believing that people in the backyard were threatening to come into the house.

He also had many lucid moments. Larry had always been a handsome man, and he took care to dress in slacks and button-down shirts. On several occasions, Mario's friends from San Francisco visited. Larry disappeared, returning with the smell of Old Spice aftershave. He always took special care with how he looked. However, his dexterity had deteriorated, and he had trouble managing his buttons or belt. Nonetheless, Larry insisted on dressing up. Tina helped him dress and encouraged him to wear suspenders, because he could no longer buckle his belt.

"No, I don't want to wear this shit," he declared as they were running off to a doctor's appointment. "Give me the belt."

"Larry, we're going to be late. Come on now. Just wear the suspenders. They are so much easier for you."

"No, no! They look terrible," he said as he fumbled with the belt.

Tina began to cry in frustration. The physical and emotional burden of caring for him had steadily broken her down.

"Why can't you just listen to me, Larry? You make things more difficult. We are going to be late," she said through her tears.

He was startled by her reaction and froze. *What have I done?* He knew she was just trying to help. She was his rock. The last thing he wanted to do was hurt her. Larry let the belt drop to the floor and hobbled over to her and took her in his arms.

"Tina, I'm sorry."

It was the first step of many in giving up control. Winter turned to spring and spring to summer with his mental and physical health deteriorating even more. Home health aides came twice a week to help Tina care for him. The aide bathed and dressed him and led him through physical therapy. Tina joined in, and they would do the exercises together.

Thanksgiving rolled back around, and the family was grateful to have Larry at the table with them. Just a year before, they had taken turns visiting him at the rehabilitation center. This time, he took his place at the head of the table with Tina by his side. The usual chaos of dinner gave the holiday a festive air despite Larry's distance. Speaking was difficult for him, and he seemed detached from conversations and the jovial interaction taking place all around him. Still, his family was comforted by the fact that Larry was right where he should be. They rested in the knowledge that even though he wasn't able to participate as he normally would, Larry was at the table with his loving family.

That year, Christmas was a blur as Larry receded further from the world. Family gatherings found him entirely disengaged and barely eating. To get his attention, one would have to sit directly in front of him and call his name. Walking became more difficult; he didn't have the strength to get from his chair to the bed. His son-in-law, David, would lift him up and carry him to bed. He had lost so much weight that he felt like a child in David's arms.

In his weakened state, Larry could not stay up to watch television with Tina. By 8:00 p.m., Larry was ready for bed. He and Tina had always gone to sleep at the same time, and he couldn't understand why she changed the routine. *Why won't she join me?* He had no sense of the fact that it was so early. To quell his concerns, she stood at his bedside, holding his hand until he fell asleep.

Standing there as he drifted in and out of sleep, she felt the strain in her back. They had rented a hospital bed, which stood much higher than their regular bed. When she attempted to sit to relieve her discomfort, or if her hand slipped away from his, Larry would awaken. As the Parkinson's continued to worsen, their days were busy with practical tasks like dressing, eating, and bathing. Tina didn't know how much Larry understood regarding his condition. *Does he realize how bad it is?* she wondered. They never discussed it, nor did they consider that he could be nearing the end of his battle. Tina couldn't let herself ponder the inevitable.

One snowy day, the school was closed, so Mario visited from New York. As he entered the house he could tell that Tina was frustrated with Larry.

"Larry, you have to eat something. Please, have a little soup."

He turned his head away from the spoon she held up to his lips.

"Ugh! At least try. What is wrong with you? You need to eat!" She was exasperated.

"Mom, let him be. Don't force him," Mario said gently.

"Look at him. He's losing so much weight. I don't know what to do anymore."

Tina walked away, visibly upset—at her wit's end. Emotionally and physically drained, she was only beginning to come to terms with his deteriorating condition. Tina could tell he was nearing his end, but she could not face it. She focused solely on his recovery. Mario sat at the table with Larry and put his hand on top of his father's. Larry was pulled from his distant gaze and looked up at his youngest son.

"Dad, what's the matter? Are you not hungry?" Mario asked.

Larry shook his head.

"How about a little water? I'm sure you're dehydrated."

He shook his head once again.

"It's okay, Pop. You don't have to do anything you don't want to. No one is going to force you to eat or drink, all right?"

Larry nodded his head. Mario turned to see Tina watching their encounter with tears in her eyes. They all knew what this meant. Mario brought his mother to the other room and sat her down.

"Mom, I know it's frustrating, but you can't make him do anything he doesn't want to."

"But if he doesn't eat or drink, he'll waste away. I can see it happening already." A single tear trickled down her cheek.

"I know, Mom." There was silence, and then he continued, "But he has to do this his own way. He's taking back control. It's the only power he has left."

Tina shook her head. "I'm standing by watching him leave me, and there is nothing I can do."

Mario pulled her close to him and said, "You can love him, Mom, as you always have. Just be with him, hold him, and tell him you love him."

Silence engulfed them as the gravity of the moment weighed upon them. Mario helped Larry to the couch and tried to reinforce the fact that he was in charge of his own destiny.

"Pop, you do what you need to do. You've had an awful year, and I know this is torture for you. You know we'll all be okay, right? We'll take care of Mom. I promise."

Larry looked into Mario's eyes, and although he could no longer formulate full words or sentences, he managed to stammer, "I, I, love…"

"I love you too, Dad, more than you know."

With tears falling from his eyes, Mario could barely see the snowy roads as he attempted to drive home. Not a mile away from Marisa's house, he lost control of the car and skidded over the curb, stopping just before a grove of trees. His body shook with the shock of what nearly happened. Then he rested his forehead on the steering wheel and cried.

From then on, Larry stopped eating and drinking. He refused to take his medication, and he became weaker by the hour. Five days later, Larry had trouble breathing, so Marisa called the hospice center. The nurse arrived shortly after and stayed throughout the night. When Larry's breathing grew more labored, the nurse turned to Tina and said, "This is what they call the death rattle. It won't be long now."

She took her place beside him in the narrow bed and held him in her arms. She could tell he was in pain, so the nurse increased the morphine drip, giving him a small dose every thirty minutes. Tina was beside him, holding his hand when he breathed his last breath. All at once, the room became quiet. The death rattle had ceased—Larry labored no more. The doctor came just before dawn to pronounce him dead. It was February 17, 2010, on Ash Wednesday.

Chapter Thirty-Three
The Funeral

Oxford, Connecticut 2010

On the morning of the funeral, Tina bent over the coffin at the funeral home. It was an hour before the funeral Mass, and the remaining time was reserved for the immediate family. Inconsolable in her grief, she placed her hand over Larry's icy hands and sobbed. She could not let go of him. All the emotions she had buried during his last torturous year came spilling forth. Tina was the rock that held her family together. In the last weeks of Larry's decline, she buried the pain of his rapid deterioration deep within. There was no room for her feelings or fears—her only task was to care for her *immenso amore,* her great love. In those final minutes before they lowered the lid of the coffin, Tina could no longer contain her sense of loss. The tears and anguish of losing him flowed like blood from a pierced heart.

Startled at Tina's grief, her four children felt the impact of her loss. In theory, they understood she would be devastated, but to see her wailing over his coffin ripped their hearts in two. Never had they seen her cry. She always remained the stalwart image of strength. But this time, for the first time, she didn't worry about anyone else. Tina gave in to her grief. The family followed behind the coffin during the processional song. Marisa and Annette held Tina up as they trudged up the aisle, with Frankie and Mario right behind. Mario had planned the music and joined his dearest friends in the choir loft to sing the psalm. Larry was always so proud of his son's tenor voice. But Mario wasn't sure he could get through the song he prepared.

"Tony, you know this piece. If I break down, please take over."

"I've got you, Mario," he said, placing his arm around him.

The family passed through the funeral Mass as if through a fog. The extended family gathered at a local restaurant for lunch as they celebrated Larry's life for the last time.

The weeks and months that followed Larry's death passed in slow motion. Tina refused to leave the house unless it was to go to Mass. She had no desire to socialize or visit with friends or extended family. However, renewed energy came with the arrival of spring. Witnessing new life buoyed Tina as buds peeked from the ends of the skeletal branches, and crocuses dotted the barren earth with shades of lavender, white, and yellow. Spring blossomed all around her, and her heart slowly reawakened. Out she went into the garden, digging in the soil, planting and feeling nature's life-giving energy. At long last, with the sun's warmth amid the blossoming flowers, the darkness that gripped her heart slowly released its hold.

By summer, Tina was out in the garden more than in the house. Marisa chided her for not pacing herself, because she worked for hours and exhausted herself. But Tina knew there was more to it than that. To her detriment, during the final two years of Larry's life, she concentrated on making him as comfortable as possible. Tina pushed herself to her emotional and physical limits. She allowed no room for self-care. On a visit to her cardiologist, she was told that she needed a valve replacement. Tina refused to have surgery, telling the doctor her priority was to care for Larry. She never told her husband of her own health issues. If she had, his worry would have precipitated his decline. Instead, she had a stent put in as a temporary fix.

By December, nearly ten months after Larry's death, the time was long past to care for herself. An appointment with her cardiologist resulted in scheduling her heart surgery. The doctor knew that she would need at least one bypass. The evening before her surgery, her children were at her bedside. Both Marisa and Annette knew the hospital staff and many doctors. This added a level of comfort for everyone. In preparation, Tina had signed a DNR, a do-not-resuscitate order. She had always been clear that she did not want to linger on life support. Tina placed her trust in God. When it was her time, she would join Larry.

In theory, her children understood the necessity of her decision. Her quality of life mattered to all of them. But somehow, her youngest son, Mario, took it hard. Not that he disagreed with the DNR. He hated the idea of her subsisting on life support. What struck him, however, was the finality of it. The gravity of her condition weighed heavily on his frayed emotions. When it came time to leave for the evening, Mario and his siblings began walking down the hall to the elevator when he paused.

"Hold on, guys. I'll be right back." Mario flew back to Tina's room, and she looked up with wide eyes. Mario wrapped his hands around his mother and looked into her eyes. Words wouldn't come. Then she spoke.

"Mario, I'm going to be okay."

"Yeah, I know, Mom, but…"

"We've been through enough pain these last months. I will not have my children lose both mother and father in one year."

Mario closed his wet eyes and leaned his head against her hands. He just couldn't tear himself away.

"*Ti amo*, Mom."

"I love you too. Now go. I'll see you tomorrow."

He kissed her goodbye, and both their hearts ached as they felt each other's pain.

The surgery proved to be more complicated than initially thought. Tina ended up needing two valves replaced. They also discovered damage to her heart wall because of rheumatic fever from her childhood that needed debridement. Despite the complications, Tina was home for Christmas. Though weak, she sat on a stool in the kitchen, watching Mario make the sauce for the traditional seven fish dinner on Christmas Eve. He dunked the wooden spoon into the sauce and held it to her mouth.

"Bravo, Mario! Just like mine," she exclaimed to his delight. No one in the family cooked Tina's recipes for her to eat. They knew no one could top her expert hands.

Her surgery was a turning point for Tina. She made a conscious decision to live again. Her children's fear throughout her surgery and recovery sent a clear message—it was not time for her to go. There was much more for her to do in life, and her family needed her. Tina took on the mantle of keeping Larry's memory alive for her children and grandchildren. She had a dogwood tree planted in the front yard and placed a stone at its base engraved with his name. Every February, around the anniversary of Larry's death, she gathered the family to attend Mass in his honor. Afterward, they'd return home for the traditional Sunday meal of pasta and meatballs.

As her grief mixed with loving thoughts of their lives together, Tina began to share vignettes of their time in New York and Connecticut. She recounted stories of Larry's childhood and their unusual courtship. Her tales spurred the family to do the same, and Larry came alive through their shared memories. Tina was finally ready to sift through Larry's dresser and give away his clothes. It was bittersweet—with each item, she felt his absence, and yet myriad happy memories danced through her mind.

While emptying his nightstand, Tina discovered a few letters in the back corner. Pulling them out, she recognized her handwriting. Orazio had safely stashed her letters from Italy for over fifty years. A single tear fell on the envelope as she pulled out her letter and read. Transported to a time before she had children, in a world and an ocean away, her own words sang of the loving anticipation of a life with her *immenso amore,* her greatest love. Page by page, Tina sailed into the past to her eighteen-year-old self, dreaming of romance in a land far from her little town of Bisceglie. Memories of family drama paled in comparison to the profound emotions written on the thin pages she held in her hands. *This is where it all began,* she thought.

Tina had saved many of Larry's letters, but she did not know that he had done the same. A man of few words and guarded emotions, Larry held his profound love for her deep in his heart. Tina was overwhelmed as a fountain of love flowed from her heart. After so many years together, she understood Larry better than he understood himself. She knew what he held in his heart. But to find these letters confirmed all that she loved about him. The letters from Italy were for nobody's eyes but his. Larry kept them as a reminder of her love, their romance, and the beginnings of a dream come true. He had found her—his *tesoro.*

During the following years, Tina's life was brimming with love. Her grandchildren, Cristina and Matthew gave her momentous occasions to celebrate. Being the bride's and groom's grandmother on their special days was a great honor for her. Witnessing her precious grandchildren grow into adulthood gave her unfathomable joy. She and Larry had done their fair share of childcare throughout their youth. As the years continued to pass, both Cristina and Matthew became parents. Tina's eyes sparkled with joy as she held each tiny miracle in her arms.

"Oh, how I wish you were here to meet your beautiful great-grandchildren, Larry," she would say each night before bed. "But I see you every time I hold them. Each carries a part of your generosity and love."

Jack, Adelyn, and Gemma became the focus of the entire family. They infused new life into their gatherings. Those energetic bundles of joy transformed Tina's family as each witnessed the pure delight of the first steps, first words, and of course, their first tastes of spaghetti. Baptisms, birthdays, and the holidays no longer marked the absence of Larry's presence. Instead, they held the promise of lives just begun and adventures not yet taken.

Letter Twenty

On the ship from Paris, en route to NYC
February 19, 1952
Mia Adorata,

I write these few lines to tell you I am well, except that my heart is broken. But don't feel bad for me. I know it will pass. I miss you so much that I rest in sadness and desolation. I don't know what to do. I can do nothing without my eyes filling with tears at the thought of you so very far away. It breaks my heart again and again. At this moment, I know the meaning of being distant from your love, and I ask you to forgive me for the times we were in Bisceglie and I said, "I can't wait to return to America." Forgive me, my love. I didn't know what I was saying. There were moments when I was anxious. But now I understand the significant loss of your presence at my side.

My love, let me know how you are feeling now that you are alone, without me. Take courage—you will see that it will pass. I feel totally powerless, and I cry often. Your absence is bitter medicine. We loved each other like two euphoric children. The two of us were so very happy, isn't that true, my love? Our love is unshakable. I look forward to the day our great happiness returns anew. And so, more than ever, we must be strong in our love.

Sending many sweet kisses, my love.
Yours forever,
Orazio

Chapter Thirty-Four
Sundays

Connecticut 1960-2004

A nd then there were Sunday dinners. Of all the memories the Dell'Olio family shared, this very ordinary ritual will be forever imprinted in their hearts. Waking to the aroma of sautéed onions and garlic, hearing the sizzle of frying meatballs, one could not mistake what day it was. Tina rose early in the morning to begin her routine. Mass was at 10:30 a.m., so she had to prepare the meal well before leaving for church. With no recipe, Tina's sauce was always the same, and it was one of the main staples of their diet. The Italian Americans in Connecticut called it gravy. When anyone in the family referred to gravy, it was tomato sauce. If it wasn't sauce, one would have to distinguish it by its color—brown gravy, which rarely, if ever, appeared on the dinner table.

The ritual was the same each Sunday. Frankie would sneak behind his mother as she fried the meatballs. As each gained their crispy caramelization, she gently turned them in the frying pan. The aroma of tomato, garlic, and freshly fried meat wafted through the house. It was the best smell in the world, and Frankie couldn't resist.

"Do you want one, Frankie?" Tina asked.

"Can I? They look so good!"

"Here, take this. But be careful, it's very hot."

She placed a meatball in a tiny dish and gave him a tiny fork to match. As he cut the meatball in half, steam rose from within. He didn't bother waiting for it to cool and popped it into his mouth. As it burned his tongue, Frankie held his mouth open to cool it off.

"Now, what did I tell you, Frankie? Blow on it first."

Frankie didn't stop at one, however. Three or four meatballs never got to the dinner table. But he wasn't the only one—all the children stole meatballs on Sunday mornings, and Tina was sure to make enough for breakfast and dinner. And those were the best breakfasts ever.

With the meats prepared, Tina transferred them to the big pot of sauce. The kitchen was usually in need of a good cleaning from splattered oil and drops of tomato on the stove's surface. Once she finished her chores, Tina took off her apron and left the kitchen to wash and dress for church. Then the family piled into Larry's Chevy Belair and made their way to St. Raphael's Church. All four children attended the Italian national parish school, and that's where they attended Mass rather than at the local parish.

With four children in the school, they actively took part in the parish life. The children often ran into classmates and chatted after Mass. Since Larry's nephew, Father Frank Dell'Olio, had been assigned to the parish years before, the priests knew the family well. Being at Mass each Sunday was like another family gathering. Familiar faces, colorful personalities, and crying babies were all part of the experience.

The family passed each season at St. Raphael's. The start of school brought excitement with the colors of fall leading into the celebration of All Saints' Day on November 1, Tina's birthday. Like the traditions in Italy, St. Raphael's School had students dress as their name saints. With excited anticipation, the children lined up around the corner, at the entrance to the school. Each was preening, proud of their costumes, and telling of their saints. Mario had been saying Mass at an altar in his grandparents' bedroom for years. Tina sewed altar cloths and a set of priestly vestments for the would-be priest. However, for All Saints' Day, he would dress as San Mauro, the patron saint of Bisceglie. Such a significant saint deserved regal vestments—cardinal red satin, velvet piping, and red lace that trimmed the sleeves and collar. On his head was a bishop's miter covered in aluminum foil with blue and gold stars forming the Chi-Rho, the P X in Greek that is the symbol of Christ. He even had a crosier, a bishop's staff. Although nobody knew who San Mauro was, he couldn't have been prouder in their procession around the block and into the church.

At Christmastime, the family arrived early or stayed after Mass to visit the manger scene at the corner of the churchyard. Palm Sunday was a regal celebration that carried its own family ritual. On those afternoons, once they cleared the dinner table and washed the dishes, Tina and the children sat at the kitchen table for hours. They fashioned crosses from the palms the priest had blessed at Mass. They placed one in each bedroom and tucked them behind each crucifix in the house. Easter Sunday brought fragrant white lilies and a visit to St. Margaret's Shrine, where Larry would take photos of the family in front of the statues. Mario had made his First Communion and confirmation at the church, and all four graduated from St. Raphael's School. It was their home for over eight years before the family left Bridgeport and moved to Trumbull, Connecticut.

Annette, Frankie, and Marisa started St. Raphael's school in seventh and fifth grades. They were the new kids when they started. As the youngest child, Mario spent all eight years of elementary school there. He grew up at St. Raphael's. Mario had fond memories of the nuns who taught them for so many years, especially Sister Kevin, who introduced him to playing guitar. At the end of each day, Sr. Kevin pulled out her guitar, sat on her desk, and led the class in song. It was always the best part of the day. Mario credits her with inspiring him to become a music teacher.

Following Sunday Mass, the family walked to the side altar in front of the church and lit vigil candles for Larry's parents, Francesco and Antonia. They always fought over who would get the taper to light the candles. Then they all loaded into the car and drove to Pacelli's Bakery. Pulling up to the bakery, the heavenly aroma of fresh bread and sweets filled the air. Larry left the children in the car with Tina as he dashed across the street to get bread for Sunday dinner. If he made the mistake of bringing them in, they'd beg him to buy doughnuts.

The order was the same each week: two French sticks, now known as baguettes. But as they grew into adolescents, two loaves would not suffice. Larry knew it wouldn't last the drive home, especially if the bread was hot out of the oven. As soon as he got into the car with the warm baguettes, the kids would scarf up one of them within minutes. On those days, Larry bought an extra loaf.

"Okay, kids, it's nice and hot. *Mangiate!*"

"But only eat one loaf. We need some for dinner, and I don't want you to fill up on bread! Then you won't eat your pasta!" Tina added.

Annette would be the first to rip the end off the crispy loaf. Frankie complained.

"Annette always gets the *culli*! That's not fair. The end is my favorite part."

"You were born too late, brother," she replied, grinning as she took her first bite.

She tore off a crispy chunk of bread and watched the steam rise from the soft white center and unceremoniously gobble it down. As they passed the loaf around, crumbs flew everywhere. When it got to Marisa, she turned to the youngest and offered him the coveted end piece.

"Here, Mario, you take the *culli*. You're always last."

She was always watching out for her little brother—she still does, supplying him with homemade zucchini bread each week. With warm, crispy bread in their bellies, they made their way home. The weekly visit to Pacelli's Bakery was one of their favorite routines. However, on some unfortunate occasions, they stopped at the bakery before Mass. It was the cruelest of tortures. Annette would hold the warm bread on her lap as they drooled, almost willing it into their mouths. Everyone knew, however, that they had to fast for an hour before receiving communion. There would be no snacking before Mass. This served as extra penance as each of them suffered through the long Mass in anticipation.

When the children were much younger, and Mario was still a toddler, Larry played Italian music on the HIFI stereo. Enrico Caruso sang opera, and Connie Francis and Mario Lanza belted Neapolitan love songs. On a blanket in front of the stereo, baby Mario became quiet while moving his arms to the music. Larry and Tina swayed to the music while Larry's beautiful tenor voice intoned love songs to his wife. Annette, Frankie, and Marisa huddled together on the sofa, giggling at the romantic scene unfolding before them. Every Sunday, they'd run to their seats when Larry pulled the vinyl album out of its sleeve and placed it on the turntable. Soon, they were humming along as they watched their parents so obviously in love.

When Mario grew older, he was not content to watch his parents sing to each other. As the youngest child, he was always the center of attention, and it piqued his jealousy. As Larry held Tina in his arms and sang to her, Mario wriggled between them, trying to sing along. Rather than shoo him away, Larry picked him up, and without skipping a beat, continued singing his love songs to Tina.

After Church

Sunday mornings would not be complete without a visit to Larry's sister, Lily. Lily and Eddie lived a block away from their home in Bridgeport. Mario bolted out of the car and ran to the back door. Without knocking, he burst into the kitchen.

"Hi, Aunt Lily! We're here!"

When Mario was very young, Aunt Lily would walk to their house to check on her parents. He looked forward to her visits. With his siblings at school and parents at work, Mario got a lot of attention. He was the youngest of all the nieces and nephews at that point and was spoiled. Lily never failed to bring Mario a treat. Eyeing her purse with anxious anticipation, Mario couldn't hide his excitement.

"What do you have for me today, Aunt Lily?"

"Why don't you see for yourself?" she said, offering him her purse.

"Really?"

"Yes, go ahead, open it, and see what I brought you."

He loved to snap open the gold clasp on the black pocketbook. Once unlocked, he gazed inside to find a chocolate treat in a shiny red wrapper. With melted chocolate smeared all over his lips and face, Mario sat contentedly while Lily visited with Francesco and Antonia. He grew very close to his aunt during his younger years, and their affection for each other never waned.

Each Sunday morning, Tina and Larry sat at Lily's kitchen table while the children ran off to play with their cousin, Eddie. But Mario always found more comfort sitting with the adults. The smell of freshly brewed espresso coffee with a shot of Sambuca filled the air. Lily set the demitasse cups on the table along with homemade cookies. But Mario's favorite was her homemade *taralli*, a Biscegliese specialty—hard pretzels spiced with anise seeds.

Every Sunday, Uncle Eddie boisterously teased everyone who came in the door. When Larry's older brother, Gianni, arrived at the door, Eddie leaped up to hold the door closed.

"Go home," Eddie joked through the door. "We don't want you here!"

"Open up, you crazy old man. Let me see my little sister," barked Gianni in reply.

No one escaped his teasing. Eddie was relentless with Larry. For the most part, Larry took it in stride, but when his older brother, Gianni, joined in the fray, it became too much. That was usually the cue to leave. Standing and grabbing their coats, Tina and Larry called to the children and said their goodbyes.

"Where are you going?" Eddie asked. "You just got here! Sit down."

"I've got to start dinner, Eddie," Tina said.

"Ten more minutes. Sit down."

"Eh, you yell at me all morning, and now you want me to stay?" Larry asked.

"No, not you. Tina can stay," Eddie responded.

"*Ma vatine via!* Get out of here!" Larry said, revealing his frustration.

It was all part of the Sunday ritual.

The Meal

Tina and Larry maintained the Italian tradition of *pranzo*—the main meal of the day served at 1:00 p.m. Every Sunday, the entire family would gather, even after their children had grown and married. As the family grew, they added another leaf to the dining room table. As soon as anyone entered the house, the scrumptious aroma of fresh tomato sauce tantalized the senses. Frankie continued to steal away to the stove with fork and plate in hand to swipe several meatballs.

"Frankie, don't take so many!" Tina gently admonished. "Leave some for everyone else."

Nonetheless, he filled his plate with three or four meatballs covered with the brilliant red sauce. There was never any fear that they would run out of food. Abundance ruled the day. Tina always made enough for a second full meal later in the week. Each time the door opened, and more people would arrive, the din became greater and greater. Joking, kissing hello, and football on the TV made for a boisterous gathering.

"Enough, someone set the table," Tina yelled over the noise. "Annette, Marisa, take the knives and forks, please."

"I've got it, Mom," Mario chimed in. "Let's use the pink dishes. I'll get them out of the hutch."

"No, no, those are for company. Just use the regular dishes," Tina replied.

"Why, aren't we special enough? We never use them. Come on, Mom."

"Fine, get the china, but be careful!"

Annette stood in the kitchen making garlic bread, which would barely make it to the table. As soon as she took the crispy loaves from the oven, a swarm of hands reached to sample it. The water boiled on the stove; Tina poured the pasta into the pot, and the anticipation grew. Everyone was famished. The usual continental breakfast consisted of coffee and several *Stella D'oro* biscuits rarely held them over until *pranzo*.

Once the pasta was ready, everything moved quickly. Tina grabbed the potholders and moved to the sink to drain the pasta. Mario laughed as steam fogged her glasses, obscuring her vision. She drained the macaroni in the colander and placed it back into the pot. Tina poured a few ladles of sauce over it so it would adhere to the pasta while the starch was still sticky from the water. Rinsing the pasta underwater would be a cardinal sin. That would wash off the salt and prevent the sauce from amalgamating with the surface of the pasta. Larry stood beside Tina, handing her the bowls, and they began a chain gang until each bowl was on the table.

There was nothing formal about those Sunday dinners. Everyone talked and ate until they were full. After they finished the pasta, Tina brought out the serving bowl full of meats from the sauce—Braciole, both hot and sweet sausage, pork ribs, and of course, meatballs. Braciole is a thin cut of beef—usually flank steak stuffed with garlic, parsley, hot pepper, and *Parmigiano* cheese. This was a family favorite. After the meat course came the palate cleanser of celery, *finocchio*, walnuts, and hazelnuts. Dessert was only for special occasions, but in its place was always fresh fruit.

"Mario, how about a peach? They're in season—nice and sweet."

"No, thanks, Mom."

The question was always the same, along with the answer. Mario wanted dessert—cake or cookies. But the tradition in Bisceglie and in many parts of Italy was to end the meal with fruit. As they grew older, they served espresso coffee to finish the meal. That was the sign that the meal had concluded. They spent hours at the table talking, laughing, and eating until they couldn't move. None of them could ever forget the aroma of Sundays—fried meatballs, fresh-cooked sauce, and garlic bread. There was nothing better except, of course, eating it all.

Those traditions, though not as frequent, still take place for every holiday and special family occasions. Many years have passed since Larry's death, but the family often repeats his stories and common phrases when they gather. It is not surprising that it is around the dinner table that he is most present. If there is one tradition that the family holds sacred, it's the ritual of breaking bread together. At ninety years old, Tina doesn't cook as frequently. She says that each of her four children has mastered one of her recipes. From eggplant Parmigiana to her meatballs and sauce, Tina has handed her cuisine down to the next generation. She keeps a close eye as her children and grandchildren cook her dishes under her guiding hand.

Seventy years after she and Larry began their courtship, the legacy they leave behind is poignant—filled with the love that brought them together. Kindness, loyalty, and love bind their family to this day. And it all started with a tiny black-and-white photo. From the very first look at a young woman strolling in the *piazza* in Bisceglie, Larry knew they were meant to be together. Their love flourished as their family continued to grow.

Theirs is a love story that began with letters from Italy, and it will never be forgotten.

Family photo: Frankie, Kathleen, Marisa, Jim, David, Gemma, Brenna, Tina, Matthew, Mario, Jackson, Annette, Cristina, Adelyn, Wayne, Charley.

Letter Twenty-One

New York City
February 6, 1950
Dearest Amore,

As you see, I write to you often, letting you know I am well together with my relatives. This way, my dear one, I hope to hear from you in a beautiful letter. You know I love getting your messages and I read them over and over again. It's like finding a beautiful trinket for my heart. I feel as if we are seated together on a comfortable couch, chatting with each other. And that is precisely why, my sweet Nicoletta, I am writing now, because I am thinking of you. I retired early this evening to tell you that, before you, I have never loved before. You are my first and my adored, the woman who will accompany me in my life.

You will see, Nicoletta, for you, I will be a good man, one you have always dreamt of and hoped for. Your wish, the desires of your dreams, will be realized as two little hearts that pray to be united. I must tell you I have always dreamed of being loved like this—to have a beautiful young woman like you. Just as you dreamed of having a dear and good young man like me, dearest love. Perhaps you believe I exaggerate. I hope you are as happy as I am.

I've enclosed a dollar for you. Please get a photograph taken of you and send it to me. I would love to place it right beside my chair to gaze on your face always. Please write to me soon, as I think of you constantly.

Sending hugs and kisses from Papá and Mamma.

I want nothing but good things for you.

Sending a big kiss to you,

Your love,
Orazio

Letter Twenty-Two
The Final Letter

White Plains, New York
June 2020
Dearest Orazio,

It has been over 10 years since you left this earth, and I can still feel your presence within me. Not a day goes by that I don't turn to ask you something. There are moments I wish I could share a thought or a fear with you and must be content with my own thoughts. I speak to you every night before I go to sleep. When I awaken during the night, I reach out to touch you, but find the empty place beside me.

We spent fifty-eight beautiful years together and raised a family that we were both proud of. I picture your face smiling at me at each special moment we shared. You promised me back in Bisceglie that we would have a home of our own that was bigger and better than the house my parents left me, and you were so proud when we crossed that threshold.

I marvel at how we first came to be. From that tiny photo your brother sent you from Italy, you chose me. What drew your eyes to me, Orazio? What was it about me that drew your attention? And what gave you the courage to write to me? So many questions remain unanswered. But what is certain is the fact that the photo transformed both our lives beyond our imaginings. The tiny image of five young people strolling in the piazza started us on this fantastic journey together.

In your letters, you wrote what you could not say in person. I came to understand who you are and what you wished for your life. In the letters you received from Italy, you came to truly know me. I laid my dreams and fears before you. I bared my heart through my written words. And when we finally met, our profound understanding of each other's hearts was greater than any couple could hope for. I will always be grateful for those letters, for they laid the foundation for our relationship and our love. We could never settle for less as we moved forward with our complicated lives. No matter what pain or struggle we encountered along the way, we met at a deeper level to face them together.

There is so much more I would like you to know about this wonderful family we raised. You were always proud of our children, and now you would take great joy in your grandchildren. Cristina is the mother of two beautiful children, and I can picture you teaching them how to eat spaghetti just as you did with Cristina and Matthew. Her husband, Charley, is as gentle and loving as you. Our miracle great-grandson, Jackson, is thriving after being born at only 26 weeks. His little sister, Addie, looks just like Cristina did as a baby with an infectious laugh and filled with life. You would be so proud of the man Matthew has become—seeing him and Brenna filled with joy at the birth of their first child, Gemma. Matthew is sensitive and kind, just as you were. You would take great pride in his dedication to Italian culture and language and, of course, his love of pasta.

Orazio, you have left an indelible mark on our family, and I see you in each of them. It is through your children that I continue to hold you in my arms. You live on— not only through our letters, but through each of them. You used to call me Tesoro, your treasure. But it is obvious where our treasure lies. It is within each of our children, grandchildren, and great-grandchildren. Our treasure lives on in our legacy that began with one tiny photograph and a romantic man with a dream.

I miss you every day, and I know that someday soon, we will be reunited. I look forward to that moment when we can simply sit and share our thoughts. How I long to hold you, to touch you, and to kiss you one more time. I will see you soon, my love.

Il Tuo Tesoro,

Tina

THE END

About the Author

Dr. Mario Dell'Olio is the author of *Letters from Italy, New Men: Bonds of Brotherhood, Coming About: Life in the Balance,* and *Body and Soul.*

As chair of the music department and ethics teacher at an independent school for girls in Manhattan, he leads choirs on international concert tours and has released numerous albums. His doctoral project examines the woman's voice in the music of Hildegard von Bingen and has published several articles.

Coming About is the main theme of a concert experience of the Empire City Men's Chorus of New York, a documentary with music featuring Mario Dell'Olio reading excerpts throughout the performance.

Dr. Dell'Olio holds a Doctor of Sacred Music, a Master of Music in Voice, and a Master of Religious Education.

Note from the Author

Word-of-mouth is crucial for any author to succeed. If you enjoyed *Letters from Italy*, please leave a review online—anywhere you are able. Even if it's just a sentence or two. It would make all the difference and would be very much appreciated.

Thanks!
Mario Dell'Olio

We hope you enjoyed reading this title from:

BLACK ROSE writing™

www.blackrosewriting.com

Subscribe to our mailing list – *The Rosevine* – and receive FREE books,
daily deals, and stay current with news about upcoming releases
and our hottest authors.
Scan the QR code below to sign up.

Already a subscriber? Please accept a sincere thank you for being a fan of
Black Rose Writing authors.

View other Black Rose Writing titles at
www.blackrosewriting.com/books and use promo code
PRINT to receive a **20% discount** when purchasing.

5/23-3

Made in United States
North Haven, CT
20 March 2023